HOLLYWOOD
IN A SUITCASE

SAMMY DAVIS, JR.

HOLLYWOOD IN A SUITCASE

WILLIAM MORROW AND COMPANY, INC.
New York   1980

Library of Congress Cataloging in Publication Data

Davis, Sammy, 1925-
  Hollywood in a suitcase.

  1. Davis, Sammy, 1925- 2. Entertainers—
United States—Biography. I. Title.
PN2287.D322A27   792.7   80-14792
ISBN 0-688-03736-4

Printed in the United States of America

First Edition

1 2 3 4 5 6 7 8 9 10

BOOK DESIGN BY MICHAEL MAUCERI

I dedicate this book to every person who has ever sat at a Saturday matinee and cheered the hero and hissed the villain. It is also dedicated to the multitude of those of you who, like myself, have become film critics and movie buffs and, last but not least, to the devoted artists in front of and behind the cameras: actors, producers, writers, technicians, and directors.

Preface

This book has been a lot of fun for me to write because movies are my passion. It may be overindulgence on my part, but I felt the need to share some of this deep feeling with other people.

I have been an entertainer for fifty years and hope I've given a little bit of pleasure to people. But others in show business have given me immense pleasure as well, and I thought it was time to pay them a personal tribute.

I did not set out to write another *Yes I Can*—my earlier autobiography—simply because I've still got a lot of living to do before writing the final chapters of my life. This is an interlude piece, a pleasurable book to write and, I hope, to read. It is a book, like a certain song, I felt I had to do.

I am deeply indebted to Simon Regan, without whom the book would never have been written.

S.D., Jr.

Contents

Chapter 1

Bogey

During that long and exciting period when I was young and brash and fighting against private and public odds to establish myself as a successful entertainer, Humphrey Bogart became my private mentor.

Outwardly I was almost as full of myself as it was possible to be. Inwardly I had all the biting insecurities of a fledgling entertainer. I knew I had the talent, but did I have the balls and the staying power to make it to the top? A pint-sized black guy with a patch on his eye, lost and a little lonely in the sprawling concrete of Los Angeles, I was constantly nagged by doubt.

In the middle of all this Bogey—and Frank Sinatra, whom I'll talk about later—grabbed hold of my hand and led me gently through Hollywood. Whatever kind of piss and vinegar I showed up front, Bogart spotted the inside of me as soon as he saw me.

I know what he did for me on a personal basis, but there is no way of knowing all the things he did behind the scenes. He put a protective and friendly blanket of approval over me when he asked me up to the house for the first time. He purposely invited other guests who would be useful to me. "You look after this kid,"

11

he would say. "He's going places." Naturally I was thrilled to be hobnobbing with people who had, up to then, been merely my screen idols. To a large extent that alone would have been a great pleasure. But Bogey's help and friendship went much deeper than smiles and handshakes at those famous Holmby Hills blow-outs.

I first met Bogart when he was in the audience on the opening night at Slapsy Maxie's when the Will Mastin Trio—my father, my uncle, and I—was headlining in Los Angeles for the first time. Slapsy's was then the most famous and celebrity-filled watering hole on the West Coast, and we were going to give them hell. The message came backstage that just about every name in town was down there waiting for us. How much of this was Sinatra's doing and how much a result of our growing reputation I shall never know. They say that evening has become a show business legend, and if you'll excuse me, I won't argue the point too strongly. Since I was three years old, I had been waiting for that night. Dad and Uncle were very pleased, of course. This was not just an ordinary show. But they didn't share with me that burning, boiling madness of ambition.

I went out there that night to give them every last drop of sweat I had in me, or I would die trying. There was no question of pacing myself, as I do today, or balancing the act to give highs and lows. I went out there to bowl them over. I danced until my feet ached; I sang my guts out; I impersonated half the audience. I had never driven myself so hard, and I probably never will. I was inspired in a way that I can't describe, and the audience picked it up.

Despite all the frenzied activity onstage, I could still make out the smiling faces below. Images of a thousand films were sitting down there, watching. There was Spencer Tracy . . . over there was Douglas Fairbanks . . . my God, there's Judy Garland . . . and there, right in the middle, sat Humphrey Bogart. Seeing him lifted me to a pinnacle of inspiration which forced me to get things out of myself which even I had no idea were there. The show ran hours overtime, and I didn't see the standing ovation because I was crying so hard. I had driven myself to the point of total exhaustion, yet I felt so elated I could have started all over again.

All the celebrities trickled backstage after the show, and I don't mind admitting I reveled in the compliments. Bogart eventually came in with Sinatra and Betty Bacall. He touched me on the shoulder and said, "You were swell." Then he turned to Frank and said, "You must bring him up to the house sometime. We gotta see a lot more of this kid." A few weeks later Betty called me up and invited me to a small party in Holmby Hills. It was the start of a beautiful friendship. In time I became a fringe member of the elite centered on the Bogart household which Betty had named The Holmby Hills Rat Pack. It had its own kinds of kudos.

Bogey cherished talent, and to him it was always instantly recognizable. He'd seen something in me, and he wanted to protect it. One of the ways in which he knew he could do this, without the slightest hint of conceit, was to give me the "Bogey Seal of Approval." He never patronized me but always encouraged—sometimes with some very blunt advice. It would not have been in his nature to try to mold my career, but he often told me where I was going wrong.

On several occasions after he had seen my show he came backstage and pointed out mistakes. The fact that he bothered at all was a great encouragement to me, and I quickly realized his blunt advice had been staring me in the face for a long time. He said I was too fond of aping performers I admired, told me to develop my own style. Even if, at first, it wasn't as good, it would be mine.

He helped me in all sorts of other ways. Even after Slapsy Maxie's, when he knew I was playing in town, he would gather up all his pals and every other celebrity he could get by phone and reserve all the front tables. He made sure all my opening nights would go with a bang. It was this kind of generous support which indebted me to him forever.

Frank Sinatra, of course, was the other person of this period who gave me the same kind of friendship and support. Frank was one of Bogey's greatest pals and a front-runner in the Rat Pack. Two of the men who had been my idols had become my friends. At that time in my life I could hardly have asked for anything more. It was also a great morale booster, in a time of great uncertainty, that I was able to give them a performance which they respected.

Bogey loved having interesting people around. He liked writers and a handful of the directors. Apart from a few other celebrities, they were the only people in the film industry he could tolerate. He selected his friends very carefully, and there was no way you could suck up to the guy. He would see through you as you walked in the door. In the main, his friends were intelligent, witty, sometimes outrageous, but always brilliant conversationalists. Boring Bogey was a cardinal sin. Generally speaking, his relationships with women were the same. He wanted broads he could talk to. Betty Bacall was the most obvious example. He had already had a tempestuous marriage with Mayo Methot. He and Mayo spent their lives together boozing, fighting, and making passionate love. Once, after the director Howard Hawks had physically separated them in a dreadful fistfight, Bogey was so sure she was going to murder him he insured his life for $100,000. The fans loved it. One day one of the celebrated fights started in a restaurant and became a running street battle. They were still fighting in front of huge crowds as they reached the car and drove off. One woman in the crowd said, "Jesus, she's tougher than he is."

Soon after they divorced, she died from alcoholic poisoning.

There is no doubt about Bogey's drinking habits. He boasted of them. But he was no born fighter. Despite his tough image, he had come from middle-class parents and, unlike Cagney, had never been near a street fight. Drinking helped his image as a rebel, but he was essentially a social drinker. You rarely saw him under the table, although after a session at his house we often found other people in a state of collapse. The Rat Pack left Sid Luft curled up on a bookshelf and went off to dine at Romanoff's. Sid didn't wake up for twenty-four hours and had cramps in his legs for a week.

Bogey's famous quote that the whole world was three drinks behind gave us all the excuse to drink far too much, and he treated his drinking habits with the same wry humor with which he handled everything else. He loved to remind us that when he made *The African Queen* on location in the African swamps, he was the only one on the set who did not come down with an ailment during shooting. "I drank so much booze during the making of that film, any bug that bit me died instantly," he said, laughing. He got an Oscar for playing the drunken captain, but very few people realized that when he looked drunk on screen, he really was. Bogey got a big kick out of that one.

Everyone in the Rat Pack, with the exception of Betty Bacall, loved to get high. Spencer Tracy was always around. Bogey firmly believed Spence was the finest American actor in Hollywood. But his drinking habits were very well known. At one time during the making of *Boys' Town* he came onto the set so drunk he had to be propped up. It took five hours for him to say a single line properly, and after the final take he collapsed. The irony of this was that Spence was playing a guy meant to be a good influence on the kids.

Frank Sinatra, Judy Garland, "Prince" Michael Romanoff, David Niven, Irving "Swifty" Lazar, and other regular drop-ins all loved their booze. Others, such as the cartoonist Charles Addams, the politician Adlai Stevenson, the writer John O'Hara, and the director John Huston were valued for their conversation more than for their drinking habits. But you rarely saw them at Holmby Hills without drinks in their hands.

We all loved Bogey's hard image, and he played up to it. Almost everyone was a little in awe of him because they either loved or feared him. When he was unkind, he was testing people or being loyal to his friends in the face of some criticism. The key was to give as good as you got. I remember when the producer Stanley Kramer was up at Bogey's house after a day's shooting on *The Caine Mutiny*. We were well into a drinking session when Kramer decided to leave. Bogart stopped him by saying, "Wait a minute. What the hell difference would it make if you don't show up tomorrow?" Everyone stood around a little awkwardly as Kramer paused and looked at Bogey.

Then he said, "Well, Bogey, I have to be up early to make sure the set is ready for prematurely balding and aging actors like you."

Bogey squinted a little, and you could see the famous quiver of the lips. Then he suddenly roared with laughter, slapped Kramer on the back, and they were the best of friends until Bogey died.

On the other hand, Joan Collins was at another party where she made a rather rude comment about Sinatra. Bogey overheard it, grabbed the front of her dress roughly, yanked her forward, and snarled right in her face, "Don't you ever talk about a pal of mine like that again."

Miss Collins wilted and never spoke to Bogey again.

This side of Bogey is probably better known than the private side. Most of the time he was a surprisingly sensitive, friendly, faithful, warm, and intelligent person. He was extremely lovable. I think it true to say he had taken so much crap that in the latter part of his life he strenuously guarded against being forced into taking any more.

Bogey could understand only black and white. There were no gray areas in his life, and he wasn't the kind of guy to go chasing shadows. He loved to take people under his wing, but his reasons were never self-centered or ambitious. He wanted to protect them from everything he knew was out there, and he wanted to buck the system. He was brilliant at both. His protection was unlimited and never sought reward, yet he got a kick out of telling newcomers to the rat race what the industry would expect from them.

Once on a trip to England he saw a bright young kid called Richard Burton playing *Hamlet* at Stratford-upon-Avon. He went backstage right after the performance and congratulated this obviously up-and-coming star. "The only thing I can say, young man," he told Richard, "is that if they ever drag you to Hollywood, just look me up. I ain't hard to find."

Burton said, "Thanks," in a way that was a little arrogant. He was full of his success at the time.

Bogey looked at him with that knowing squint and said, "Believe me, kid. You're going to need pals. Talent like that's got to be protected."

For my own part I did not have to run the Bogey gauntlet. Maybe he spotted my vulnerability, for Bogart was never a bully for the sake of it. I could hold my own in any conversation, but an element of the awe I had for him must have crept through. My testing ground—for there always was one with Bogey—must have been the stage itself. Frank's wholly benevolent attitude toward me may also have helped. All I can say is that from the very beginning Bogey treated me with the greatest of kindness and affection, and in turn I tried to be as personable as possible at his social gatherings.

I have read a lot, but I am not well read. I have traveled a great deal without being worldly. I have had almost every kind of human experience, yet in middle age I've just become adjusted to myself. I am very proud indeed of the varied talents God bestowed on me, yet I have always been keenly aware of my limitations. So, in such brilliant and gracious company as the John Hustons, John O'Haras, and Humphrey Bogarts of this world, I had to fall back on my other abilities. To hold my own with such a distinctive set of characters and personalities, it was necessary to extend my role as entertainer. I tried hard to be amusing, good company, erudite and knowledgeable about the things I knew about. I wanted to be a gracious guest, fully appreciative of the fact that I was there at all and responding to the good humor all around me. I like to think I succeeded. There was a lot of me in those days that could have been picked on and exploited by a man with the abrasive perception of Bogey. He never tried.

When Bogey and Betty Bacall met and fell in love on the set of *To Have and Have Not,* I think Bogey realized just how much of his life he had wasted with other women. She did not drink much, and she became a great and stable influence on Bogey. She was his natural partner. She was big enough and intelligent enough for him, without ever wanting to swamp or control him. He always told her, "If you want your coat held up, then don't act like a fella."

Before the shooting of *To Have and Have Not* began, Howard Hawks got hold of Bogey in front of everybody and told him, "This girl is new. But she's got something. She's the only actress I know who can get away with being more insolent than you. Don't try to browbeat her because I'm going to make sure she's ruder than you. You are the most insolent actor in the world, but this girl is going to walk away with the show."

Bogey scoffed, "Fat chance!"

Howard put his foot down. "Well, Bogey," he said, "every scene you play with this dame, she's going to leave you with egg on your face."

Bogart went on the set clearly bemused and curious. At the end of a single day's shooting he went over to Hawks and said, "I see what you mean. She's some dame."

I think the film stands as a celluloid record of the kind of relationship they had. The hard cynic met his match and finally succumbed. She played it as tough as Bogey, and he saw he was faced with one hell of a broad.

In fact, Betty and Bogey were alike in everything, not just pure temperament and intelligence. They were of the same breed. They both were outlaws and continued to suffer for it for the rest of their lives. Jack Warner was as abusive to Betty as he had been to Bogey in the early days. He went out of his way to make her feel unwanted and unimportant. After the sensational success of *To Have and Have Not,* he went to great lengths to turn Lizabeth Scott into a "second Lauren Bacall." Maybe it was because he could never forgive Betty for falling in love with Bogey. Bogey was plenty for him to handle at one time without any complications.

Betty was left out in the cold for many years. But this was partly because, with Bogey's full blessing, she would never compromise. Both of them were always being suspended, and this didn't help after Bogey died and Betty wanted to resume her career. Before that she had clearly been more interested in fulfilling her marital ambitions as Mrs. Bogart than she had been in competing with Lizabeth Scott.

Bogey, along with the handful of the Hollywood greats who were of his caliber, was a director's dream because there was no need ever to direct him. Because of this, it often seemed as if he were a one-dimensional actor who played every part the same way. Someone once said to John Huston, "But he can only play Bogey."

Huston gave one of those sardonic smiles which was always curiously intellectual, yet down to earth, and said, "What the hell's wrong with that?"

Obviously the public agreed with him. In fact, it was the people themselves, despite all the odds put up by the industry, who made the whole Bogart syndrome possible. And the key to the entire thing was the film *Casablanca*.

Right in the middle of movie history, *Casablanca* straddles the entire industry like a colossus. Most people agree it is one of the ten best pictures ever produced and a cornerstone of moviemaking. It made Bogart the star of the decade, and it still hauntingly reflects the early forties. Yet the film itself emerged through a whole series of accidents and was given a B rating by Warner Brothers. Only one person on the set had no doubts about the movie when it was being made—Bogart himself. When I eventually met him, it was almost the first thing I asked: "What was the exact moment you knew *Casablanca* was going to be a classic?"

Bogey didn't reflect at all. "The minute I walked on the set," he said. "No one else had any idea we had a winner until the first box-office returns came in. They'd put it out as a typical low-budget B. But I had a feeling for it right away. For one thing, I knew Michael Curtiz, the director, was a genius. Secondly, they loaded that picture with talent. They didn't consider me box office, and they wanted to offset that risk with triple protection. So they put in all the brilliant character actors they could find. They got Sydney Greenstreet, Peter Lorre, and Claude Rains.

With guys like that backing you, you couldn't fail. Right away I recognized Ingrid Bergman's talent. She was a natural. But Warner's still thought I might scare the audience off, so they hunted around to give the film something more. They came up with the Dooley Wilson piece which set the mood for the whole picture. Warner's wasn't going to take any chances with me. It was the story of my life at the time."

Nowadays you only have to hear a few bars of "As Time Goes By" to get the image of the hat, the bow tie, the lisp, the cigarette in one hand and a scotch in the other.

Bogart knew the inside story of *Casablanca* perhaps better than anyone, and I never tired of talking about it with him. Although he was outwardly cynical about everything, the film had a place in his heart because it marked the first time that the audiences themselves recognized his genius with their nickels and dimes. Even with them his attitude was always: "I don't owe you anything but a performance." Yet the soft part of his nature knew perfectly well that had it not been for the public, the industry itself might have kept him in obscurity for the rest of his life.

The movie was born at a script conference at Warner Brothers some time early in 1942. Everyone was doing quick patriotic films at the time, and the vogue was to make them as topical as they could. That morning's papers were full of an obscure Moroccan town on the Atlantic coast. Someone said, "So how the hell can we make a film about a place called Casablanca?"

The studio heads repeated the name several times and then admitted, "I suppose it has a certain ring to it. Let's give it to the writers and see if they can come up with anything." The idea was handed to Julius and Philip Epstein, two contract writers, who chewed it around for a couple of days and produced a two-page idea. Eventually, this was to win them and Howard Koch, who joined them later, the coveted Academy Award.

Originally Warner's saw it as a vehicle for Ronald Reagan and Ann Sheridan. But Curtiz knew Rick, the hero, had to be a sardonic tough guy. The studio asked George Raft, who said the immortal lines "Whoever heard of Casablanca? And anyway, I don't want to star opposite an unknown Swedish broad." He was suspended for the umpteenth time and had the grace to admit, years later, "It was the biggest mistake of my life."

It wasn't until they had considered five other leads, including Errol Flynn, that someone remembered Bogart was hanging around the lot, waiting for work. They dubiously agreed to try him out.

Bogart had, after years of abuse, become completely disenchanted with Hollywood. It looked to him as if he had missed the boat. He had tackled everything thrown at him. He was hungry for work. For a third of his career he had played third, fourth, and even tenth lead in low-grade B movies. He had arrived in Hollywood in 1930 with trainloads of other actors. He hung around for a long time before making eight films in two years. He even made a horror movie. Believe me, you have to be the most ardent Bogey fan to sit through it. It was awful. Years later, when someone referred to the film at the Bogart homestead, Bogey said, "So, now you know why I've got a fuck-you fund. Anybody asks me to make another lousy movie I can tell them where to go."

He was earning his money—often shooting two films at a time. Despite this, Warner's decided the $750 a week it was paying him as a contract actor was too much and, in 1935, refused to renew his contract. No one at the studio could see his potential greatness. Everyone had decided that his stiff upper lip, partly paralyzed in a childhood game of tennis (though the publicity men called it a "war wound") was simply unsalable as a sex symbol to their predominantly female audiences. At this point, Bogey booked his return to New York.

Luckily fate, in the person of Leslie Howard, was standing by to pull him sharply back by the scruff of the neck. Howard was one of the hottest properties on the Bel Air circuit. He could name his own terms, and he insisted Bogey repeat his stage performance in *The Petrified Forest*.

Warner's attitude was: "What the hell. It's no big deal. Put Bogart back on the payroll for forty weeks."

His part in the film called for few words, yet he dominated most of the scenes, and he was an immediate and overwhelming success with the public. The film was box-office dynamite. Yet, he told me later, "Warner's thought it was a one-shot. They told me they'd keep me around in case the Big Three—Cagney, Edward G. Robinson, and Raft—got out of line."

But if Jack L. wouldn't explore Bogey's full potential, other people could. The tempestuous director Raoul Walsh was one. He had liked Bogey in *The Roaring Twenties* and demanded him for *High Sierra*. Warner reluctantly agreed.

Finally, when *The Maltese Falcon* came along and became overnight dynamite—and a trend setter for decades—Jack L. grudgingly admitted that Bogey might have a future with the studio. This film endeared Bogey to the director John Huston.

When Ingrid Bergman finally knew she was going to play opposite Bogey in *Casablanca*, she went to see *The Maltese Falcon* a dozen times just to get acquainted with his acting style. That was the mark of a real pro, and one of the reasons they hit it off so well on screen was that she had done her homework.

With all this behind him and with Bogey by now commanding an almost fanatical nationwide fan following, it seems incredible that Warner's should have put Bogey at the bottom of the list when they started casting *Casablanca*.

By the time of the first day's shooting, Howard Koch had been brought in to help with the script. The screenwriters worked on it each day for the next day's shooting. At one stage an intrigued Ingrid Bergman asked Curtiz how the film was going to end. He rebuked her with: "Don't ask questions."

When they did finally think about how it was going to end, the last page of the script called for Rick to die. Bogey went into complete revolt. "Get George Raft to die. I don't want to die just yet." Curtiz insisted his version be shot. However, when Jack Warner saw the uncut film, he was impressed enough to remark that there might be a sequel. Curtiz hurriedly reassembled everyone and shot an alternative end.

The whole film looks, and is, a Warner Brothers set piece. It was shot in six weeks flat, on a shoestring, and was shoved into distribution only a few weeks after the actual Moroccan town had ceased to be covered daily by the newspapers.

The various accidents and quirks of fate which brought Humphrey Bogart to *Casablanca* were only a little more intriguing than the final selection of Ingrid Bergman as the heroine, Ilsa. The early history of Miss Bergman's life in Hollywood was that she triumphed in parts that had been created for someone else. *Casablanca* was no exception. She stepped into the part created for Ann Sheridan.

On the set Bogey and she created a whole mood between them. Yet curiously, and untypically, they had no real interest in each other, and when Curtiz said, "Cut," they both would go brood in their separate trailers. Gary Cooper once said of Ingrid, "No woman has loved me more than Ingrid Bergman when we worked together. Yet the day after the film ended I couldn't get her on the telephone." According to him, Ingrid always fell in love with her leading man.

When Bogey woke up to find himself a living legend, he decided that the only real advantage was that he could now tell the studio bosses to go to hell. Consequently he was always being suspended. But to Bogey it was no hardship at all to sit by the swimming pool rather than make another lousy movie. His attitude toward suspension drove the studios crazy. He followed the advice he gave liberally to everyone else: "Hold out at any cost. Mortgage the house, drive a cab, stop eating; but never let them see you running. Just remember there's always a script in someone's desk and you're the only guy who can play the part. When they bring it out, they'll come running back."

During the filming of *Dark Passage* in 1947—a full five years after Bogey had become Warner's leading property—he found he was losing his hair. In the film he played an escaped convict hiding out at Betty Bacall's place while undergoing plastic surgery. Only he and Betty knew at the time that he was wearing a toupee. In the final scene, when he had a fight under the Golden Gate Bridge in San Francisco, the director, Delmer Daves, began telling him how he wanted the fight to go. Delmer said, "You gotta win this fight, and after you've hooked with the left, I want you to lead in with the right."

Bogey looked at Betty for a second, and both of them knew his toupee wouldn't have much chance of surviving. "Wait a minute," he told Daves, "I'm no fighter. Get John Wayne to play it. If you want me to fight this guy, I can only do it sock by sock."

Later Delmer heard about the toupee and thought the story was hilarious, but at the time he told me shooting the film was like piecing together a plate of spaghetti.

From then on, every time Bogey got up in the morning his pillow was covered with hair, and at first he looked with alarm at the growing nakedness of his scalp. Eventually, with his usual realism and humor, he accepted the fact and took his wig off as soon as he left the studio gates. It wasn't long before Jack Warner heard about it and summoned Bogey in for an examination. He deliberately left the toupee at home and sauntered through the Warner lot with his dome gleaming in the sunshine. He had combed his remaining strands of hair right back to give the worse possible effect.

He never tired of telling us, back in Holmby Hills, what happened next. "Warner just sat there in a state of total apoplexy for several minutes with his mouth wide open and his hands gripping the table in front of him. Then he exploded with a great spluttering sound and ran from the room. He didn't come back. I think he's been on special pills for his heart ever since."

Warner was a feisty man who had a gift for upsetting most of the people he met. Very few of his big stars had much to say in his favor except that they recognized his genius for moviemaking and star spotting. He lived in the decade when movies were a compulsion for nearly the entire population, and he had an uncanny knack of knowing what and who they wanted. He was also, in his way, one of the most progressive of producers, always having a "nose" for the next trend. It was he, after all, who had produced the first sound movie, *The Jazz Singer.*

Bette Davis, James Cagney, Edward G. Robinson, and an array of other greats had long and bitter fights with him and constantly accused him of treating them like cattle. But it was with Bogey that he had his longest-lasting and best-known running battle. And, let's face it, they were big enough for each other. To be the enemy of either would have spelled disaster for lesser men.

Forming a private company to make *The African Queen* became Bogey's final snub to Jack Warner, who never forgave him. The film's total success, which included Academy Awards, merely rubbed salt into the wound he had inflicted by going out on his own.

He tended to walk through most of his movies in the latter years of his career with a sense of humor and a nod and a wink to Betty, who knew him better. But Bogart walking through a part would have been a star performance from almost anyone else. When he made *The Big Sleep*, for instance, he refused to take the film seriously, yet this in itself helped make the movie into a classic.

There is a particular scene in which he has to walk into a bookshop and ask about a certain book. The bit was crucial to the plot but utterly boring as a piece of cinema. Nothing really happened during this dialogue to keep the audience awake. They made several takes before this dawned on them, and Bogey jumped up and said, "Just a minute. I've got an idea. Let's see if it works. Run it through again."

The cameras started rolling, and a perplexed Howard Hawks watched Bogart suddenly pull out a pair of dark glasses and put them on. He went into the shop and hammed it up in an effeminate way. It was utterly comedic. He turned a full three minutes of film into a classic cameo, all with a little inspired improvisation.

Bogey didn't go to the sneak preview, but Howard Hawks did. He told me later, "It really worked. We could have sat around for days dreaming that one up. You could feel the audience catching on to it as soon as he put the glasses on."

When Warner's spies reported the incident back to their boss, he sent a terse memo to Howard Hawks: "Word has reached me that you are having fun on the set. This must stop."

Bogey's last real-life performance was his greatest. In the three months before he died everyone could see he was wasting away. Just before the end he was little more than a skeleton. Yet that twinkle remained in his eyes, and his brain was forever active and intelligent.

His valet would help him up and dress him. They'd put him in the "dumbwaiter" and send him downstairs. Betty would fix him a very large, very dry martini, light a cigarette, and prop him up in one of his favorite chairs. Then the old buddies would drop by. Only a few of the close outsiders had the privilege of visiting him. His many cursory acquaintances were gently turned away. Bogey didn't want any but the people he really loved to see him die.

To the very, very end he was a sociable man who had to keep up with everything that was going on. He spent his last days with his chums, still drinking, smoking, conversing, and arguing. He maintained that cancer was at least a "respectable disease." Bogey was the kind of guy who met the end with a curl of the lip. He'd been there so many times on celluloid, and he knew how to play the part.

One of his last acts, as he sat there in the morning sunlight on the porch in his robe, was to raise his glass and say, "Well, Jack L., I guess that sooner or later we'll be getting together again."

The great Jack L. Warner died in 1978. When I heard the willful old mogul had finally gone, I fixed myself a double shot of bourbon on not much ice. I found myself looking out the window and reflecting for a moment. It's always bad when a legend dies, and I had no gripe with Jack L., but I couldn't keep a little smile from breaking out on my face as I thought, Well, Jack, I guess you're finally going to meet Bogey face to face on equal terms.

Chapter 2

Liz and Richard

Richard Burton's fame and fortune for most of his life in Hollywood have been so intricately linked to Liz Taylor's that it is difficult for most people to see them as separate forces in movie history. I have known them both for a long time. I was first introduced to Burton at what was then Ciro's Restaurant in Hollywood when he was making *The Robe*. Naturally I accepted an invitation to go on the set, and Richard and I became firm friends very quickly.

I had known Liz Taylor since she made *National Velvet* when she was twelve. She was always one of the most eternally beautiful women. She came up to my house with her secretary a little while ago. I've got a pretty big place, even by Beverly Hills standards. Elizabeth filled it with her presence. She is full of bubbling good humor, and she never fails to try to con my diamond rings from me. She also has a marked weakness for southern fried chicken. On this trip, when she wasn't trying on all my diamonds and hinting madly about how lovely they were, she was also devouring a huge platter of fried chicken.

She is a deliciously greedy person in the best sense of the word.

She is opulent in her tastes, and when she likes something, she likes a lot of it. Both on and off screen she exudes an incredible mixture of absolute bravado and total insecurity. It seems as if nothing could conquer her, yet she remains attractively vulnerable. This is the reason she quickly wins over all her costars. They feel her power as an actor and are reassured by it. Yet something in her calls out your protective instinct; you feel she needs looking after. It is an incredible contradiction in her personality which makes her very much a man's woman.

When Burton is being brilliant on a stage, there is virtually no one alive who can get near him. This made it all the more sad for his friends when he made a series of toilet movies. Everybody is entitled to do a picture which looks excellent on paper but just doesn't work on the screen. But there were times when Richard hardly knew which picture he was making because he had so little interest in them; he was walking through them, suspecting they were shabby before he read the titles. His friends found it difficult to forgive him for wasting himself like this because they knew the range of his talent and potential.

Burton has had several down periods, when everyone who knew him has said, "Richard, what the hell are you doing to yourself?" But he has always come to his senses. He invariably wises up and floors us with something—because Richard has to be accepted back in the fold. He needs the respect of his peers, and he has to keep getting his reputation back on the line. He needs that Oscar, too. It was stolen from him in 1978, when he was nominated for *Equus*, but sooner or later Burton will do something that simply cannot be ignored. There is a complicated key to his apparently seesaw career. But his up periods always recur when he returns to the stage. It is his spiritual home, and Burton is one of the few actors who can continually and successfully go back to it.

After one long bout of downers he came back to Broadway with his experimental *Hamlet* and stunned the world. He had, of course, already mastered the Shakespeare play in London a decade before. When he was asked to revive it for America, he was worried that there was nothing more he could do with the part. So he decided to have fun with it, even giving it shades of dark humor. He turned it into a personal theatrical exercise in which he tried to find out how far he could stretch the part. He used it like a rubber band. No one could catch up with him.

Most nights when he was onstage Elizabeth would be my guest. We saw *Hamlet* about fifteen times, and I never tired of it. Sometimes I would take Liz to dinner, and we'd catch the last act. Or we'd take in another Broadway show and meet Richard backstage or later at a favorite watering hole. When he was onstage, Richard knew that Elizabeth would be properly looked after when she was with me. I had my own haunts, and I always had bodyguards with me. All my guys are keyed up to moving celebrities around and looking after them without problems.

More than anything else in the play Richard reveled in the very last scene, when he had a sword fight with Laertes. Wherever we were, Liz and I would try to hurry back for the last ten minutes just to catch the line "Give us the foils" because Richard never did it the same way twice. I don't think Richard would ever have seriously competed with Errol Flynn or Stewart Granger as a movie swashbuckler. But he had perfected stage swordplay into something unpredictable and exciting. He really did make Laertes fight. He did the double fight with the sword and dagger, and it was absolutely believable because it was real.

There was nothing ungainly about Richard during that last scene. He moved incredibly well, even though he came offstage in a film of sweat. He made Laertes follow him all over the place. They'd go through the rehearsed routine, but the actor was always wary that Burton would try to pull something on him, and Richard always did. Then Laertes would get all fouled up trying to keep up with him. Richard had him all over the stage, practicing all sorts of improvisations. He went too far one night. He had insisted that the points of the foils should not be blunted— to give the fights that added "edge." That night he got Laertes in such a state of confusion that the foil was going in every direction, and Burton was severely slashed across the arm. Only a few of us knew it was not tomato sauce seeping through his blouse, but Laertes was in a state of panic. Richard let the whole thing calm down, and they finished the fight as rehearsed. At the end Burton staggered offstage, took a long swig from a bottle, and laughed his head off. Laertes came storming off in a rage, but Richard soon calmed him down. We had his arm bandaged, and we all went off to a place in New York called Himself, which was one of Richard Harris's many East Side watering holes. Burton was full of the fight. "I wonder how many people noticed how really close that was," he said.

Richard had become an expert stage swordsman over the years because he understood and had developed the rhythm of a fight. He used his foil the way Buddy Rich plays the drums. He knew exactly what he was doing all the time. Things went wrong only when the guy he was fighting couldn't keep up.

The restaurant was crowded, and Richard was explaining all this in a fairly excited and loud way. He suddenly leaped up and said, "The foils, give us the foils." He then grabbed some of those extra-long breadsticks you get in some restaurants and threw me one. I caught it and decided to go along. I'm a mover, a dancer, and a mimic. I'd watched every decent piece of swordplay on celluloid and I'd studied Burton onstage. I felt confident that despite the unlikely setting, I could keep out of his way. "*En garde*," he yelled as we reached the small dance floor. The waiters looked on apprehensively, and most of the other customers were suddenly speechless. They hadn't expected a floor show.

Before I knew where I was, Burton was all around me, his breadstick jabbing at me from every direction. My reflexes are excellent, and I was able to parry with him for a while. The breadsticks broke every minute or two, and we had to keep grabbing more off the other tables. Elizabeth was in fits of giggles, and we were all a little high. Burton had altogether too many tricks up his sleeve. He was running rings around me.

"Stop anticipating," he yelled breathlessly as his breadstick slashed at my buttons. "Stop trying to guess my next move while dealing with my last . . . ah . . . see . . . got you again . . . try to go on the offensive [slash] . . . thrust at me . . ."

By the time the "fight" was over we had broken every breadstick in the joint, and they lay littered all over the tables and floor. We got a standing ovation from the rest of the customers, and a worried manager waited a little while before he brought out some more breadsticks from the kitchen.

One day I'm going to take fencing lessons and give Richard what the British call a sound drubbing.

By coincidence I was in Rome when the whole Burton-Taylor syndrome started. At the time I was still married to May Britt, and we were visiting Italy, where she had started her career and where she was still extremely popular. She introduced me to an Italy I did not know existed, and we both developed a deep affinity for the place. We had heard the faint rumblings of The Romance from afar, and by the time we got to Rome the whole *Cleopatra* company was sitting on a time bomb.

Eddie Fisher, whom Elizabeth had married when Mike Todd died so tragically, was on the phone day and night, trying to find out what was going on. As the story spread, he was getting a lot of sympathy from their mutual friends, and a few of them were turning against Liz. Sybil Burton, who had been married to Richard for some fifteen years and had shared all the lean times with him, was not making much of a fuss. She always was an extremely civilized woman. But this in itself only increased the vitriol against Elizabeth. The producers of *Cleopatra* were getting nervous. To date it had been about the most lavish and expensive film ever made. The moneymen back home wanted guarantees on their investment. No one needed a big brouhaha. In 1963 the Swinging Sixties were in their early days, and scandals were still scandals. While Liz and Richard were careful not to shove the romance in anyone's face, it was getting more and more difficult for them to hide it.

Many stars have fallen in love while making a movie. It is a constant occupational hazard and occasionally inevitable. When two good-looking, talented, often sexy people with strong personalities are thrown together in the madhouse of a working movie set—and then go through all the minor offstage dramas together—falling in love becomes unavoidable. They relax over lunch one day, the chemicals start working, and sooner or later the sparks ignite. One of the first things a good director has to learn is the warning signs. The next is how to deal with the situation. He must know how to keep the production going during the obvious traumas of a love affair. If he is clever, he can even learn how to exploit all that emotion for the good of the film. The only thing which is new about movie set romances is that these people invariably fall in love while fifty technicians are examining them in every detail. When the reality takes over from fiction, a few dozen people will be intimately aware of it. Laurence Olivier and Vivien Leigh fell in love while making *Fire Over England*. Carole Lombard and Clark Gable lit each other's fires when they starred in their only film together, *No Man of Her Own*. Steve McQueen set his sights on Ali MacGraw while filming *The Getaway*.

Yet while certain aspects of the romance on the set of *Cleopatra* were predictable and typical, it was quickly obvious that this one had a lot more going for it than a simple screen flirtation. Liz and Richard were so deeply in love that when the filming stopped, they hardly noticed the silence. They both seemed almost overawed by what had happened to them. This didn't stop them from laughing a lot. And I think it is this that enabled them to keep on loving each other, through so many traumas, for so long. They were always laughing, normally at their own expense. When they did fight, it was always real dynamite. But it never lasted long, and after they made up, they loved each other harder than ever.

When May and I first arrived in Rome, Burton's name was mud with Twentieth Century-Fox, which saw him compromising their multimillion-dollar investment in Elizabeth. Liz herself was big enough to take everything they could throw at her. Burton had not yet, by any means, established a secure base in the industry, although everyone recognized his great acting ability. In several ways Liz had to protect him. She threw caution to the Roman breeze, ignored all the critics, and defiantly asked what business it was of anyone else. The liaison did not affect their working relationship except in the best possible sense. They sparked each other in a unique way that made both roles more exciting. But a lot of people began to ostracize them both, and only a few of the old buddies were willing to help form an umbrella for the emotional storm. I like to think of myself as one of them.

As the film more or less finished on schedule and the general hubbub subsided into vague rumblings of discontent, the great courting days began. The industry soon accepted the romance for what it was, and now that the film was in the can, the moneymen began to appreciate just how much publicity had been generated. So now Richard and Liz could carry on without worrying about anyone else. Richard was full of excitement and roaring good humor. He was drinking, of course, but magnificently. When they were together, it seemed as if two huge forces had fused into one great, bubbling caldron of activity. Liz is never happier than when she is handling great big beautiful diamonds or when she has just fallen in love again. It brings a new dimension and radiance to her already scintillating personality, and it affects all those around her.

When this overwhelming lady met the animal magnetism of Richard Burton, there was an immediate clash of wills and personalities, but these two very separate characters shared a massive dose of mutual sensuality.

We all split up when May and I came back to Hollywood and Liz went off to make *Reflections in a Golden Eye* with Marlon Brando. Richard went with her, and off the set, the situation became a riot. They were besotted with each other. Richard got along well with John Huston, the director, and this helped the general ambiance.

Only Brando seemed completely unmoved by the chaos around him. His professional relationship with Liz was a strange one. Maybe it was because he was psyched up, playing a homosexual army officer, or maybe he merely found the whole hullabaloo a little disturbing. Liz and Marlon had an immediate and complete professional respect for each other but absolutely nothing to do with each other off the set. While Liz and Montgomery Clift spent long hours discussing their parts and socializing at restaurants and other places, Brando kept completely to himself. They would rehearse and then shoot the scene, then Brando would go back to his trailer and sit there alone. Both Liz and Richard praised Marlon's performance, but neither was able to befriend him.

Richard, like his buddy Peter O'Toole, is a compulsive charmer. In many ways he lives his whole life on a stage. He is a master of the anecdote and will turn his throaty intensity on any lady present, with a total disregard for either her age or her marital status. He is always on the make. He lives for it, almost as a drug. This has nothing to do with actually falling in love, which, when he does, he does to excess. It is because Richard gets a feeling of power from seeing a lady wilt under his charm. When he turns it on, it is something to behold. He is articulate, brilliant, smooth, witty, affectionate, flattering, extremely persuasive, and utterly beguiling.

Richard and Elizabeth went on to make many brilliant movies together, others that were made from wishful thinking, some that were rather mediocre, and a few that were downright bad. But considering the sheer number of films they made, one after another, I think their track record is more than fair. If they had done nothing else but *Who's Afraid of Virginia Woolf?* they would have established themselves in movies as a marital *tour de force*. Their performances had a little of each of us, and Burton was especially brilliant because *Virginia Woolf* was a movie of a stage play, and he is the master of any stage.

Richard's classical background is, of course, superb, but it has led to the belief that he taught Liz Taylor a lot about acting. I think this is absurd. People forget *Cat on a Hot Tin Roof* and a host of other brilliant films she made before she had ever heard of Richard Burton. At first she may well have been a little in awe of his experience on the stage, but there was nothing Burton could teach her on a film set. Richard was always a great actor in a movie, but he was never a great movie actor. There is a big difference. Liz, on the other hand, was very much at home in front of a camera, and there is little doubt in my mind that she was responsible for introducing Richard to new concepts of movie acting.

In *Butterfield 8*, for instance, Taylor gave a performance which was a definitive piece of movie acting. It is true that Liz has always privately maintained that she got the Oscar for the film only because Hollywood people thought she was dying in a London hospital. I suppose this could have tilted the balance in her favor—there may have been some sympathy floating around—but the Academy Awards aren't that simple. If Elizabeth had been basking in radiant good health, her performance in *Butterfield 8* would still have been the strongest of contenders.

In fact, Liz never wanted to make the movie in the first place. She was contracted to make one more film for MGM, and the studio made it plain she would never be released to make *Cleopatra* unless she made *Butterfield 8* first. She finally agreed but told the studio she'd walk through the part. Some walking. In fact, the main problem turned out to be Eddie Fisher, who kept insisting they rewrite the script to give him a bigger part than Laurence Harvey. Every time Eddie turned up with a rewrite the producer, Pandro Berman, threw it in the wastepaper basket. Liz herself remained very well behaved, although she couldn't wait to get the filming over.

Apart from the animal lust she seems to bring out in every man who sees her on the screen, Elizabeth Taylor has brought a unique vision to many of the parts she's played. A good example was in

X, Y and Zee with Susannah York. Susannah had already played a fairly explicit lesbian scene in *The Killing of Sister George*. Robert Aldrich had directed it in a very clinical way, and it was effective. But neither Susannah nor her costar, Coral Browne, recognized the finished film. Despite Aldrich's cool-handed approach, there had been a lot of embarrassment on the set, especially between the actresses, and as a result, the scene never quite worked. So when Susannah was approached to do another lesbian scene, this time with Liz Taylor, she was naturally a little worried and hesitant.

The difference was that Elizabeth, the complete professional, knew how to handle it. She got rid of the clinical approach by popping a crate of champagne and getting everyone high. By the time they were ready to roll they were giggling like hell, and the whole set was relaxed and bubbling with good humor. The booze helped radiate a feeling of warmth which was easily translated into sexuality. The scene worked like a dream, and the number of takes was reduced to a handful.

Both Elizabeth and Richard wanted me to play the part in *The Sandpiper* which eventually went to Charles Bronson; we were all very good buddies in those days. They were enthusiastic about the picture because they thought it reflected parts of their own love story. I signed the contract at the William Morris agency, and we had long conversations about the story and the film. Then the agency told me *Golden Boy* was opening earlier than expected, and since I was committed to it, I had to drop out of the running, to my deep disappointment. Elizabeth was upset and tried to find a way in which I could do it, but MGM wouldn't buy it. So Charlie Bronson got the part.

Years after *Hamlet*, Burton went through another long period of inconsistency, both privately and professionally. Then he went back to the stage for his brilliant interpretation of *Equus*. He is perhaps one of only three actors in the world who could do complete justice to the part. I'd nominate Nicol Williamson as another. And of course, Alec McCowen introduced a marvelous *Equus* on the London stage.

It so happened that my wife, Altovise, and I were in New York again at the time, and it fell to us to look after Elizabeth throughout the rehearsals. Despite the fact that they were by then not completely happy together, Richard was in top form. I nearly lost all my jewelry again, but we were happy to resume escorting Liz around town, and generally we had a ball.

Richard was magnificently successful, and it rubbed off on all of us. The critics raved, and so did everyone else. He beamed; he was full of life and laughter. For those of us who had watched while the industry had flushed him down the toilet and pulled the plug out, those days in New York were full of joy. He was back showing them all just what real acting was all about, as he had done so many times before.

Burton is flamboyant, larger than life, capable of incredible feats of artistic intensity. On the other hand, as with any great artist, when he does have a downer, he tends to sink to unimaginable depths. Richard and I have often discussed this and decided the one thing we had very much in common was our attitude to personal advice. Neither of us could ever take advice even if it was very much in our interests to do so. In effect, we both are stubborn individuals who resent any interference, however well meant. On our periodic journeys into self-destruction, no other person is able to pull us out of it. It has to come from ourselves. When everyone started telling Burton he was drinking too much, his attitude was: To hell with them. Didn't he always learn his lines and turn up on time? At the same time my closest friends began telling me I was destroying myself with drugs. I was stubborn and wholly self-centered and firmly believed I could do it all. The crunch came with Burton and me when we both realized that our performances were suffering. We couldn't have a policy of suicide through overindulgence *and* a professional career. That self-realization counted for more than every piece of advice ever given to either of us.

Our problems were very similar, and we dealt with them in much the same way. I woke up one morning and discovered the house full of people I hardly knew. I was disgusted with myself and with them. People were flocking to the house for a free turn-on. I would go off to do a show, feeling awful, and come back to find them all still there. My performances were mediocre at best, and I was using tricks and gimmicks to get an audience response. People were still buying it, but I knew inside that I was letting myself slip. I was also extremely difficult to live with. That morning, when I woke up in disgust, I simply said to Altovise, "That's it. No more. I don't need this shit."

The first thing we found out was who our real friends were. Nowadays anyone who comes up to the house fully understands that drugs are banned. They can turn on before they get there if they want to. But they can't bring it with them. In recent years I have also moderated my drinking and feel a lot better for it. I have paced my performance now to the point where I don't think I've ever been better. But for a time it was touch and go. As an entertainer you know full well that you can only get away with less than the best for a very short time. Sooner or later people stop coming to see you. If you are a true professional, that message is enough to get you back in line.

With Richard Burton, the stimulus is a little different. For a start, he is a self-confessed alcoholic, and when he goes on the wagon, he needs a great deal of self-control. My drug taking was a passing fad that I didn't really need. Secondly, Richard has an overwhelming need to be praised by his peers, but only when he himself has become dissatisfied with his work does he put himself under strict restraint. It is during these periods that you will see the true genius of Richard Burton. When he is trying to get back in line, he is unsurpassed as an actor. And he does it all himself. The one certain way to make Burton drink too much is to tell him he's drinking too much. Everybody, including Liz, eventually learned that the more they ignored his boozing the more likely he was to check himself.

His constant method of rehabilitation is to return to the stage. When *Equus* was such a resounding success, Richard was tickled pink in a way that is difficult to describe. It was part sheer elation, but there was an undercurrent of "I knew I still had it in me" in his emotions.

Richard has often said that when he was first married to Elizabeth and they got their amazing traveling circus on the road, he was too quickly overexposed. He accepted everything offered, almost without question. In fact, there were not enough suitable vehicles around at the time, and Richard was too easily persuaded to make films that were at best indifferent. "It was very difficult for a working actor who had known many hard times to refuse work," he told me. "I was still hungry as an actor and believed I had no limitations. It just wasn't in my nature to turn down offers, especially as they became so lucrative. But there is no doubt that many of the films I made were mediocre, and my reputation suffered because of it."

Burton will keep working until he dies because he is an actor and he has to. Work is a drug for him. Most actors would have rested on their laurels if they had accomplished a fifth of Burton's brilliant track record, but he will be back to floor us all again. And again. And again. I just want to be there on that day he meets Oscar. The two of them were made for each other.

Chapter 3

Spooks

On the night I saw my first movie we were playing somewhere in downtown Chicago. The Will Mastin Trio did four acts a day, and it was midwinter. As usual, the Chicago winds were howling across the lake. It was an old and eerie theater, very typical of the vaudeville of the period. Between acts Uncle and Dad could rely on three shots of whiskey to keep warm. I just had to keep moving.

I was the most pint-sized, wide-eyed kid you ever saw. I never did grow too much, but in those days my size added to the act because the people thought it was cute. Onstage I danced my feet off, so there was no trouble keeping warm. But between acts I had to hang around the theater, mainly in the dressing room, trying to amuse myself. I guess I was lonely enough sometimes, although, as usual when you try to think back, I can remember only the good times.

I can recall that night as if it were yesterday. It was early evening, and my dad was going out for a couple of hours. Probably for a drink, but he might have found a game someplace. Before he left, he gave me a warning, and I noted a mood of seriousness:

"Now don't you let me catch you going downstairs to see these moving pictures things. You stay right here. They're for grown-ups, you hear me. If I catch you down there, I'll whip your hide."

Papa then gave me a wink and closed the door softly behind him. I sat for a few minutes in a state of some bewilderment. The concept of moving pictures was completely beyond my under-standing. The only actual pictures I'd seen were in cheap comics Dad sometimes bought me. It seemed absurd, yet fascinating to me that pictures like that could "move."

When Papa told me I mustn't go near them, of course it fanned my curiosity. I began to feel a strange compulsion to disobey him. The old man could be awesome when he got angry, and he had a strong right arm. I'd known his wrath more than a few times, and some stinging lessons on my backside had taught me not to pro-voke him if I could help it. But I realized he'd be away for an hour or two, and I knew the theater inside out. I quickly planned a clandestine route down to the stage. I gave him a few minutes to get clear of the building and peeked out the dressing-room door. There were a couple of guys hanging around, but they wouldn't stop me. They had no reason. The fact that I was being bad gave me the old exciting feeling in the belly that only fear can bring.

I slipped down the backstairs, running my hand along the grimy walls, and through the seedy area where the props were kept. I kept in the shadows and dodged into the security of the heavy black curtains on the side of the stage. The film had started, and images were already flickering over a huge sheet temporarily placed right where my family and I had done our act. I was just five years old.

At first I was merely full of curiosity, and I clutched the curtain because I feared discovery. I'd already worked out an escape route back again, just in case, but I snuggled into the folds of the cur-tain, fairly sure I could remain unseen.

Because of what Dad had said, and because I knew it would have to be something special and new, I thought I was ready for anything. But I was not prepared for what did unfold.

There on the screen was a nightmare which kept me riveted to the spot for the next eighty-five minutes. I had chanced upon the original Bela Lugosi *Dracula* for my initiation into movieland, and it held me immediately with so much fear that I could not move. My spine tingled, and the muscles in the back of my neck started making my head shake. My mouth opened even wider than my eyes, and my body shook uncontrollably.

Every shadow and cobweb in that dusty, cold theater seemed to become part of the unfolding drama. Years before CinemaScope came along I knew what it was like to be surrounded, literally, by the screen. As doors creaked on celluloid, wind whistled through the backstage props. The fiendish fangs of that dreadful Count gleamed amid the hanging ropes and dark lights of my hitherto-innocent vaudeville life. I stayed to the end of the film only because I would have fainted if I had moved.

As the lights went up, I quickly scampered upstairs. Dad had not yet returned, but when he did a few minutes later he knew immediately I had disobeyed him. He took one look at his tiny son, cowed, trembling, eyes nearly popping out of his head, and guessed where I had been. I was in such a state of shock that he thought I had been punished enough. He roared with laughter and gave me a little hug. "That'll teach you," he said, and, still snickering, began to change for the next act. Soon after, Uncle Will came in and joined the frivolity. Dad told me he had forbidden me because when he saw the film, he'd been scared to death himself.

I had been on the road with the trio for two years already. That was half a century ago. Since then I've probably spent a third of my waking life watching movies. My father had been completely wrong about one thing. *Dracula* was no punishment. I reveled in the utter fascination of it all. The film had been the greatest single discovery of my youth, a youth filled with a thousand exciting memories.

Dracula played two or three times every day, and I watched all the performances until the end of our run. I soon knew every last action of that immortal spine chiller, and it hasn't stopped fascinating, terrifying, and thrilling me to this day. Now that I have built my own screening room it was among the first films I acquired for my collection, and every now and then I pull it out and run it again. The experience is an exercise in nostalgia, but it still gets the old spine tingling away.

My informal education on the road with Dad and Will was split almost evenly between what I could learn from fellow vaudeville performers and the gems I could pick up on the screen.

Because, from the moment *Dracula* scared the pants off me, no express train could haul me away from the movies. Both asleep and awake I lived all their dreams and dramas. No one can change the history I learned from them, even though it might not be according to the facts. To me Robin Hood and Abe Lincoln were equally important to the development of mankind, for I believed everything I saw on film. I learned all my vocabulary from Clark Gable and Errol Flynn. In all my waking hours, when I was not onstage or eating I was hunting down another film to see.

John Huston was once asked how much truth there was in his westerns. He thought about it for a moment and said that whenever he was given a choice between fact and legend, he always went for the legend. So do I. I can see "real" life all around me, but when that projector starts whirring, I want to sink into that adventurous oblivion only movies can bring. It's the ultimate luxury.

Because of that first experience, I have always remained faithful to Bela Lugosi's famous and definitive interpretation of the Dracula role. The film industry has done a lot since with Bram Stoker's Gothic tale of the Transylvanian vampire, some of it excellent and some of it embarrassingly dreadful. But every minute detail of the original is implanted firmly in my head.

When the time came for me to set out on my own and make it in Europe, I knew I would have to add several dimensions to both my act and my life-style. Europe beckoned like the sirens in *The Odyssey*. But unknown to my advisers, who saw only an expansion of my personal audience and financial market as an entertainer, I had many other motives for crossing the Atlantic. The prime one had been an obsession with me for several years. I had to go see the studios where they made all those Hammer horror productions which, for a decade, had become the natural successors to the Lugosi legend.

I was the ultimate sucker for Hammer Films. They were tailor-made for me, and I had seen every one many times before hitting the tarmac at London Airport. Just about the first thing I did was fix up a visit to the studios. I had been around such places as the MGM lot a few times, and I was expecting something similar. When the car stopped outside the Hammer building, I just didn't believe it. I thought it was the reception area.

Christopher Lee and Peter Cushing ushered me in, and I suddenly realized this actually was it. I found Hammer had done all those films on one and a half stages and had to get out at midnight so that someone else could start shooting at dawn. The entire operation would have fit in an MGM parking lot.

I was enthralled as I saw one of the low-budget blockbusters being made. The whole thing was incredible. Hammer was making millions, but at the studio you would have thought they were producing a low-budget educational film. They would churn out a whole film in days, not only one version for the British market but two other versions for the rest of the world.

I watched as they shot a fairly sedate scene for Britain. The makeup man came along with a little brush and splashed red paint onto Christopher Lee's lapels. Then they shot the American version. The same guy came along and threw paint all over him.

They stopped for a minute, changed clothes, and got ready for the Far East version. This time whole tribes of special effects guys came on with buckets of red paint and sloshed it everywhere. You'd have thought they had shares in the tomato industry the way they used that ketchup.

Later I had lunch with Chris and Peter, and they found my incredulity amusing. I couldn't get over it and finally said, "Well, no wonder you make so many millions. You just don't spend a penny."

Both of them looked at each other and then back at me. "What do you mean, millions?" Chris asked.

"Your last movie made ten million dollars in America alone," I said. "You must be very rich young men."

They looked at each other again, and I could see Chris's upper lip quivering as it does when he smells blood. "Ten million?" he said, and it was his turn to be dumbfounded.

"Sure, what's your cut?"

Both of them started fidgeting, and Peter Cushing said, "I was paid fifty pounds a week, and I'm the established star. What about you, Chris?"

Chris said, "Forty-five pounds, and I thought it was marvelous to be able to pay the rent again."

Their entire vision had been confined to that tiny little island known as England. They had shot three versions, all in the working day, but once they had gone home, they had forgotten about the rest of the world. I was glad to put them right on the facts, although I realized I was upsetting them considerably.

I don't begrudge Hammer Films their "cheap-film" reputation at all. They worked under such idiotic conditions and produced such marvelous films they deserved all they got. Even today the first thing I do when I get to London is call up and get them to send over the latest films, and a few of my old favorites as well. They know I am their number one fan. After a while I got to know everyone at Hammer and started collecting bits of scenery, props, costumes, and even masks and fangs. Often, when they delivered them, the whole cast would turn up direct from the set complete with makeup and costumes. When they arrived at the May Fair Hotel in a fleet of taxis, they used to scare the hell out of everyone. It was always an excuse for an instant party.

Chris Lee became a special friend. Obviously, with my own great personal affinity with Count Dracula, he was one of the first people I wanted to meet when I got to Europe. But our friendship really blossomed when he moved permanently to Hollywood. He and his family are always coming over to our house. They are very special people. After watching every Hammer production a thousand times, I think I know Chris's face better than he does.

My wife, Altovise, is as scared at horror movies as I am, but she never gets the same enjoyment out of this fear. She simply will not sit through a spooky movie. This comes in handy if you want to get rid of your wife for a while, but in reality it means I rarely play horror films at home. One occasion she felt she had to sit down and put up with it was when I showed Chris Lee's second *Dracula* movie, *Dracula, Prince of Darkness*, during one of his many visits. Chris, of course, kept saying things like: "Oh, God, do we really have to put up with this? Is it really necessary?"

As the film started running, I could feel Altovise fidgeting, but the rest of us settled down to enjoy it, and after about fifteen minutes we were completely engrossed, although poor Chris kept muttering and groaning at certain scenes. At the point when the screen Dracula "dies" in the ice, he said, "Thank God it's nearly over." Hammer had run out of ideas for killing Christopher and had spent ages devising the ice-death sequence.

When the lights finally went up, we had forgotten Chris was

in the room; it was quite an experience to find him sitting there. We got over it only when someone poured him a glass of red wine and pretended it was blood.

Chris, of course, has many times pounced at me from dark corners in his full Dracula regalia. At one point he had scared me so successfully so often I decided it was my turn to scare the daylights out of him.

I planned it meticulously. I went to my dentist and asked him to make me the "perfect" set of fangs, ones that were actually molded into my mouth. Cost was no object, and he spent a great deal of time making them absolutely "authentic." I had many dress rehearsals with various friends and probably put as much timing into the act as for any professional engagement. To rile Mr. Lee, the whole thing had to be perfect.

My chance finally came when he visited me in the penthouse at the May Fair Hotel. I got him to the bar and mixed him a Mexican Mary with tequila and lime juice. I said it was a specialty of mine and wanted his opinion. I was so enthusiastic about it that he was eager to taste it.

I made a great play of mixing the drink, so the act would grab his interest. As I handed him the glass, I guessed I would have two seconds to slip my fangs in. Then I put on my most horrendous glare and shoved my face right over the bar close to his just as he looked up, saying, "*Ummmmmm . . . rather nice.*"

It worked like an instant nightmare. Chris flew out of his chair screaming. He turned livid and yelled, "Sammy, don't ever do that to me again. I nearly died."

I have had a few standing ovations in my time, but scaring Dracula right out of his pants was probably my greatest single theatrical achievement.

Chris, who comes from a decent middle-class family full of colonels and bishops, drifted into acting almost by chance when a cousin suggested he try becoming a "Rank Starlet"—a bit player for the J. Arthur Rank organization. He made a living of sorts for ten years before Hammer offered him a part.

He specialized in dying because, years before, Peter Cushing had said to him, "Become a type and do it well. There's always employment for types." So Chris had become a "dying type." There was never anyone who could die the way he could. Whenever a scriptwriter thought up an ingenious way for someone to

die, the studio yelled, "Send for that Lee chap." Dying gave him
a reasonable living, and he eventually caught the eye of Hammer,
which was casting *The Creature*, a remake of the old Frankenstein immortalized by Boris Karloff. At first the critics were cool.
They said, "Young Christopher Lee looks as if he has been in a
road accident."

At one point the Creature got shot in the eye and Chris had
to slap "blood," which he had hidden in his palm, right into his
face. The screaming that followed was for real. Chris later told
me he'd stuck the acrid blood—Hammer people called it Kensington Gore—right in his eye and thought he'd gone blind.

His pay for the film was $1500. The total budget was $200,000.
Chris was glad of the check at the time. So far the film has
grossed $25 million and, in terms of cost versus profit, is the
most successful British film ever made. Christopher Lee had
finally been established as a "type."

Lugosi had originally played Dracula as a melodramatic but
wily scoundrel. The first film version, which I had chanced upon
in the Chicago theater in 1931, established the Count, along
with Superman, Sherlock Holmes, and Tarzan, as one of the
great folk heroes. Dracula has since caught the public imagination
in more than 200 films in ten countries, and the original novel
has never been out of print.

In 1943 Lon Chaney invented a tough, fleshy Count Dracula,
and Boris Karloff introduced John Carradine as the most gentlemanly and debonair of counts in *The House of Frankenstein*.

But it was Chris Lee who brought the story back as a vogue
when Hammer started making Dracula movies in 1957. His
gentlemanly, yet evil and chaotic, sadoerotic character, who managed to be elegant and deadly at the same time, gave the Count
a new breath of life. Chris always used to tell me, "Dracula had
something for everyone. But what gave him his real potency was
that no one could entirely discount the vampire belief."

None of the people in horror movies liked the word "horror."
Lon Chaney, Boris Karloff, Vincent Price, and Christopher Lee
all preferred to call it the Theater of the Fantastic.

One of the reasons Hammer was so successful in this kind of
film was that it had a brilliant special effects man called Les
Bowie. He was the real Dr. Frankenstein because he would create
incredible monsters in ridiculously primitive conditions for next

to nothing. Dozens of eerie scenes of castles and misty forests were, in fact, only Bowie's mat paintings. His genius dumbfounds any casual visitor from Hollywood. In *One Million Years B.C.*, for instance, he created the world in six days and nearly got fired for going $200 over the $2,000 budget. The whole thing was crazy. He used oatmeal for lava and an ordinary water faucet to represent a vast prehistoric deluge. Bowie even parted the Red Sea for just $150, using every trick in the book to save money.

Bowie was also around when Boris Karloff was riding high in the monster genre. Boris, one of the greatest, finally decided there was nothing more he could get out of the part, or add to it, so he just gave up. In many ways good monster movies were never the same without him. In those days, if you got no satisfaction out of the job, there was very little reason for continuing. Being a monster of any consequence was the most arduous part in the business. When Fredric March, for instance, made the original *Jekyll and Hyde*, the studios had none of the makeup techniques of today. His mouth was puffed out with padding, and his false teeth were clamped onto his gums. The makeup people stretched his eyes and stuffed unimaginable things up his nose. Sometimes they pushed acrid putty up there which burned and made his eyes water. Suffering horribly like this, Fred played one of his most incredible roles, managing to make the definitive Jekyll *and* the definitive Hyde.

Anyone in the horror-monster business had to get used to being dreadfully abused by the makeup and special effects men. Vincent Price was another who was no stranger to having his face caked and stuffed. We all automatically think of him in the chiller role because he did it so well, but in fact, only a fifth of Vincent's 100 films since 1938 have been horror movies. He coined the characters of the wicked, aristocratic cheat and the deceiving, often demented psychopathic killer. Yet audiences enjoyed a certain sympathy for him because he managed to combine a commanding physique with a mild, suave manner. It is the touch of sophistication, laced with sharp, even dark humor, in all his characters which has established him firmly in the public mind.

He is, in private life, one of the most civilized men in the world, with a cultural side to his personality that most fans don't see. He has a fascinating knowledge of a whole range of things, including food and wines. He is an excellent raconteur and a gifted writer, and his knowledge of art borders on genius. When he discovered I had not read his brilliant book, *I Know What I Like*, he kindly sent me a copy. He didn't know I had set up a red alert all over the town we were playing to try to find one. In fact, my search was so successful that I ended up with six.

Vincent came into his own in Hollywood when the American equivalent of Hammer, American International, began specializing in Edgar Allan Poe stories. Until then AIP had only done cheaply made, and often dreadful, monster films. Poe handed the studio a gold mine and quickly established Vincent as a household name. Horrible chillers and thrillers found a fantastic medium in celluloid. Clever directors devised all sorts of tricks and gimmicks to exploit a torrid tale. Visually movies could often outdo the original stories, frightening people in a grossly entertaining way. They were fun, but it was easy not to take them too seriously because they belonged to the world of fantasy. Nightmares perhaps, but as with dreams, people woke up from the spell as they left the movie house.

Alfred Hitchcock, on the other hand, used many of the same tricks to create dramatic fear and tension from real-life situations. When audiences left a Hitchcock movie, they would often translate those fears to the dark shadows cast across the streets where they lived. *North by Northwest* displayed several typical examples of his brilliant ingenuity. When the villains are tracking down Cary Grant, they chase him into an auction room. Grant gets out of a seemingly hopeless situation by bidding ridiculously and being thrown out by the police, who then protect him. Later the script calls for Cary to meet his killers. The cliché would have been a dark doorway with a single lamp, a cat mewing, and a lot of shadows. Hitchcock said, "I want bright daylight in the open country."

The audience is always given all the information in a Hitchcock film. Hitchcock lets you know all the answers; that adds to the suspense. In *North by Northwest* the audience knew Cary was in a spot, but no one could imagine where the trouble would come from.

A car rumbles up and a man gets out. He stands there for a moment and says, "That's funny."

"What is?"

"There's a crop-duster over there dusting a place where there are no crops."

We all knew suddenly where the trouble was coming from. That's the kind of moviemaking which adds up to genius, and Hitch has done it often. I can't remember the times I've had to keep the lights on and the radio playing all night because I'd just seen a Hitchcock movie.

Hitch is one of those directors who like to have every last detail on paper before they start shooting. He invented the whole windmill scene in *Foreign Correspondent*, for example, while sitting in a small office in Los Angeles. Hitch asked himself, "What have the Dutch got that we can use dramatically?" Color was not used freely in those days and he didn't think tulips were dramatic enough. So he came up with windmills and sat down and wrote in the whole sequence.

Hitchcock is also the world's greatest artist with double exposures and back projection. *The Birds* used lots of trick photography of one sort or another. In *Lifeboat* only one shot was taken outside the boat. The rest was all back projection. Hitchcock always maintained he could make a film about a man in a telephone booth. In *Rear Window* he almost achieved this, using the camera to pick up every detail.

Hitch was always having rows with David Selznick about what spies should be chasing. In fact, when, two years before the atom bomb, Hitchcock said they should be chasing uranium in *Notorious*, Selznick lost his cool and sold the whole package to RKO for $800,000 and half the profits. "What Selznick failed to realize," said Hitch, "is that *Notorious* was not about uranium at all. It was a love story. The public are never interested in what the spies are chasing. It could be anything. It is the people who are of real importance."

The film was probably the best Ingrid Bergman ever did for Hitch. Better even than *Spellbound*, for which she did her homework in a mental home. *Notorious* was her final film with Selznick and her last successful film for a decade.

Within Ben Hecht's incredible script framework the chemistry between Cary Grant and Ingrid really ignited and generated a whole sense of erotic tension. This hadn't happened since *Casablanca*, arguably the only finer film she ever made. *Notorious* had so many of those magic moments. The close-up, for instance, of Bergman's hands nervously clasping and unclasping the key to the all-important wine cellar; "the longest kiss in history," in which the two stars move into several different situations still kissing; superb, masterly cinema. As a real-life sidelight to all this on-screen tension, Hitchcock's amiable inquiries into exactly what plutonium really was, and his excellent grasp of the facts, led to a full, clandestine FBI investigation.

My own favorite Hitchcock movie is *Rope*, which, considering the all-time classics he made, is thought a strange choice by some people. But the film has all the ingredients for me. One of the first Hitchcock color films, made in 1948, with an all-star cast headed by James Stewart, the plot follows two college boys who unemotionally kill a boy for fun and delight in confusing the police. It was brilliantly constructed. The whole New York background was a model and took up more space than the set itself because the crew had to shoot it from every angle. They had clouds of spun glass floating around all the time. They numbered all the clouds on the back and just hung them around, changing the position on every reel. When they came to dub Farley Granger playing the piano, they found he had no idea how the instrument should be played and his hands were straying everywhere. After the film was in the can, they had to get one of the music guys at Warner's to study Farley's fingers and rewrite the music to fit the action.

I remember when Hitchcock's *Psycho* first came out, we were playing just outside Boston. We all went to the movies in the afternoon and the film had us spooked for the rest of the day. Even after the show, when we went to a show business hangout called the Waldorf, we were still dodging the shadows. Murphy Bennett, who was then my road manager, couldn't stop talking about the movie. Michael Silver, our drummer at that time, kept giggling at his fears. I didn't let on exactly how scared I had been myself. But I had done the show with my heart in my mouth.

When we got back to the hotel, we separated, and I didn't get to my room for a while. When I did, I immediately went into the bathroom, and I knew Michael Silver was hiding in there. He wore a very distinctive after-shave lotion, and the smell was so strong I could actually trace him to the shower. Even though I knew it was him, a shiver went down my spine. It is an accolade to Hitch's greatness that to this day I can't go into a bathroom without pulling the shower curtains back.

Showing an unnatural calmness, I turned on the tap and left the water running. I crept up to the curtain, and I was mad, with both fear and anger. I turned my glass eyeball around and put on my most menacing gaze. Then in one quick movement I pulled the curtain back and screamed a terrific roar. Michael was crouching down. He shot up in the air and jumped about three feet. His arms went up, and I thought his eyeballs would pop out. I cannot repeat the torrent of bad language which accompanied this in case any lady or child might pick up this book believing it worthy of family reading. But amid pants and groans he went through just about every Anglo-Saxon swearword ever invented. Plus a few more on top.

I gave him a large brandy to calm his nerves and had a few myself for the same reason. Even so, I slept with the light on and locked the doors.

After beating him at his own game, I thought I had heard the last of it, but Silver wanted to get even. The very next night, as I was coming out of the elevator, he was hiding on the side of my blind eye, and I thought I was alone in the corridor. A voice said, "Room for one more, guvnor?" It was Silver's turn to see me jump to almost my own height.

"OK, Michael," I screamed. "You got me that time. But this is war. I am going to scare you absolutely shitless. I mean it, Michael. From now on you ain't going to know where I am. But you're sure going to find out. This is it, Michael Silver. You'd better sew yourself into that skin because I'm gonna make you jump right out of it."

Michael started pleading: "No, no, no, Mr. D., don't do that. I didn't mean it, Sammy. Don't do it to me."

But I was angry. I told him, "You shouldn't play this *Psycho* game with me because I'm better at it than you. You've got a lesson to learn around here."

For days he went around turning on lights, locking doors, walking with other people, giving a wide berth to corners, going to bed early, and constantly looking over his shoulder. The rest of the gang thought this was a great laugh and reported his antics back to me. But I had patience. I was going to wait for this one, and I let it go for a full week. I treated him normally, and we went about the daily routine of putting on a show. He began to relax, as I knew he would eventually. I wanted to set this one up perfectly. I sent for the mummy's mask from the old Hammer productions which the guys had given me a year or so before. I smuggled it into the house while Silver was eating. Then I bided my time.

I spent an hour getting my act together. I pushed a pillow up the back of my shirt, arranged so that I looked a genuine hunchback. I had the mask fitted perfectly and the lighting in the hall fixed so that it would give the best effect. Then I went into action.

I had chosen this moment because I knew he had a chick in the room and he would be at his most vulnerable and defenseless. You don't go out to scare the hell out of someone who is expecting it. This was war, and he was going to lose his skin.

We all crept up to the room, and I got Murphy to stand on one side with me behind him. A few others were hiding down the corridor. Murphy knocked.

"Who is it?"

"Murphy."

"I'm busy right now, Murph. I got a lady in here."

"I gotta talk to you right now. It's important."

Silence. A little rustling. We knew he was getting into his robe.

"OK. Wait a minute."

He opened the door, and Murphy said, "I got to talk to you about tomorrow."

"I can't talk to you now. I got a robe on, and besides, my gal's getting cold."

Murphy was moving just a little away from the door so that Silver had nearly come into the corridor. As Murphy turned and moved off, with Silver's eyes right on him, I pounced.

It was one of those Superman leaps from nowhere right in front of him. The man became demented immediately. He went up against the wall, and he had real terror in his eyes. Then he backed into the room, still swearing profusely, and actually peed.

There were no hard feelings. Michael knew he had it coming to him. But he never did try one on me again. We called a truce and shook hands on the deal. Neither of us wanted to go around for the rest of our lives waiting for the next heart attack to come bursting out of the shadows.

I don't even like nice surprises. It's a golden rule with anyone who knows me that nothing should be sprung on me. I like to be prepared for all eventualities. Surprise eliminates preparation. Second—and I admit it freely—from the moment I saw that first *Dracula* I have been spooked. This made every horror and monster film, every Hitchcock, every murder mystery, every spooky movie, and every frightening drama, from the original *Jekyll and Hyde* through *Rosemary's Baby* to *Death on the Nile*, very special for me. I live it every time for what it is. It *scares* me, and I love it. But I don't translate that fear out of the magic of the movies into my everyday life. There're enough scaring things to cope with without personal theatrics. I get frightened at all sorts of things without anyone's bothering to set them up. Altovise is the same. We can cope when we know what's going on. We don't mind when it's on celluloid, but there are too many people out there ready to get you without anyone making a game of it.

Altovise knows that when she's in the house, she has to make a noise as she's walking around, just so I know it's her. A couple of years ago I went into the bedroom and called her and wandered around, wondering where she was. Someone must have told her I was calling because she came looking.

By then I had examined most of the annex where we sleep, and the lights were down. Because I lost my eye in a car accident, I have only part vision, and we have very soft carpets in that area. When I suddenly did a half turn and she was there, it sent an immediate shiver down my spine. She had inadvertently crept up on me. She knows better now because I hit the roof. I was genuinely in a state of immediate and blind panic.

Altovise gets scared even faster than I do. All I have to do when she is in bed is drag my feet along our wooden floor. I make one step and drag the other foot up to it. That's all it takes to make her quake with fear. I come along the corridor, and she says, "Davis. I know that's you. Stop it, Sammy. I know who it is. Sammy, don't do it to me."

She knows it's me, but she's never quite sure. So we get: "Mr. Davis, if you don't show yourself, I'm going to cry."

And I know she means it. So I show myself, and we cuddle up, and that's one of the few times neither of us is scared of anything.

Chapter 4

Sportin' Life

Back in the late fifties I was convinced the Will Mastin Trio had exhausted what it could achieve as a black song-and-dance act, and I knew that sooner or later I had to get into the movie game. I was, and always wanted to be, an all-around entertainer, and as a movie buff, I just had to face the cameras myself. So I began seriously casting around for the right vehicle.

I found it eventually in *Anna Lucasta,* and I'm extremely proud of that film. It launched a particularly productive decade of my life, in which I eventually made nine movies. It had a lot of things going for it and at a very exciting time in movie history. The old studio system was breaking up fast, and all the established filmmakers were setting out for Europe to spend what was left of the studio money. Over the years American movies had made millions over there, but the studios couldn't transfer the cash back home because of local currency restrictions.

The great exodus soon became a tidal wave. Pundits predicted the end of Hollywood. But there had been a lot of very gifted guys hanging around for some time. At last they had a chance to jump into the void left by the film establishment. They started off as independents, and soon a new wave of creative talent began to show itself. When *Anna Lucasta* came, I was sitting happily on its fringes.

The movie was based on the Philip Yordan play and was directed by Arnold Laven. Eartha Kitt and Frederick O'Neal starred with me. It tells the story of a promiscuous Eartha leaving home when her boyfriend finds out about her love life. It never got the rave reviews we all yearned for, but it was by no means badly received, and the film went on to make a lot of money over the years. It had a very small budget from a pilot company, so we all were rather pleased with it.

For me, the whole thing was a new adventure. We leased Goldwyn's studios, and there was a great pioneering atmosphere on the set. If the film had taken off, we all planned to go into independent production. Maybe, with hindsight, this was a little ambitious, but that was the feeling of optimism at the time.

It took me a couple of very nervous days to settle down on the set. I tried hard to get on with the crew, and they returned this by being especially kind to me. This was my debut, and I was having to learn new techniques very quickly and work with experienced movie actors. They indulged me in the kindest possible way, and I like to think I lived up to everyone's expectations.

I was a rapt student, learning everything I possibly could. I had seen many hundreds of pictures being made and picked up all the tips available. Now I could put them to practical use. It seemed to work in *Anna Lucasta,* and this gave me a great deal of self-confidence. So, when I knew they were looking around for a guy to play Sportin' Life in *Porgy and Bess,* I pulled out every stop to land the part.

I don't mind admitting I got all the pals I could muster—Sinatra, Jack Benny, George Burns, and guys like that—to root for me with Goldwyn. I nagged the William Morris agency to make it a top priority. I think Goldwyn must have finally got sick of the sound of my name because he appeared at the door of my dressing room at the Moulin Rouge nightclub one night and said, "Mr. Davis, you are Sportin' Life. The part is yours. Now will you get all these guys off my back?"

I learned later that Goldwyn had watched *Anna Lucasta* and then gone directly to the Moulin Rouge. He had not been to a nightclub for five years. Luckily he had been suitably impressed.

The William Morris boys had hastily to rearrange my schedule for several months. This was going to be the Really Big One. Everyone but Will and Papa, who couldn't understand my desires, had been waiting for it, and I wanted everything to be perfect.

I know they've said a lot about Otto Preminger's being a son of a bitch to work for. At one time you could rarely pick up a movie paper without hearing some actor or actress moaning about the dreadful life they had under Otto. Maybe he can be a tyrant, but I never once saw that side of him. Sure, he was a perfectionist, and he would never tolerate anything but the best performance. He used to say, "You are paid a very great deal of money to act. Now please get on with it."

We all gave the film everything we had in us, and I think he appreciated that. My own relationship with him couldn't have been more pleasurable. When everything settled down to its day-to-day routine, he and I started developing a repartee which kept the whole set giggling for days. When the cameras were whirring, I would give my very best, but between takes I played the comedian. It made the set a very happy place to work. I found I was the only one who could talk back to him, and he let me get away with murder.

We also socialized off the set. He seemed to be attracted to the kind of life I had carved out for myself. I always made sure I was in the center of the action. Almost every day we lunched together, and we'd hit the nightclubs most nights. All he ever wanted to talk about was broads. He never tired of the subject. As I could always muster up half a dozen good-looking ladies with a couple of phone calls, I soon found I couldn't get rid of Otto even if I'd wanted to.

I was having a very deep and emotional affair with Kim Novak at the time, and when I was not available for some reason, he would sneak off to lunch with her. Sometimes he would look after her over dinner. Then he'd say to me the next morning, "You're going to get into a lot of trouble with this girl."

I used to dismiss him with: "You sound like you're still doing those Nazi parts."

He was right, of course, but I didn't ever listen to that kind of advice.

Most nights we would go out with a bunch of broads until the early hours. In those days I could take it, almost forever. But Otto soon began to wilt. We'd both have hangovers in the morning, and he always blamed me. He pretended he was going to give me a hard time.

"Mr. Davis," he would bark, "why aren't you in costume already? What's the matter, can't you keep up with an old dog like me?"

"I'm not in this scene, Mr. Preminger," I would answer. "Look at your schedule."

"If you are not in this scene, Mr. Davis, what are you doing hanging around my set?"

"Because, Mr. Preminger, I like to see a genuine Nazi at work."

"Well," he rejoined, "that seems like a pretty dumb reason."

And so it went on.

In fact, when we were filming, Otto left me almost completely alone. If I wanted to do something my way, I checked with him. But he never gave me the thumbs-down on an idea. That whole cameo when I did the walk and struck a match on the wall was a Davis invention which Otto approved of. I tried to turn it almost into a pantomine.

I was so naïve in those days I had no idea that the "happy dust" Sportin' Life was using all the time was actually cocaine. I used to ask people, "What the hell is this happy dust I'm selling?" I thought it was some magic potion. Everyone, including Otto, would tell me everything but the truth. There comes a time in the film when I offer some to Bess. I tempt her and tempt her until she finally succumbs. When she takes it, she shows her back, and her turn-on is left to the imagination. I had no idea how to open the packet and how to deal with it. They all had to demonstrate.

It was only years later, when the whole of Hollywood was turning on to "coke," that I fully knew what Bess was doing. The laugh was on me. After all these years I suddenly realized this folk opera for family audiences was actually into pushing drugs. I can imagine Otto, with the Germanic giggle of his, still laughing his head off at that one.

Nowadays, of course, you wouldn't miss it. You go to almost any Hollywood party, and there's a little booze left on the side for the alcoholics. Nearly everyone else is standing around the table, dishing into two big bowls. One carries the caviar, the other, the cocaine. But in the *Porgy* days, I had absolutely no idea what the "white dust" was.

Sportin' Life was the epitome of evil, and that made the part a great challenge. People had to hate him, yet he had to be a little lovable as well. He was the rogue, the man you booed in burlesque, the lighthearted wickedness seeping out of him. "Evil is as evil does" in every sense of the phrase. He was the ultimate opportunist and the cat who rolled with all the punches. So although he was bad, really bad, a lot of people could identify with him. The attitude was that a pimp can't operate unless a guy wants some pussy. He could not have existed unless there were evil all around him. He wove in and out of all the corruption. If you want to get deep into it, he was the devil. The devil doesn't have a job to do if everything is pure. He was temptation, continually stirring it all up and walking away from it leaving behind his evil. We all should hate and fear the devil, but that doesn't stop us from being tempted. In this way the devil is something we live with and can sometimes even find attractive. Sportin' Life never put a razor on anyone. That wasn't his brand of evil. He had it all figured out. And I never tried to hide his badness.

I worked it so that I never simply walked on or off the set. I would leap on or suddenly appear from nowhere, giving that shazzam quality of the appearance of sudden evil. And I got off the set like a whiff of smoke. Puff . . . gone, leaving only the mists of evil. Sportin' Life was the great survivor because people felt a strange attraction for him. While Crown was heavy and bad and could consequently get killed without anyone's batting an eyelid, Sportin' Life was allowed to survive.

It was the fifties, and I was full of piss and vinegar, and I think that helped to make it work. Also, I had a lot of advice from Robert Breen, who had produced the stage play. When I approached him, he was kind enough to explain every nuance of the role. I knew exactly how I wanted to play it long before the cameras rolled.

Originally Breen was to be the movie director, but for various reasons it didn't work out. He had produced the play in Europe to sellout audiences and even taken it to Russia. *Life* magazine had featured him on its cover. I don't know why he was taken off the picture, but I do know that he was big enough to feel no resentment. He spent hours with me, day after day, giving me a brilliant conception of the whole thing, not just how Sportin' Life should behave but his whole relationship with the other players. It was invaluable. If my Sportin' Life was the definitive version, I owe Bob Breen a lot of thanks.

However, within the framework of his guidance, I like to think I accomplished much innovative material myself. I introduced the long brown cigarette, which became a symbol of the part. I invented a special walk and many other little touches which seemed to fit the role perfectly.

I knew the part was working for me after only two weeks' shooting. All the rushes were put together, and we looked at them for the first time. André Previn, who was musical director, whispered to me, "You're going to steal this picture." It was a statement which I didn't really believe until the critics agreed with him.

Preminger got me to one side after the showing and said, "You are very *gut*, Mr. Davis." Otto never said words like "great"; being "very *gut*" was part of the job. The rushes told me that at least I was doing the part right. Because I had only a very few lines, I was pleased that Sportin' Life was emerging as a major character in the movie. It took only a couple of takes to finish "It Ain't Necessarily So," which was a record for the film. Otto more or less left me alone.

I naturally met Samuel Goldwyn several times while making *Porgy*. He invited me to his house for an excellent dinner. He was a marvelous old man who had forgotten more about motion pictures than most people would learn in a lifetime. He loved films and he loved great artists. He adored the Leslie Howards and the Oliviers of this world. And they responded to him. They would work for him when they turned down everyone else. He respected them for it. He made it simple for himself, of course, by buying up the best of everything: the best actors, directors, cameramen, and writers—the cream. He got very upset by certain aspects of *Porgy*. He had a vision of the film which he didn't think Otto Preminger was holding to. There was always a clash of opinions—not personality clashes, professional ones. I think he knew that *Porgy* would be one of the very last things he would ever do, and he wanted it right for him.

Preminger and Goldwyn were such giants in their way that it was difficult for one of them to put the other down. Preminger tried several times. He made it clear he didn't have much respect for Goldwyn, and it occasionally got a bit embarrassing. After Goldwyn had seen a set of rushes, he told Otto, "They are beautifully photographed."

Otto said, "Why don't you tell Shamroy, the photographer?"

Goldwyn came back as quick as a flash, right in front of Leon Shamroy, "Why should I tell him? I pay him enough!" It was a very typical Goldwynism.

Goldwyn was always asking Otto questions to test the director's knowledge of filming. Otto used to get frustrated because he thought Goldwyn didn't know the answers himself and felt he shouldn't be producing films at all.

There were many stories floating around the set which had probably been started by Otto. Billy Wilder had told him before the shooting started, "Look out for you. This is Goldwyn's last film; you don't want to make it yours as well." Later we were all out on location when Goldwyn called and told Otto some shots done the previous day didn't match. Preminger rushed back to the studio and found they matched perfectly. Goldwyn was again trying to find out whether Otto knew his business.

Once Preminger went up to Goldwyn's house and commented on a beautiful Picasso over the fireplace. According to Otto, Goldwyn quickly said, "It belongs to my wife."

Preminger said later, "He was afraid he might have to give it to me."

But I think the thing which rankled most was that when Preminger had been engaged to make the film, his brother had been acting as his agent, and when Goldwyn offered the director a profit participation of 10 percent, the brother turned it down as too small. Preminger had said, "Tell Mr. Goldwyn that when the picture is finished, we will leave it to him."

Otto reasoned that he would get at least the original 10 percent but hoped Goldwyn would be so impressed he would increase the figure. When the film was finished and was being acclaimed everywhere, Goldwyn was asked about the profit participation.

"What profit participation?" he exclaimed. "He left it to me? Then no profit participation."

He was proving, if it ever needed to be proved, his own great adage: "Verbal contracts aren't worth the paper they are written on."

Personally I got on with Goldwyn extremely well, and one reason I value the film is that I came into close contact with him. He was a slender, dapper man who never carried anything—not even money—because it might ruin the line of his suit. He may have been a tyrannical movie mogul who upset many people, but I found him a shrewd, extremely able man with a lot of nerve and an acutely brilliant mind. He told me I had carte blanche to come up to the office anytime I wanted if I needed something or if there was a problem on the set. Very few people had the open door to Goldwyn's office in those days. Most of them had to go through his deputy. But he knew the only reason I would ever want to see him was to avoid problems, not to make them, and told his secretary to let me in without question whenever I turned up.

I didn't go up there very often, but sometimes there were hot personality clashes on the set, and I knew Goldwyn was the only person big enough to cool them down. The picture was loaded with strong stars who wanted things done their way. Pearl Bailey was very outgoing, like me. Sidney Poitier was all inside himself, bottling up most of his emotions. He got very much into the part. Dorothy Dandridge was simply out on another plane somewhere, and none of us knew where she was heading.

She was beautiful, and she was a brilliant Bess, but sometimes it seemed as if she weren't there. I remember one day Dorothy walked off the set in a big huff. The photographer, Leon Shamroy, had cursed like a trooper about us all, and it upset Dorothy to the point where she couldn't go on working. Leon was, in fact, as temperamental as anyone in the acting profession, and he wasn't talking only about Dorothy. He started hitting out at everyone. Dorothy took it personally, went into her dressing room, and cried. She was really hurt. I went in to talk to her, but she refused to come back onto the set.

She wanted Shamroy to apologize and promise not to scream abuse anymore. The whole production stopped because Shamroy refused to say a word. Goldwyn eventually heard about it, as he always did, and called me in to see him.

"What does the girl want from me?" he said, with that accent which he always exaggerated. "Shamroy talks like that all the time. But he photographs beautifully. You want me to lose him?"

I said Dorothy was like Loretta Young and Merle Oberon. She was sensitive and hurt easily. She didn't have a broad back like the rest of us.

He said, "You know, whatever I say, he will never apologize."

I said, "Well, Mr. Goldwyn, you may have to close the picture down."

He looked as if he were on the point of tears and said, "I simply don't understand actresses. Why do they do this to me?"

This went on for about twenty minutes. Then he said I should send up the art director, Serge Krizman. I don't know what plot they hatched together, but it took all day to sort out. We all were eventually sent home.

When we had the set call the next day, there were about a hundred people around, and Shamroy was getting ready as usual. You could have cut the atmosphere in half. But he suddenly turned around and addressed everyone, saying, "Listen, you guys. Yesterday I went crazy. I thought I was making a marine picture. If all the ladies will forgive me . . . and the fellas have heard it all before, so I'm not going to apologize to them. But for the ladies, maybe I went too far. . . . OK, shall we go back to work, everybody?"

A great sense of relief swept over the set as we all got moving again.

Goldwyn must have gone to Cleveland and back, via San Francisco and New York, to get that set moving again, but somewhere along the line it had worked. Shamroy didn't lose face, and he managed to keep his temper throughout the rest of the picture.

In retrospect you realize that these things were no real problem. They happen every day on every film set. Goldwyn must have seen them a million times. But to me, at the time, they seemed both dramatic and traumatic.

Most of the time we had a ball with that picture. Pearl and I got along beautifully. Sidney and I cemented an acquaintanceship into a strong friendship which has lasted to this day. I was living the life-style which I can afford now. The only trouble was that, then, I couldn't. I lived it up way past my means, and no one, including myself, knew where it was coming from. I always had the booze going and the records and girls in my dressing room, so

Van Johnson and Bogey.

Frank Sinatra and Betty Bacall visit my dressing room and Frank shows
me how to do an impression of Edward G. Robinson.

With Elizabeth Taylor and Richard Burton.

Liz Taylor, Liza Minnelli, and Altovise at the premiere of *That's Enter-tainment*.

Visiting Elvis on the set of *Loving You*.

Frank Sinatra and Nat King Cole.

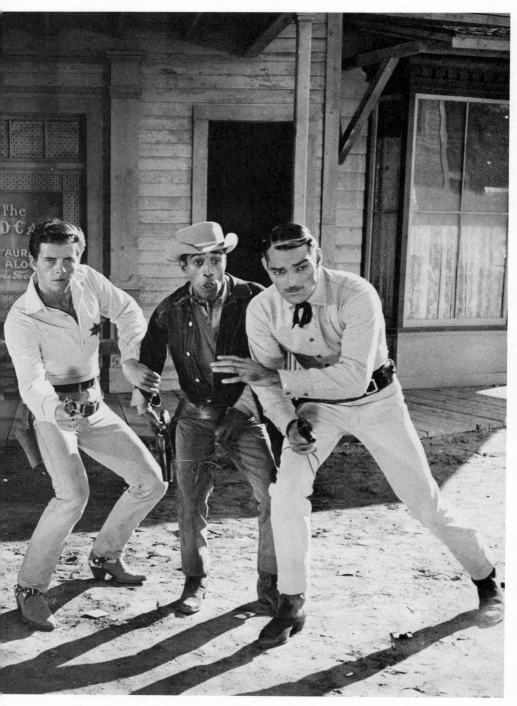

On the set of *Lawman* at Warner Brothers, *left to right*: Peter Brown, myself, and John Russell.

With Dan Rowan on *Laugh In*.

Frank Sinatra, Dean Martin, and me.

With Frank at a SHARE benefit immediately prior to his first "retire-ment."

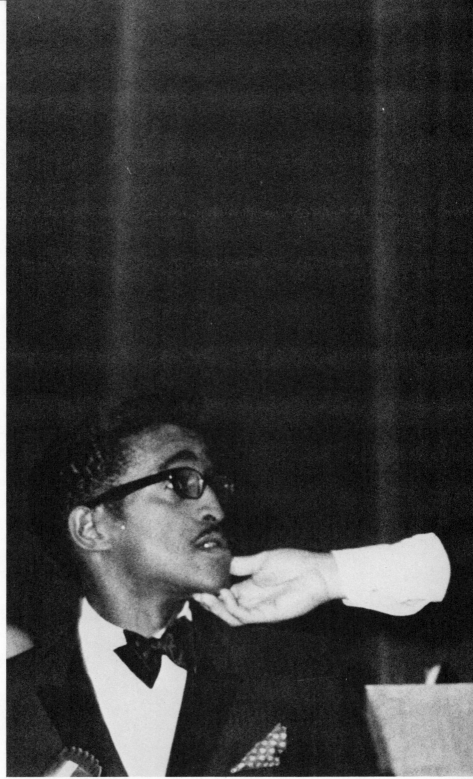
Being serenaded by Frank.

I had nothing to do in this scene, but Frank insisted I be there to "add a little color."

it became a sort of Mecca for the whole set when they wanted to relax and enjoy themselves.

I was very happy at how things were working out, and everyone was being kind to me. I think it is ultra-important for any all-around entertainer to have one really good classic film part behind him. If you can do it several times, like Sinatra, well, that's beautiful. But my finest piece of movie acting was Sportin' Life, and if I make nothing else, I'll let that stand on my record without a shadow of regret.

The reaction to the picture was very good for me. Critics were even kind enough to say things like Sammy Davis "steals" the picture. I hoped it would be the same in Europe. I couldn't do the normal publicity tour because I was working, but when I finally got over there, they wanted only Sportin' Life from me. It was as if I had done nothing else. I had to rearrange my show to include all the numbers from *Porgy*. I still have to. It seems that if you once do something really special and people pick it up, they will remember you for it for the rest of your life.

When we had finished shooting, there was a big fuss over my billing. Goldwyn thought I had a good chance of getting an Academy Award nomination. The William Morris agency had insisted, when I got the part, on the studio's giving me star billing, and at first I had been enthusiastic about that. But when it came to the crunch, we knew I would never get the nomination for Best Actor because I was by no means the leading player, so Goldwyn wanted to downgrade me to "supporting" actor because he felt that the nomination would be in the can. He was eager because Sportin' Life had got the only significant world reviews. They had raved about the part in both America and Europe. In the end it was the lawyers who decided. They said we couldn't start changing the billing after the film had been released. So the only possibility I ever had of meeting Oscar was plucked away.

It was the first of a handful of great disappointments in my life. The second was when it was seriously suggested that Elvis Presley and I should play the leads in *The Defiant Ones*, later cast with Sidney Poitier and Tony Curtis. Both Elvis and I were anxious to do the picture. But Elvis's manager, Colonel Tom Parker, thought it was "controversial" as a vehicle for his "boy" and turned it down. We both put up a terrific fight, but by the time everything got settled we had gone on to other things. It was a shame because both of us would have been wonderful in the parts, and we all would have recognized at last Elvis's burning ambition and ability to act his butt off.

Presley was always an enigma. He had a great talent as a screen personality, and a couple of the things he did, like *King Creole* and *Kid Galahad,* showed genuine promise. But they put him in that million-dollar-a-picture mold for the teenyboppers, and Colonel Tom wouldn't let him change. I know that Presley got fed up with it. After twenty or so pictures he refused to make another one. "I've done it all already. I can't go on making the same film over and over again," he told me.

Presley had serious but gradual ambitions to become a "real" actor. He became extremely frustrated when no one would let him. A year or so before he died we regularly sat all night together in Vegas, and he'd pour out his heart about how he wanted to do a film without a single song. He was a great movie buff, and we'd sit from midnight to dawn, showing old movies. His own library was equal to my own, and he had a wonderful ability for impersonation. His Bogey was better than mine.

Elvis had exactly the same problem as Jerry Lewis. He'd created an artistic niche, and people were buying it. Everyone implored him not to change it while the money was rolling in. With both of them, the artistic urges began to take over, and they were desperate for change. They wanted the public to know they could do something else. Remaining the teenage idol when Presley was forty didn't work. Yet when he tried to change it, he upset his loyal fans. Presley had to continue being the plump, middle-aged, wrinkled teenager, and Jerry had to continue being the nut.

Presley was philosophical about his artistic frustration. "How can I moan when I'm still making ten million dollars a year?" he said in Vegas. "I'm still packing places. I've got no right to bitch." He couldn't fight it and go out and do two shows a night.

I don't trust the spate of books that came out after Presley's death. They showed him as a morose man, bedeviled with fears and doubts. That was certainly not the Presley I knew. He had a great sense of humor, and he was always full of fun. I guess all stars have their down periods, even deep depressions, and I don't think he was any different. But when I was around Elvis, they all were good times. We had a ball. There were no brooding depressions. He was the original average guy made good. He really was a plain, openhearted country boy. His only frustration was that he needed to stretch himself more. After his entourage and the public between them had forced an image on him, he had to lock himself into a private frame to be himself. Unlike me, he was never allowed the flexibility he needed as an artist.

Chapter 5

The Clan

For as long as I can remember, Las Vegas has been my spiritual home. My act was tailor-made for the town, and in turn the place was built for my kind of life-style. I am a night person, and Vegas never sleeps.

Years before *Porgy*, I had got tired of hanging around the Vegas bars and casinos between shows, so I hired a projector and a hotel suite and had dozens of 16 mm prints flown out from Hollywood. I started showing two great classics a night, and it got to the point where the gypsies (the show-biz nickname for dancers) were coming from all over town to sit in and watch along with the other stars and celebrities and the waitresses and barmen. Everyone was welcome. Clubs like the Stardust would call up to find out what was playing that night. They'd put it on the staff bulletin board, and for a very long while it became part of the whole Vegas scene.

Word would get around the tables, "Hey, he's showing *Robin Hood* tonight," and the girls were even splitting from their "mixing dates"—a mandatory part of a show girl's life in Vegas, when they come down after the show to mix with the gamblers. Eventually I had to hire a huge suite to accommodate everyone. Even

80

then the room would get so crowded stars were falling over one another, trying to find space on the floor. Someone like Paul Anka would light a match, trying to see the way, and everyone would yell at him.

There was no greater relaxation for me than sitting around with a bunch of pals, watching the great old movies. I laid on food and unlimited drink, and there is one thing you can guarantee about a show girl—she'll always be hungry. One night things got a little wild, and a whole plate of stew was spilled over a white sofa, so then the management asked us to drop the food.

At first the casinos loved the film shows because when we finished running two movies, it would be around 5:00 A.M., what they call the dead hour in Vegas. The girls would liven everything up when we all emerged down in the bar for a liquid breakfast. It was a good, healthy, happy thing. There was rarely any hanky-panky, although a lot of people would have liked to believe otherwise.

But gradually the whole thing got out of hand. The big boys, including Howard Hughes, got the Hotel Owners' Association to look into it. They were worried because all the girls were disappearing so early in the evening. Traditionally they should have spent a few hours out with the gamblers—especially if there were a few high rollers around. It added glamour to the night's gambling. The owners themselves were coming up to see the films as well. But they liked the stars to mingle with the high rollers to give the atmosphere some class. When they found guys were calling up and saying, "I hear you're running *Gunga Din* tonight, Sammy. We're playing a late show; can you show it second on the bill?" I think the Hotel Owners' Association felt I was managing too much of the action.

I used to get notes and gifts from Hughes, who was later responsible for putting in my $10,000 projection room at my home in Beverly Hills. But Howard wasn't too happy about my film shows in Vegas, so eventually we had to control them and allow in only a few close friends.

But in the good old days we had a lot of fun. Those big 16 mms came in two or three reels, and every fifty minutes or so the lights would go up, and you would always find someone groping someone else. I used to yell before turning the switch, "Anyone who's involved . . . I'm turning the lights on," and hear shuffling all over the place. One day this led to an embarrassing incident.

A journalist and his wife, a well-known English actress, came by one night, and obviously they both had had a lot to drink. The guy just fell into an armchair and started snoring. His wife was swaggering around loaded to the gills. Just then a really beautiful and slender boy dancer came in and sat near the woman. He was only a teenage gypsy, but he was extremely good-looking. The woman just flipped over this kid.

We started running the film, and I became completely engrossed, as I always do, in what was unfolding on screen. Suddenly I became aware of heavy moaning and groaning just behind me. The projector was making noise, but this obvious lovemaking was loud and clear above it. I sneaked a look and saw, right behind the projector, the couple leaving nothing to the imagination.

The guy was oblivious to what was happening around him. The girl was making all the action. The reel came to an end, and someone turned the lights on. The couple carried on for a while as if nothing had happened—they were so engrossed. Suddenly the lady realized, with a terrible, overpowering sensation, that the entire room was looking at them with complete fascination. And I must say, we were. It wasn't so much that we all were interested in a free porn show, it was just such a totally bizarre sight. POW. She shot up like a bullet and adjusted her dress as she fled from the room. The poor kid was just at the point of a terrific orgasm, and he had to put it all away. We all felt for him.

She had left the room, and no one said anything for maybe half a minute. The husband was still happily snoring away, oblivious to everything. We showed the next reel and tried to forget the whole thing. At the end of the film the guy stumbled around, looking for another drink, and finally went back to his wife. The next day he told me, "Sorry I fell asleep, Sammy. My wife tells me it was a great movie."

My only regret about this incident was that it was the end of a good friendship because the woman never spoke to me again. I don't think to this day the husband ever discovered what his wife had been up to.

In those days I was between marriages, and I was pretty good at hanging around with attractive ladies. I was never the swinger some people like to think, but I didn't do badly. I know how to have a good time. I would think nothing of taking two or three girls out at one time, even though I knew that was the worst thing to do if I wanted to score. It didn't matter that much to me. I liked to move with attractive people.

Vegas was always full of classy dames, and I never tired of the town. Luckily Vegas seems to feel the same about me. The newspapers there used to say that when Sinatra or I was in town, we brought in more trade than three conventions. It was Peter Lawford who suggested to Frank that we round up Dean Martin and Joey Bishop and the five of us would make a film in Vegas and play the Sands cabaret each evening. Vegas has never been the same since and neither have I. We worked from the crack of dawn on the film, *Ocean's Eleven*, meeting for a conference in the steam room in the early evening, and then going on to do the shows. But more than this, it was such a ball with all the guys around. I was playing hard, too. I was drinking a great deal—a prerequisite for being a Clan member—hanging out with the gypsies, playing the tables, and every night was New Year's Eve. After eight weeks I finally keeled over and spent a week in the hospital with nervous exhaustion.

One evening Senator John F. Kennedy came with a party of people to catch our show. Kennedy had already set his sights on the presidential nomination, and he was big news. Frank, who was fully committed to the Kennedy cause and had pledged all his support, introduced him. He rose to take the applause, and Dean Martin staggered onstage. Dean, well known as the soberest lush in the business, asked Frank, "What did you say his name was?" Then we all went out front and started clowning around. Dean suddenly picked me up and carried me across the stage. He pretended to hand me over to Frank. "This has just arrived from the National Association for the Advancement of Colored People," he said.

Despite the work and the tiredness, we sat up that night and several other nights with Kennedy talking about his presidency. Many schemes were discussed, some of which came to fruition, and we all agreed we would try to lead the show business support.

That was in January 1960. Frank's plan was twofold. First, we would root around and get all the pals to do benefits to raise money for the senator. Secondly, we would try to get the support of all the major stars for Kennedy rallies. Kennedy was excited and grateful for this support.

On the night of July 10, 1960, we put our promises into actions. We went to the Democratic Convention at the Beverly Hills Hotel. There were so many people there they needed two ballrooms to put on the show. We all entertained in both rooms. Frank did his piece, then I, Judy Garland, Mort Sahl, Joe E. Lewis, and, of course, Kennedy's brother-in-law Peter Lawford.

Judy and Frank later sat on the dais with Kennedy, Lyndon Johnson, Adlai Stevenson, and Eleanor Roosevelt. It was quite a lineup. We all called Kennedy Jack, and the whole thing was very pally, more like a star-studded party than a convention. And of course, Jack carried the day.

I don't know how much voting power we added to the Kennedy circus. It might not have made a lot of difference, but during those nights of animated conversation back in Las Vegas, we certainly *thought* we could make a big difference. We got caught up completely in the Kennedy optimism, and it was an exciting time for all of us, especially Frank. It was very much Sinatra's baby, and he played it to the hilt.

In fact, when Kennedy left Vegas, it was a bit of an anticlimax for a couple of days. But we soon got back in the swing of things when the filming started again and life resumed its normal chaos.

One day Frank laid it on the line. "We're not setting out to make *Hamlet* or *Gone With the Wind*. The idea is to hang out together, find fun with the broads, and have a great time. We gotta make pictures that people enjoy. Entertainment, period. We gotta have laughs."

That really *was* what the Clan was all about. We never discussed money, neither how much we made from the film nor how much we might be losing by canceling other dates. Money was not the motivating force. Frank made all the arrangements. He always had a brilliant business mind and an excellent set of advisers. When he showed me the contract, I saw my salary was to be $100,000, which was then extremely good money unless you were a leading star. In 1960 I needed it. By my third film my wages were upped to $125,000. But it was never discussed. Frank just fixed it, and that was that. I was naturally grateful, but I would have made those films for next to nothing. It was just nice to have some cash rolling in as well.

No one would suggest that any of the Clan films were artistically important. But none of us was ashamed of them. They made a great deal of cash, and they still turn up in the annual *Variety* list of all-time money-makers. People took them for what they were—good, amusing entertainment. They picked up the fun we were having, and it was infectious.

Frank was very easy to work with. He was always at the helm, and we kept it that way. He made the actual filming as painless as possible because he got bored easily and couldn't bear hanging around the set. When we worked together, there was a feeling of camaraderie, and we seemed to move as one force. We managed to carry that onto the screen. None of us Clan members had ego problems with the others. A few of the people on the fringes came with their problems hanging all over the place. They weren't invited again. That wasn't the name of the game.

I don't mind admitting that Frank Sinatra looked after me like a mother hen. The other Clan members didn't need it as much as I did. Dean Martin was riding high in the nightclubs, and Peter had carved a very comfortable niche on television. Joey Bishop was very much his own man. But I was still trying to climb the ladder of success, and I could do with a helping hand. Frank was incredibly protective toward me, long before it was fashionable to be so. I didn't have enough reputation to demand things. I never asked Frank, but he demanded things for me. Sinatra would be at a script conference, and the casting director would say, "We've got to have a young guy to play the second lead."

Frank would say, "Sam will do it."

"But, Mr. Sinatra . . ."

"You hear me, Sam will do it. That's the end of it."

It would be fixed just like that. It was the end of the matter. There was never any argument when Frank wanted something done his way. When everything had been signed and sealed, Frank would walk out and say, "Let's get going." The next thing I knew I had been cast for something.

I have never hidden the fact that I have a very deep spot in my heart for Frank. He was always very much the big brother looking after my welfare, even when sometimes I didn't deserve it. He's a great guy's guy and an exceptionally charming man around the "dames." He is the best kind of buddy you could have, never failing to surprise you with some new act of kindness. He swings easily with a lot of things, but he cannot suffer fools gladly. I

fully support his feelings. Frank was never knowingly nasty to
someone who didn't deserve it. He takes a lot of things, but there
is a point sometimes when he's had enough. When he gets to that
point, it is silly and unwise to continue arguing with him. He
raises his hand and says, "That's enough," and he means it. You
either fall out with him or accept his position.

I've never seen him really angry. I've seen him fed up with
someone, and I've seen the old flash of temper in the eyes, but he
is certainly not the vindictive, angry, fighting, and belligerent guy
some newspapers like to paint him.

Frank, who'd had a great deal more movie experience than I
did, helped me professionally as well. He humored me when I
tried to learn how certain scenes should be played. He had an
instinct about how some things would look on the screen. In fact,
he was very much an instinctive actor in every sense of the word.
That's why he became known as One-Take Charley. Frank figured he had to play it straight off the cuff.

There was a point in the first Clan film when I didn't know
what to do with my hands. Most of my life as an entertainer had
been dominated by my holding a microphone. I felt a little
naked without it. In fact, the more I got into acting, the more I
realized props were unnecessary. But in those days I needed something, so I decided to hold a cigarette, one of the oldest props in
the business. Frank understood my problem but told me a cigarette was not the answer. "Well, Frank," I said, "that's how I
want to play it."

"OK," he said with a resigned air. "Do it your way. But mark
my words, you'll regret it." I didn't know what he was talking
about, so I lit up. But the scene needed four or five takes. In
every shot the cigarette naturally had to match. I could not be
seen in one early shot with a short cigarette, a second later with
a long one. So we spent most of the day burning cigarettes down
to the same size. Frank watched with some amusement. He never
did say, "I told you so," but I said it for him.

"OK, *Mr. Sinatra*," I said eventually, "how would you do it?"

"Simple," he said, and immediately lit up a king size. He went
through the motions of my act, came in front of the camera, and
stubbed the cigarette out. "You can't take one of these from shot
to shot unless you're Bob Mitchum," he said.

Frank's advice to me was highly constructive, from a guy who knew most of the tricks of the trade to a guy who was still learning. He also gave me practical advice about camera angles: how to keep in range even when the camera is concentrating on someone else, perspective, catching the light, and framing a shot. I had picked up something from my visits to film sets, but Frank was the only one who had ever bothered to take me to one side and give me the benefit of his experience. Since then I have never had any qualms about asking an actor why he did a certain thing in a special way, and because of this, I think I now know most of the tricks. But it was Sinatra who was the first to hold my hand on the film set.

It was he, for instance, who showed me there is a special way to ride a horse in a western which is nothing like the way you would ride if you were out for a Sunday jaunt. To make it good for the camera, you have to sit high and straight on the saddle. He knew that slouching on the screen looks dreadful. You tighten up the stirrups so you don't bounce up and down. You also try to hold the saddle horn, especially if you are riding away from the camera. Getting on and off a horse is more important than anything else. It can be extremely undignified unless you have the knack. Some people could never master it. When George Stevens wanted a particularly spectacular leap onto a horse from Jack Palance in *Shane*, he had to film him leaping off the horse and run the film backward.

The next film the Clan did together was *Sergeants Three*. We all trooped over to a place in Utah and met up with the producer, Howard Koch. Frank has made seven films for Koch, and they have remained good friends. Howard always understood that Frank needs excitement. He doesn't like hanging around, waiting for things to happen. But he also knew Frank is highly conscientious. *Ocean's Eleven* was a lot of fun, but I think *Sergeants Three* was the best film we ever did together. It was a good story with a lot of fine points, and we packed it with action.

The film was, of course, a second remake of the immortal *Gunga Din*, first made in 1939 by George Stevens with Cary Grant, Douglas Fairbanks, Jr., and Joan Fontaine, and we were fully aware that we should not try to copy the original. We changed the setting from India to the American West and turned the heroes into cavalry officers. I played the Gunga Din part, originally done by Sam Jaffe. Although we departed from the

Rudyard Kipling story, we kept to the basic outline of three soldiers saved by a nondescript water boy. John Sturges directed our
version, and the whole thing came off with a lot of laughter on
the set. I think it was infinitely better than the 1951 remake, *Soldiers Three*, with Stewart Granger and David Niven.

The last movie we all made together was *Robin and the Seven
Hoods*, which was a great spoof film and very well received.
Again, we all had a ball, and while it didn't set out to rival *A
Man for All Seasons*, it entertained people. By this time I really
felt I was getting the hang of this acting thing and was becoming
more and more confident in front of the camera.

By now the Clan had developed a magnificent rapport, which
has lasted to this day. Even now, when Sinatra and I get up onstage together, something very special happens. The audience
picks it up immediately. They sense the electricity we can gen-
erate between us and the relaxed fun we always have together.
I walked onstage when he was appearing at Caesar's Palace recently, and we sang "The Lady Is a Tramp" together. The place
just fell apart.

We've had a few difficulties over the years, some heated words
and a few cross exchanges, but it never got to the stage when we
couldn't call each other up and say, "Sorry, pal." We always remained supportive and protective toward each other, even after
a blazing argument. Each would find out how the other guy was
doing, for neither of us is the kind of person who holds grudges
for long. Because of Sinatra's tremendous international influence,
if he ever were vindictive, he's powerful enough to arrange that
the person, whoever he is, never does another day's work. Frank
would never have to resort to violence. All the picking on his
negative side is just so much bull. He'd lift the phone and say,
"I don't want him in Vegas," or wherever. It would be enough.
Frank is genuinely that big. A lot of people think they're that
big, but Frank actually is. Yet he has never done it. However mad
he got, he was never vindictive.

In the late fifties Frank and I did fall out over a film he wanted
to make called *Never So Few*. Our fight was about how my part
should be played, and we had entirely different concepts of it. As
usual, Frank was in charge of everything that went on and defi-
nitely had the last say. We both realized neither of us was going
to change his opinion, so Frank pulled me out of the deal and put

in Steve McQueen. It helped make Steve a superstar. I wanted to make the picture very much, but by then I had a considerable amount of experience in movies, and I was sure how I wanted to play the character. Frank disagreed with me. That was the end of that.

So we parted company for a while. It was one of those perfectly legitimate, but mundane, buddy-style disagreements, yet in time it left no bad feelings.

Sinatra and I still bump into each other from time to time, and we remain warm friends. He doesn't hang out with show people much these days. He lives a quieter life, playing golf with his buddies.

I have the definitive collection of Sinatra records, real collector's paradise. Frank calls me up occasionally and says, "Hey, Smokey, what's on the other side of that little number so-and-so I did with Dorsey?"

I can get hold of it while he hangs on.

While we were making those Clan pictures, the whole industry was going through another change, so that in a way marked the end of the era. When eventually we passed on to other things, films like *M*A*S*H* had crept up to create a new impetus in comedy. Donald Sutherland, Elliott Gould, and Jimmy Caan then became the new core who managed serious subjects in a comedic way.

The Alan Arkin *Up the Wall* pictures were close behind, and that trend, in turn, gave way to Mel Brooks, Woody Allen, and Gene Wilder. What swings around comes around, and the changing emphasis was typical of what always happens in Hollywood. This era started with Chaplin and ended with Brooks. In between, the Clan had its day.

We got under the wire just before that kind of humor became unfashionable, and in 1965 we decided to call it a day. I was getting ready for *Golden Boy*, Frank had some other film commitments, Lawford wanted to get into producing, and Dean was striking it big in the nightclubs. We didn't so much split up as drift apart.

I was happy when I was offered a cameo part in a more serious film called *Johnny Cool*, with my old Clan buddy Joey Bishop. Henry Silva, who starred as a vicious gangster seeking revenge, specifically asked me to do the part. I had been trying to play a heavy for years and leaped at the chance to do a small but important character study. I wasn't on the screen for more than ten minutes, but I was extremely flattered when I went to Paris a few years later and found I was billed as the main star.

Johnny Cool gave Elisha Cook, Jr., just about the only positive role he ever played—as a Mafia leader who survived to see Silva delivered to the gangsters. Until then Elisha had always taken the rap or played a sniveling hotel clerk, as he had in *Hot Spot*. He got in the way of Mickey Rooney's guns in *Baby Face Nelson* and typecast his career as the cringing coward when Bogey took two Lugers away from him in *The Maltese Falcon*. In *Johnny Cool* he seemed six feet tall for the very first, and last, time.

I went on to make *A Man Called Adam* in 1966. Leo Penn directed, and Frank Sinatra, Jr., Mel Tormé, and Peter Lawford costarred. That great old jazzman Louis Armstrong had a wonderful cameo part. This time we tried to tell a story in a new, interesting, but serious way. Despite this, when we hit New York, we all managed to have a ball together. I played a failed trumpet player trying to find a purpose in life—a combination of many jazz musicians we all had known.

We were trying to make an "adult" film long before the phrase was invented. It was probably before its time. We took the cameras out into the streets, almost unheard of in those days. We let them run on authentic backgrounds, with believable people and real traffic noises, daring and experimental for its time. The critics were kind to me personally, but the film itself was totally misunderstood. I decided it was time to rekindle my reputation back in the nightclubs. I had deserted my traditional audiences long enough. I gave them everything I had for the next two years.

By then Peter Lawford and I had enjoyed working together in four films, and after several years of talking about it, we decided to make a couple more. I was going to London, his old hometown, and we knew we could find all the facilities there if we could come up with the right vehicle. We cast around and eventually found *Salt and Pepper*, which seemed to fit our particular talents and characters.

As soon as I got to London, I moved into my old luxury suite at the May Fair Hotel. It cost a fortune, and I could never stay a day in London without spending money. So even though as coproducers Peter and I paid ourselves $75,000 and were each to take 50 percent of the profits, I had to do a TV spectacular and a stint at the Talk of the Town to pay my way.

We did most of the filming at Pinewood Studios, which were small but functional. The only things we objected to were the rest trailers, which were like matchboxes. We eventually scoured the country and found two huge American-style trailers, which we quickly installed on the lot. Everyone came running over to look at them in amazement. In turn, this amazed us. It was less than we expected on any American film set. The rent was astronomical, but worth every cent. We could cook, entertain, and actually move around while handing out drinks from a well-stocked bar.

Richard Donner directed the film, and we brought in just about every established British character actor we could find. We set out to make a light but broad comedy which exploited our personal talents to the full. In effect we played ourselves and acted almost exactly as we did together in real life. That is, we had a gas. We played two innocent nightclub owners embroiled in a huge spy plot. It was a spoof, of course, and we borrowed ideas from the James Bond syndrome then enjoying its heyday. I still like that film. It had much of both of us in it, and audiences took it for exactly what it was—a lot of fun. We were so pleased with it we decided to make a sequel, *One More Time*, two years later. I even persuaded Chris Lee and Peter Cushing to do a couple of cameo roles, and we brought in Jerry Lewis as director. We were extremely happy with this picture when we were making it. It was even better than the original. But it got completely murdered by the editors and distributors.

Jerry was a brilliant director. He did all his homework meticulously and knew exactly what he wanted before he reached the set. He was a very talented young man in those days. It was a crying shame to see what happened to the film after it left his hands. Jerry did not have the final cut, one of the most important aspects of production. Whoever did finally cut it cut all our throats along with the celluloid.

When we finished the last take, I decided to throw a party for everyone and asked Mario and Franco, the famous Italian chefs from the London Trattoria, to cook up a splendid banquet. We were at Shepperton Studios at the time. Franco came out to the set to make final arrangements but got completely lost. He was in an Italian temper when he arrived and said, "I cannot put on a party if the place is unfindable." So we moved it to his Kensington restaurant. The invitations said, "From 7:00 P.M. to unconscious time"—a lovely Franco and Mario touch.

Later on poor Peter became ill with a bad pancreas and was in the hospital for about fifteen weeks. Just when he thought he was recovering, he went back in with a mild flare-up. He had many friends, Liz Taylor, Jack Haley, Jr., and me among them, but when he went back in, an incredible thing happened. The industry decided to put him in a coffin and crossed his name off the list. It was ridiculous. They made him "disappear" from the face of the earth, and none of us could do anything about it.

When he finally recovered, he was living in some *Catch-22* situation, saying, "Look, everybody, I'm still alive." But no one would give him work. It took him years to get back on his feet. It was Jack Haley, Jr., who finally broke the spell. He asked Peter to present some of the Academy Awards. Suddenly everyone woke up and said, "Jesus, it's Peter Lawford. Where the hell's he been?"

Today he is on top again, almost wholly on television, where he does just about anything. Peter's the kind of guy who will never go hungry, but for a while it looked as though his life had been taken away from him.

Chapter 6

Class

Salt and Pepper was a good reason for going to London, but by no means the only one. I had the itch in a big way, and Europe was still unconquered. All entertainers get that overriding feeling from time to time: "Don't stop moving while you've still got breath." So it was time to move on.

One of the great aspects of being a Clan member was that among us we knew almost everyone in show business—and a lot of other people on the fringes as well. It was a heady experience. People would be jetting in from all over the world to see Frank at Palm Springs. Lawford, as President Kennedy's brother-in-law, was suddenly moving in circles which were not normally open to entertainers. Frank had been moving around Europe and quickly became pals with the international jet set. People like Ava Gardner were storming through Paris and Madrid. Worldly citizens of those crazy capitals were pouring into America, many of them finding their way to Kennedy's summer home via Peter Lawford. So I was constantly meeting interesting people whom I would probably never have met if I'd stayed all my life in vaudeville.

For my first two visits to London I played the nightclubs. I didn't feel ready yet to take on the Palladium, one of the world's most justly celebrated variety halls. Of course, since then, both the town and the theater have become second homes to me. Now I have almost as many buddies in Paris and London as I have in New York. But years ago, when I was feeling my way around Europe, I depended on friends to show me the sights. I found that in London and Paris they knew me mainly from *Porgy*. The traffic stopped, and people would yell, "There goes Sportin' Life." The Clan pictures added only a sprinkling of glamour and kudos to the original image.

Sinatra's philosophy of "fun with everything, and I mean fun" had rubbed off on us all, and I left for Europe with a mixed bag of emotions: excitement, fear, awe, and ambition. But above all, I wanted it to be fun. I'd give the very best I could, but I was going to play hard as well. Consequently, whenever I hit town, I found out who else was around and whether we could get together.

Even today, when I meet interesting people who have something to say for themselves—and I have been very lucky to have known a handful or two—I am very quickly influenced by what they have to say. I have always suffered from a terrible craving for new experiences, in life and work. There has to be a new interest continually, a new sense of purpose. Once it was golf or photography. Today it's cooking. I've seen just about every hotel menu from Vegas to Vietnam. One day I met some people who were "into food" and realized just how much pleasure I was missing by always ordering hamburgers from room service. Now my traveling library includes almost every cookbook and gourmet guide in print, and I'm as happy to talk to you about *Larousse Gastronomique* as about my golf handicap.

It was very much the same with my unusual interest in bullfighting. I had never even remotely considered going to a *corrida*. The idea didn't grab me at all. I'd seen Valentino's 1922 *Blood and Sand*, and although I don't argue about Rudolph's performance, it didn't exactly make me rush down to Mexico to pick up the next Sunday fight. Nor did the Tyrone Power-Rita Hayworth remake twenty years later. But because of Hemingway's *The Sun Also Rises* and Ava Gardner's friendship with the great matador Dominguín, there had been a general interest in the subject in both Hollywood and New York.

In the end my friendship with Miguel Luis Dominguín was a big influence on my life. He was one of the first people who took me under his wing when I got to Paris. It was an unlikely meeting and an unlikely friendship, and naturally, Ava was the connection.

I had, of course, met Ava with Frank, and when she came to New York to publicize *The Barefoot Contessa* in 1954, I met her again. It was during one of the difficult periods with Frank, and he had stayed in Palm Springs. The Will Mastin Trio was generating a lot of excitement at the Apollo Theater on 125th Street, and Ava tended to gravitate toward excitement, even if it was far uptown. She came to the theater, and naturally enough, it sent a buzz all over Harlem.

It was a wonderful gesture for Ava to encourage us, and she was about the most elegant lady I had ever known. Later United Artists suggested we do a publicity picture together. They were anxious at the time to cultivate black audiences. Ava was gracious enough to do the shots, and they got very wide publicity. I also wanted a shot of us together for my own collection. These other pictures were very innocent stand-up shots, but unfortunately they were exploited by the press, which managed to get hold of them. It was very embarrassing for us both because magazines like *Confidential* were making all kinds of innuendos which not only were in appallingly bad taste but were completely untrue. Ava was sweet about it, and we have met over the years and remained friends. She was always a remarkable woman and a tremendous actress.

Ava Gardner had been around for seven hard years before she exploded into superstardom. She arrived in town when she was still a teenager from a poor family in North Carolina and was found, in one of those classic Hollywood "discoveries," by a photographer who was courting her sister. By 1949, the MGM Silver Jubilee year, she was possibly the hottest property in town. In the famous jubilee picture showing fifty-eight of MGM's top-liners, she is sitting in the second row between Gable and Judy Garland, whom she would eventually replace as Julie in *Show-boat*. A young-looking Frank Sinatra sits two rows behind. They began a closer friendship later in the year. MGM was by now pulling out all the stops for her. She was starred with Gregory Peck in *The Great Sinner* and later with James Mason and Barbara Stanwyck in *East Side, West Side*.

It is well known that Frank and Ava fell in love but were not able to marry until 1951, the year in which Ava made *Showboat* and then *Lone Star*, again with Gable. She and Frank were still very much in love when they went to Africa two years later so she could film *Mogambo* with Gable and Grace Kelly. All this time Frank was fighting for the part of Maggio in *From Here to Eternity*, which was to give him back his rightful place in show business —at the top—and for which he got an Oscar.

Ava never fell out of love with Frank, but during the making of *The Barefoot Contessa* she began to fall irretrievably in love with Europe—first France, then Italy, but finally, most of all, with Spain. She was still developing this passion when Frank went to Spain to film *The Pride and the Passion*. Ava, in fact, found the splendid ranch where they stayed.

All this time Frank and Ava were building up solid friendships with people who mattered in Europe. But although they did not divorce until the following year, both of them began to realize the marriage was not working out. Frank flung himself back into glorious bachelorhood; Ava met up with Dominguín after several visits to Spain and brought him to Nevada, where she had set up a temporary home. Their close neighbor in Nevada was Rita Hayworth, who was herself getting divorced from Aly Khan. Later Howard Hughes piloted them over to Cuba to meet Hemingway. By all accounts it was during this trip to meet "Papa" Hemingway that Ernest became convinced Ava should play the part of Lady Brett Ashley in *The Sun Also Rises*. He had, of course, been a close friend of Dominguín's for many years.

In this film set during the bull-running fiesta in Pamplona, Ava Gardner showed she was a very substantial person. To a great extent she had been an enigma as an actress. It was sometimes as if she had wanted to call the whole thing off, and years later she often said she didn't care about acting. Maybe she didn't, and maybe she didn't have to. No other actress in the world could have played either the barefoot contessa or Lady Brett quite as she did because there was simply so much of her in both. She *was* Brett Ashley, the aristocratic playgirl in a spider's web of strong male characters. When Ava walked around Paris, people greeted her as they would have greeted Lady Brett. The waiters would rush forward to find her the best table; every man in the room would be tantalized by her. She would kick off her shoes and down a large scotch. When she left, half the café would leave with her. Yet it was all done with such class. *The Sun Also Rises* was wonderfully cast for every leading actor. Tyrone Power surpassed himself. For Errol Flynn, the disillusioned, broke, drunken cynic, it was probably the meatiest part of his life, and he gave it everything, including much of his real self. They all gave different dimensions to the Hemingway classic, and it worked. But Ava was extraordinary. She has always been a gracious and talented lady with qualities worthy of any part she ever played, yet they were rarely worthy of her. When she did get a goody, she was able to pour a great deal of her own experiences into the character. She could translate her own personality into the part. This is always the prerequisite of the great actress.

It would be wonderful if Ava would throw herself back into her work so that she could show some of today's younger actresses just what the hell movie acting is all about. There's a lot of talent in town, but many of the kids are getting there too fast, too easy. They start thinking they're the screen idols of all time before they're out of diapers. Ava Gardner is one of the few ladies around today who could still show the whole world what a real star is. Why doesn't she play *Sweet Bird of Youth*, *The Sea Gull*, Martha Mitchell, Golda Meir, *Come Back, Little Sheba*? There's no dearth of material around for a gifted middle-aged actress.

She and Dominguín were an electrifying couple. Miguel Luis was in Paris when I first went there, and we met for a meal. He was a fascinating man, but I never did see him fighting. I eventually planned a tour of Spain so I could, but before I could get there, he had received the fatal horn.

I have known a few celebrities in my life, but I had never seen absolute reverence for a man until Dominguín and I entered a Spanish restaurant in Paris. The Spaniards were in total awe of him. If he was not quite God, then at least he deserved the recognition of a saint. I was immediately, incomparably, impressed by his dignity and serenity. Until that moment he had just been Ava's bullfighter. After that lunch I wanted to know how and why that man could be treated with more respect and reverence than any superstar. What made this thing called bullfighting bring out a respectful admiration in humble waiters that no stage act could ever produce? It was then I determined to learn a little more about the *corrida*.

I subsequently met Dominguín a couple of times in Paris and became captivated by his charm and elegance. I didn't meet him again until he got to New York, where he was almost completely unknown. By then I had bought many books on bullfighting and had begun boning up on it. Obviously I started with Hemingway's *Death in the Afternoon*. By the time I met Dominguín again I had a fairly good technical knowledge of bullfighting and I'd seen a couple of fights in Mexico. I'd also gotten to know Barnaby Conrad, the American bullfight authority. Even more important, I had made it my duty to get to know the great Mexican bullfighter Carlos Arruza. During the next year Arruza became one of my closest buddies, and we would sit all night drinking tequilas or brandy. He gradually enlightened me about the *corrida*. I say "gradually" with great reverence for the "game." It is easy to see a few fights and read a couple of books and think you know all about it. At the start it was all fresh and new to me, and I made the mistake of equating it with show business. For a novice that was easily done. It was years before I became a true *aficionado*. And let's face it, I had the greatest teachers in the world.

Dominguín was still crazy about Ava and consequently kept coming to New York or passing through on his way to see her. Sometimes we'd all go out together, and on those occasions there wasn't much bullfight talk! During the three years after Manolete's death, Dominguín was the greatest bullfighter in the world—probably one of the five best ever. After the show at the Copacabana we'd hang out with each other until dawn. No one was bugging him in New York, and very few people recognized him. I was by then beginning to be a familiar sight at the Copa, and we could sit and schmooze all night in comfort and seclusion.

My memory of those evenings was that underneath the playboy image Dominguín was a deeply serious and emotional man carrying an almost unbearable burden. This tonnage on his back was twofold. He carried Manolete's death around with him like a cross, but he also knew that sooner or later his time would come, too. They had fought to the end as fierce competitors—but their common enemy was the bull.

By now, of course, I had devoured every detail of the great *mano a mano*. Both of them had the magic. Manolete had had the age and experience, but Dominguín had had the youth and the ambition. He eventually forced Manolete to do impossible things in the ring, to take ridiculous risks, just so he could stay on top. And eventually the risks had become too great, and the man had taken the horn during probably the greatest fight of his career. That fight haunted Dominguín because although they had rarely talked, they had deeply loved and respected each other. When we left the Copa for breakfast some mornings, he would have a forlorn, sad, almost lost air about him. He had won the duel, but part of him had died during it, and the tragedy hung around him just as the smell of garlic hangs around the bars in Jerez de la Frontera.

He could do the playboy bit right up to the hilt. With Ava, or any other woman he met for that matter, he was always the picture of charm. His English was impeccable, and he was forever the perfect gentleman. His smile was intensely sincere, yet it also seemed laconic. You could see how vulnerable he really was. Yet, unlike the case of James Dean, you didn't feel the need to run over, put your arm around his shoulder, and protect him from all the hurts in the world. This was something that only Dominguín could deal with. He walked very much alone; however much actual contact one had with him, he remained strangely untouched. His confidence was supreme, yet he was fatalistic about his death. As the man who had beaten Manolete, more was expected of him every time he put on his suit of lights. He knew that no man could take the art of bullfighting as far as he had and live for very long. There was a feeling of finality about him so that when he got that final horn and, as it happened, it was a particularly clean finish, he seemed to look at everyone as if to say, "Well, now you've got what you want, I can rest in peace." It was as if only death itself could take the burden from those slender shoulders. The same look would come over his face sometimes when I would be talking with him in the early hours of the morning and he would become lost in the detail of some fight he was describing. This tremendous weight would seem to fall away from him. Then his eyes would sparkle. He would gesticulate all over the place, occasionally jumping up to demonstrate a movement—with all the waiters still standing in the shadows, watching silently but, even in New York, with a peculiar respect.

Then he seemed alive again. He would talk endearingly, almost lovingly about the very great bulls he had killed. He could bring the whole emotional, sun-drenched atmosphere of the *plaza de toros* into a New York nightclub at dawn. He would use table knives to demonstrate the placing of the darts, tablecloths as a *muleta,* and the waiters would even sometimes double as the bull.

Carlos Arruza was never as great as Domínguín. He ruled Mexican bullfighting for a decade, and every time he went to Spain he was begged to stay. They both were a special breed of men, but Domínguín was in a class by himself. I saw the fights in Mexico whenever my schedule would allow, and of course, I never missed Carlos when I could make it. He became a constant visitor to our house in the Hills. Consequently we became close buddies, and, when he died in the *corrida,* as we all knew he would eventually, his wife gave me his favorite suit of lights. Later I completed the set by acquiring the *muleta* and sword he was using when he died. I have a houseful of very sentimental possessions. That suit is among my most precious.

Bullfighting and entertaining have one important thing in common—both can create magic. You always knew Domínguín would give you a perfect fight—as perfect as he could make it in the circumstances. But sometimes bullfighters can go beyond perfection into the realms of the impossible. You would gasp—and know that he has reached the absolute brink. Then he takes it even farther. At that point it becomes a true form of art. In bullfighting the appearance of magic is often more obvious than it is on a stage. In a theater a guy is rarely playing with his life. But sometimes great entertainers can take a performance beyond perfection, and you get a gut feeling, and the tears well up with stunned emotion, and you know you have seen the same kind of art.

Soon after Domínguín died, I was due to play Madrid, and I wanted to develop a fight sequence for my act. Carlos demonstrated the principal passes and rehearsed me until I was confident I could take on the greatest bullfighting capital in the world. I perfected the routine in nightclubs all over America, but I couldn't wait to spring it on them in Spain. As soon as the audience heard the opening trumpets and recognized the beginning of the *corrida,* they went crazy. I did a complete sequence comedically and, in no time at all, the first *olé* went up. I played up to it, and eventually the whole audience rose to their feet, just as they do in the real fights.

It was all in pantomime, but the people caught every move until it seemed as if a real bull were passing the cape. Then, when I went into all the special passes which famous bullfighters had developed, the audience knew I was an *aficionado*. Of course, they recognized the passes, and they started calling out the names of the men who had made them famous. They knew I had been to the fights and appreciated that. I can tell you it is a marvelous feeling to get people on your side like this when you don't even speak the same language.

Barnaby Conrad and I remained friends, even after the deaths of our two friends, and I have always kept up a lively interest in what is going on in the bullfighting world. Barnaby and I were sitting by the pool in Beverly Hills one day chatting about old memories, and we discussed Sinatra's interest in the fights. He was into them for a while, although he never became the great *aficionado* he might have been. He had a very good working knowledge and appreciation of fighting. He had seen Manolete fight several times. In fact, he could impersonate him perfectly. One of Frank's great party pieces before Manolete died was to put on a false nose and strut around arrogantly—he was the spit and image of the great matador. He had the same build, and it could easily have been Manolete walking around the room. I told Barnaby of this, and he said, "Are you kidding? What a wild idea!"

We discussed it some more, and I was swept along by Barnaby's enthusiasm. "Why didn't I think of it before? Sinatra as Manolete. It's just got to be the greatest idea. If I bash out a twelve-page outline about the last days of Manolete, can you get it to Frank?"

"Are *you* kidding? Of course I can. Can you write it tonight? I'll fly down to Palm Springs tomorrow. I can be back for the show. It's a great idea."

So Barnaby got down to it and worked all night. By the time I rose a secretary was typing and he was drinking coffee as if there were no tomorrow. He looked tired, but he didn't look drained. He'd got a real kick out of the whole idea.

Later that day I watched Sinatra read those pages, and I could see a look of interest in his eyes.

When he finished, he put the ms. down on the coffee table and went over to the window. I suppose he seemed a little wistful as he turned to me and said, "I'd like the part, but the American public doesn't like bullfighting. I don't want to be in anything the American public won't buy. You need too much going for you if you start off with a loser."

I remonstrated with him. "But, Frank, there've been a good few bullfight movies. Look at Mel Ferrer in *The Brave Bulls.* You would be the definitive Manolete. He's still fresh in the public's mind. It's gotta be a hit in the rest of the world. Can't you see it? It's you, Frank."

"No, Charley," he said kindly. "I know what you're talking about. But this one's not for me."

We left it at that. Maybe the subject brought back memories he wanted to forget. If that was the case, I respected his feelings. But to this day I wish he'd done that part because it was made for him. Sinatra had known the tragedy. But he'd also experienced the kind of emotion, respect, dignity, and adoration accorded to great bullfighters. He is one of the few actors who could have delivered that on screen. The only guy today who could play the part is Robert De Niro, but I doubt if the time will ever be as right as it was then. Anyway, Sinatra turned it down and we, again, went our separate ways.

Knowing Dominguín had been a revelation, and I was always grateful for his personal introduction to Paris. But he was by no means the only person to have looked after me in those early days when I needed inspiration and friendship. When I was playing the Olympia in Paris all sorts of people gravitated toward the show itself and either came backstage at the theater or looked me up at the Plaza Athénée. I went nightclubbing every night, and soon we were all swinging. Paris is not short of hot spots, and we hit them all.

It helped that the show was getting rave reviews. For a start, it reinforced my confidence; it always does. But secondly, I was hot in town, and people went out of their way to drop by. One of them was the great playboy Porfirio Rubirosa, who quickly decided to take me under his wing. Guys like Rubi and Dominguín come along once in a lifetime, a unique breed of men who touch your life in a special way. If you are lucky enough to get to know them and, more important, to learn from them, your world is never the same again.

I admit that I have always tried to be the world's snappiest dresser, and I will go to almost any length to look good, even at home. Dressing the part is fundamental to being a star. I have spent fortunes on clothes, hats, jewels, and other accouterments to make sure that, even crossing a hotel lobby, which is an extension of the stage, I look and feel at the top of my profession.

But Rubirosa made me feel as if I'd fallen off a garbage truck.

He was the most elegant man I have ever known. He was charming, erudite, highly amusing, debonair, extremely attractive, but, above all, without doubt the world's best-dressed man.

His life read like a scenario for every Errol Flynn movie ever made. The film of *The Adventurers,* based on the Harold Robbins novel, was supposed to be based on his life. Believe me, it had nothing on the real one. After all, not only had Rubi married five of the most beautiful women in the world, but two of them had also been the richest. As I got to know him, I could see at first hand the spell he must have cast on not only them but a host of other beautiful women, including Ava Gardner, Kim Novak, Zsa Zsa Gabor, Jayne Mansfield—a whole tribe of goddesses. The world was literally his playground. He was the last of the playboys, and when he died early one morning in his Ferrari in the Bois de Boulogne in Paris, the last of a unique breed of golden studs had passed.

We used to have get-togethers after the show in Paris, and he would introduce me to his favorite Parisian restaurants. He was happily married to his last wife, the delectable French actress Odile Rodin. I was crazy about another French actress at the time, and we all had some fun evenings together. We would eat and drink until seven or eight in the morning. After that I just wanted to crawl back to the hotel room and fall into bed.

Rubi would look at his watch and say to Odile, "I'll drive you home, darling. I have an appointment at nine." Then he'd turn to me. "See you for lunch, Sammy. There is this marvelous little place on the Left Bank I've just got to show you."

He had been boozing with me, drink for drink. When I later staggered out of bed to keep the appointment, I would look and feel like the bottom of a dung heap. Talk about hangovers—a subject I know far too much about. An expert, you might say. I never had bigger lulus than when I'd been with Rubirosa. I'd down what the British call a heart starter, try to pull myself together, and crawl to the restaurant, often late. Rubi would be standing at the bar looking like a million dollars. He'd bathed and changed, kept his appointment, and here he was without a wink of sleep, ready to get going again. It would drive me crazy. I thought I was the original night person able to catnap for weeks without getting a really good night's sleep. In Rubirosa I had clearly met my match.

At the bar, I'd prop myself up and say, "How do you do it, Rubi? What's the secret, for chrissakes?"

He always had one of those oracular answers like: "Life is too precious to ever feel bad." Or he'd raise an eyebrow and say, "It's nothing. Your profession is being an entertainer. Mine is being a playboy."

And play he did, fanatically. Frank once asked him in Palm Springs, "Have you ever actually worked, Rubi?"

He said quickly, "Work? I have no time to work!"

As son-in-law to the Dominican Republic's President Trujillo, he took himself from being a junior officer in the Dominican Army to a diplomatic post in Paris. There he quickly found himself invited into the best drawing rooms—and bedrooms—in Europe. His first wife tired of his exploits and returned to the Caribbean, leaving Rubi to marry the most beautiful French actress of the time, Danielle Darrieux. That also lasted five years. After a few flings with Zsa Zsa Gabor he hit it rich by marrying the tobacco heiress Doris Duke. After another five years (Rubi never waited for the seven-year itch), she left him with his first fortune of about $1 million. By then Rubi was news. He was notorious; that gave him his credentials for the jet-set. The gossip columns tracked his movements through Monte Carlo and St. Moritz, at the tables in Cannes, nightclubbing in London, and dancing at the Waldorf in New York. He was constantly being cited by irate husbands in divorce cases. He capped this off by marrying Barbara Hutton, the Woolworth's heiress, and she too (but this time after only seventy-two days) left him with another million. He spent it all very quickly.

Rubi was a professional boxer, a tennis star, he had driven at Le Mans, he kept his job as a diplomat, and become a treasure hunter, an adventurer, soldier, a gourmet, and a world-class polo player with his own team and string of ponies. He dodged the Nazis during the war, rode the Castro storms in Cuba as Dominican ambassador, and endeared himself at every rich socialite gathering in the world. After the breakup with Barbara, Frank

Sinatra said to him, "Who's your next wife going to be, Rubi, Fort Knox?"

Rubirosa and Frank had gotten to know each other when Frank and Ava were gadding around Europe. Rubi looked after them both in Madrid and Paris, and Frank didn't forget—he never does. He soon invited Rubi to Palm Springs. From there Rubi, never one to let an opportunity slip by, went with Peter Lawford for tête-à-têtes with the President and Jackie at their summer cottage at Hyannis Port. Rubi was always acting as "fixer" for some business deal or another. Money just gravitated toward him, and while he never actually did any work, he was constantly putting people in touch. His visits to America were always lucrative for him— both in bed and for his pockets, which seemed bottomless.

He never once denied his reputation as the world's greatest lover. His philosophy on women was plain: "Always treat them as if they are the greatest woman in the world. Love them. Treat them as idols. Make them feel beautiful, and never disappoint them in bed." Observing him at play with the ladies was always a treat. Watch some men when a lady comes to the table. They get up as if their flies were caught in the napkin. Rubi glided up, always the first to greet the lady because she naturally seemed to come to him first. He was irresistible.

Once I kissed a lady's hand in front of him. At the time he frowned slightly, and later, in the washroom, he took me to one side. "Sammy," he said a little reproachfully, "there is a very special way of kissing a lady's hand. It is done with the eyes, not with the mouth. If you are being polite to the girl but are not attracted to her, kiss her hand gently but keep your eyes on her hand. If you wish to extend the liaison, look her in the eyes as your head goes down. If you wish to sleep with her without delay, also look her in the eyes as your head goes up. On the way down give her a touch of promise; on the way up give her a touch of lust. It makes her think her hands are sexual. But never bend more than a little way, or it won't work. Always bring her hand a little way up to your lips."

Now you know why Rubi—and the other great European playboy, Gunther Sachs—wrote the definitive book on sexual exploits, *How to Seduce Women.*

This amazing lesson, from the world's self-confessed greatest lover, amused me at first. He was so natural about it. He wanted to help me, and probably only Casanova himself could have been a better qualified teacher. It was one of the many lessons he gave me, both directly and indirectly, not just about love and the ladies but about how to be a more sophisticated and worldly person.

He had a fatherly attitude toward me, and I never resented it. On such matters he was clearly an authority. I remember when the affair I was having—she was just about as hot in France as you could be—was getting deep. I was going crazy about this lady, and Rubi could see it. Again he took me to one side and, with that soft South American accent, said in glorious understatement, "Sammy, believe me, I am not unexperienced in these matters. This girl is lovely, she's adorable, but she will drive you crazy. You will not be able to sing, you will not be able to dance, you will not be able to act because she will want to devour your talents. She is a woman with whom any man would adore a . . . ah . . . light affair . . . but love, my dear Sammy, is out of the question. I implore you not to get too serious. These things must be finessed. In such matters you must remain in control."

I thanked him for his advice and promptly continued with the love affair. It was just too fantastic to be sensible about. And just too hot not to cool down, as Cole Porter would say, because, months later, I rued the fact that I hadn't listened to Rubi. The woman *was* driving me crazy, my stage performance was suffering, and it took me weeks to get over it. The next time I saw Rubi, I think it was in New York, I said, "You were right, you son of a bitch. I should have listened to you."

He didn't exactly say, "I told you so." Rubi was far too gracious for that. But he did gently murmur, "The head must rule the heart at all times, but never let *them* know it."

Rubirosa dealt with every woman as if he were Boyer courting Lamarr in *Algiers*, which, coincidentally, was a remake of the famous French movie *Pépé le Moko*, which had starred his second wife, Mlle. Darrieux. There is a scene when Boyer tells Hedy she *is* Paris. She reminds him of the Métro and the cafés, and suddenly, as he is talking, she can hear the trains running through the tunnels. It must have been very like the moment when Rubi, in war-torn Paris, courted the real-life Danielle.

He kept his life-style up wherever he was in the world, and I learned a few lessons from him about staying power. Even though he always seemed to be on the move, indeed in the center of everything, he knew how to pace himself. He was very like Jackie Gleason's Minnesota Fats in *The Hustler*. Fats loses a few thousand dollars while Eddie Felson (Paul Newman) thinks he owns the table. But that old Minnesota Fats knows he has the staying power. He looks after himself and paces himself accordingly. At the end of the game Eddie is drunk on the floor. Minnesota Fats goes over and casually washes his hands. He walks out looking immaculate. He has class.

Rubirosa had that same class. He was physically in perfect health, and he looked after his body. He never had bags under his eyes, however late he'd been up, and he would go to infinite lengths to make sure his clothes were always perfect, his nails beautifully manicured, his shoes shined, and there was a fresh carnation in his buttonhole. He knew that if you look good, you are more than halfway to feeling good.

I can't help going back to Paris. Things always moved for me in that town. They still do. I never did attempt to tackle the language, and I never really got into French movies because I don't like the hassle of reading subtitles when I want to concentrate on the action. Dubbing, even if it is good, hurts the sensibilities, and you can guarantee that something is lost in translation. But I always feel at home in Paris.

My wife, Altovise, shares this affection. For her last birthday I presented her with a first-class round-trip ticket to Paris, a suite for two weeks at the George V, and a blank check for a shopping spree. What more can I say about my love for either my wife or that city?

Domingúin, Rubirosa, and a host of others aren't around anymore, but they managed to show me a unique side of Paris life, and I am very, very glad that I had the good fortune to know them all.

Chapter 7

Judy's Pendulum

On Academy Awards night in 1954 there was a crazy flurry of activity in two small rooms on either side of America. On the West Coast a dozen technicians were working at Judy Garland's hospital bedside in frenzy. It was the day after Judy had given birth to her second child by Sid Luft. Though she was still weak, she was enjoying all the mad hubbub around her. On the East Coast it was early evening, and a heated and excited discussion was under way in my dressing room at the Copacabana. Crates of champagne were stacked outside both rooms, ready to be iced. We all were waiting to celebrate Judy's winning an Oscar for her performance in *A Star Is Born*.

The scene backstage that evening was one which occurs in most American homes on Oscar night—and certainly in every dressing room in the land. Like everyone else, I was rooting for my favorites, though, as far as I was concerned, the whole thing was a foregone conclusion. *On the Waterfront* had to win the Best Picture, and Marlon Brando would walk away with the Best Actor Award. This was his fourth nomination in almost as many years, and it was a *fait accompli*. Looking at the women,

I knew Judy was up against some heavyweights. Audrey Hepburn had been brilliant in *Sabrina*, as had Jane Wyman in *Magnificent Obsession*. In any other circumstances I would have loved Dorothy Dandridge to win for *Carmen Jones*, but musicals seldom rate in the awards. I admit I didn't take Grace Kelly's performance in *The Country Girl* very seriously, set against Judy's tremendous *tour de force*. In my own mind I was convinced Judy owned that Oscar. She had given the definitive performance of her long and brilliant career in a movie where she had finally been allowed to use the full range of her fantastic talents. Now, before it was too late, we were at last going to say, "This one's for you, Judy."

In those days playing the Copacabana in New York was about as near to heaven as I'd ever dreamed of. I was still with my dad and uncle, and the club was one of the places we had always used as a yardstick of success. We were getting rave reviews, and there wasn't a night when the place wasn't packed with celebrities. On Academy Awards night they still flocked in. I had arranged to be informed of the winners as they were read out in L.A. It would be part of the finale of our act, and I wanted to create some of the razzmatazz of the actual awards. Winners' names would be put in separate envelopes and we'd open them up with all the anticipation of the real event. We rehearsed the theme music from all the probable winners, and I got a whole lot of special numbers together because at the end of the evening I was going to say, "Hey, listen, Judy, down there in that hospital. You got two awards in two days. Now we're going to play it all for you."

When I hit the boards that night, I built the entire atmosphere of the show around Judy's winning the Oscar. It was very obvious from the start that the audience was rooting for her. Every time I mentioned her name there was a spontaneous roar. We knew that the TV people had set up a portable studio by her bedside, confident that when the time came, they would be able to switch her through direct to the master of ceremonies, Bob Hope. This was to be Judy's moment. Show business owed it to her.

I wanted to know what Judy said on TV, so I could relay it to our audience at the Copa. I wanted them to luxuriate in every glorious second of it. When the time came, someone signaled me from the wings, and I worked around to the conclusion of the first part of our special show. Then I primed the orchestra and lights for the great announcement. Of course, I was right about Brando and *On the Waterfront*, and we all were very happy to pay tribute to a great movie and a great performance. Then it was time for Best Actress, and I just couldn't keep a smile from breaking out on my face, as if to say, "This is it, folks."

They all were calling Judy's name, almost chanting it. Under the spotlight I carefully opened the envelope and pulled out the little slip of paper. The name clearly written on it hit me like a terrible slug in the belly. For a moment I thought I must be mistaken, and crazily I turned the paper over to see if Judy's name was on the other side. The audience caught my disappointment as if I were handing out the plague. I hovered for a moment, not able to even pronounce the name. Then it became quiet enough for me to say, in an ordinary voice, without a microphone, "Grace Kelly." I could feel the gasps. You could have cut the atmosphere with a four-letter word. I did my closing number and walked off the stage.

I've walked off a dozen stages with tears in my eyes, sometimes because of frustration or occasionally anger, but usually because of the great buzz I got when the audience responded to the show. This time I fled upstairs to my dressing room, hardly knowing which way I was going and crying in a way I had never recognized before: a whole mixed bag of emotions, part overwhelming dejection and part sheer, naked anger. I was twenty-eight at the time and very emotional and headstrong. I've seen enough surprises since at Academy Awards to realize that anything can happen. But then it seemed simply inconceivable to me that Grace Kelly could have stolen Judy's Oscar. I knew how much it would have meant to Judy. She told me later that as soon as the people found out that she hadn't won, "They sure packed up quick and got out." One thing's for sure, neither of us touched a bottle of that champagne.

But I couldn't bring myself to call her that night and didn't, in fact, see her for some time. She put a brave face on it. She mentioned her disappointment almost in passing. There was certainly no personal resentment against Grace Kelly. She would shrug it off with: "Some you win, some you lose," or crack a few typical self-deprecatory jokes and leave it at that. But in reality, the incident knocked her sideways for a long, long time.

The Oscar would have meant everything to her. It would have made all the bad times worthwhile. I paced around until dawn, not able to live with anyone, even myself. I was firmly convinced that if the Oscar that year hadn't actually been fixed, there was some undercurrent going on which I didn't know about. Some people, somewhere, didn't want Judy to win it. Yet the industry had made millions out of her. It wanted to go on punishing her for the indignity of wearing herself out while it could still make a buck or two. A lot of people made excuses later, but by then it was too late. Judy didn't have the time left for them all. This had been her last shot and someone had blown it for her.

I remembered when the film was being made how we got the buzz very early on that something was happening. Hollywood's a small place, and it soon got around: "Boy have we got one coming." Naturally enough, whenever I was in town, I was down on the set every day. Sid Luft was ecstatic. "She's never been in better form," he said. He could not hide his excitement, and it was catching. Judy was in superb shape. There had never been anything like it for her, and she knew it.

I watched one of the scenes and realized immediately that this was the quintessential Garland. It was the great acting scene where the studio boss comes in to see her. She has her makeup on, but she's worried about Norman Maine and can't get the act together. She shoots half the number and everyone knows she's down that day. She's sitting in front of her mirror, and Charles Bickford comes in and tells her he's checking up on things. She gradually breaks down and starts crying, all in one scene.

She knows she's got to go back on the set and she's messed up her eyes, but she pulls herself together, and they do the whole production number. It was Garland at her peak, and I don't think there was a dry eye on the set. People—and, let's face it, cameramen and crew have seen it all—were crying openly. When the scene was over, Sid simply put his arms around Judy's shoulder and didn't need to say a word. They both knew she had just given the best performance of her life. Sid took hold of my arm and said, "You see what I mean, they've really got it coming this time."

Within weeks of hitting the screens *A Star Is Born* had a cult following. This was despite some awful drawbacks, none of them

Judy's fault. Halfway through the initial shooting of *A Star* the original CinemaScope film, *The Robe*, had taken Hollywood by storm. I first became friendly with Richard Burton when he was working on it and consequently saw a lot of it in the making. It was an exciting time, though many people had mixed feelings about this new movie concept. Most of the directors were fascinated but cautious because there was so much more screen to fill. Judy had been working nonstop on *A Star* when the studio suddenly decided to remake it in CinemaScope. It was the first of several traumatic episodes, and the film took many more months to make than originally scheduled. But the real crime about the movie at the time of the Academy Awards was that by then there were several versions doing the rounds and none of them was what Judy or the director, George Cukor, originally had in mind. It is a typical example of what can happen to a film when the bankers take charge and the director loses the final cut.

As a sort of glorified screen test for the main film Judy had shot the twenty-minute number "Born in a Trunk." Nowadays people like to think it summed up Judy's whole life story, and maybe it did, but it had precious little to do with the film itself. George Cukor put the sequence to one side and made the film to his—and Judy's—satisfaction.

When Warner's came to distribute it, it decided to get its full pound of flesh out of its property and chuck this sequence back, right in the middle. It didn't fit, there or anywhere, but it stayed. Then when the film went into general release, the theater owners complained it was far too long. At 182 minutes they couldn't fit in three shows a night. Warner's took it back and snipped out 22 minutes—still leaving in the lengthy "Born in a Trunk." But by then the film had already acquired its cult following, and the fans were going crazy about the cuts. So Warner's had to put everything back in. Very few films could survive this kind of mauling, and it stands as a monument to Judy that the film is still brilliant despite its checkered history.

The original had been made by David O. Selznick in 1937 with Janet Gaynor and Fredric March. Janet Gaynor was past her prime by this time, but it was such a hit she was able to go on making films for several years. Two decades later Sid Luft was trying to arrange a "great comeback" for his wife, who wanted to work with her old friend James Mason, at that time about the biggest name in town. Sid packaged Judy, James, and Cukor and sold Warner's the idea of a colorful remake. They spent ten months and an awful lot of money on it. (Cukor, in fact, tried to cut down on expenses by using shots of the premiere of *The Robe* in the opening sequence.)

Judy soon realized it was the most demanding part she'd ever had to play. If there had been nothing else in the film, the two great numbers "Somewhere, There's Someone" and "The Man That Got Away" proved she was at her pinnacle. And I speak not just as a friend who knew her throughout her ups and downs but as a critical fellow entertainer. It was professionally probably her greatest singing achievement. She wrung every emotional note out of a song which was just as distinctive as she was and never once overdid it. She touched the whole "torchiness" of the lyric. There is one moment of pure Garland magic when she wipes out the entire brass section with a downsweep of her hand. Judy spent years before she learned how to stage-manage herself like that. I know, like a million others, that it was a performance which thoroughly deserved an Oscar. And as all this went buzzing through my head that night in the old Copa, the longer I sat sullenly in the dressing room, the more I wondered how it had all happened.

Judy and I had been great pals since the old Rat Pack days at Holmby Hills, and she had later become an honorary member of the Clan. At some stage or another I'd bounced all her children on my knee. I dried her eyes a few times when she was down, especially at the end of her various marriages, but most of the time we had a ball. This friendship had been extended to include Liza Minnelli, who at one time was more often in my house than her own. Mother and daughter craved deep affection and friendship, and both were very special women.

So I was ready to admit freely I was biased, but I still couldn't stop asking myself: How could Grace Kelly have got it?

Before *The Country Girl*, Grace had made only three movies. Her debut in *Fourteen Hours* was particularly unmemorable. When she made *Mogambo* with Ava Gardner and Clark Gable, the critics merely talked about a "new blond actress." But in her seemingly insignificant role in *High Noon*, the now classic western, we see how far Hollywood was prepared to indulge her.

It was very clear to anyone who had anything to do with the movie that the director, Fred Zinnemann, had a crush on his new star. When they finished shooting, the film was roughly double its final length. All the extra material involved the love affair between Gary Cooper and Grace. Zinnemann really lavished his camera on her. There were endless close-ups from every angle. As a sort of funny sidelight to all this, Coop's ulcer was acting up on him and rumbling at all the most romantic times. He just couldn't stop burping.

Anyway, the uncut film got booed out of the Riverside sneak preview, and the producer, Stanley Kramer, reported to the studio that it couldn't be released. Only after some bright editor had cut the film in half did it see the light of day. The editor, within a few days, made the clock into the real star, his floor covered with miles of Grace Kelly profiles. Once the romantic angle was dropped, Coop's ulcer even added to the ultimate suspense. But it is true to say that *High Noon* became a classic only after a brilliant editor had all but ousted the female lead and replaced her with an inanimate object.

Grace Kelly's essential appeal was based on that rare effect of class which allowed her to float through films as if in a dream sequence. She was always extremely watchable, but she rarely needed to act. Her image was enough. She had drifted into films after being born very rich and becoming a top model. She made eleven films over five years before marrying her prince. It was as if her Hollywood career had been part of the rigmarole of life as a top debutante, her Oscar something to place beside her trophies from the tennis club. *Mogambo* was typical. She was the supreme cool, intellectual actress, doing it all with the mind and the pose. You knew that however long she had been living in that jungle, she would never smell of sweat.

As a film *The Country Girl* was not at all bad. It told the story of an alcoholic singer, played by Bing Crosby, and how he tried to deal with a comeback. It was a strong part for Bing, and they worked well together. But I don't think there is a single scene which will be remembered as definitive cinema.

Because of the award, Grace Kelly became big box office. But I would stake my life on the fact that she could not have sustained that terrific interest unless Hitchcock had come on the scene. During 1954 MGM virtually turned its hottest new star over to him. It wanted him to exploit her upper-class charm in three vintage Hitchcock classics. Grace turned in good performances. In both *Dial M for Murder* and *Rear Window*, Hitch's magic with thrillers got the best out of her cool countenance. But it wasn't until they had really come to know each other that she made the only exceptional film in her life. She played opposite Cary Grant in *To Catch a Thief*, and no one can say she wasn't brilliant. Hitchcock could by now mold her like putty, and Cary Grant always inspired his leading ladies.

After this she left both Hitchcock and Cary Grant and acted in only two films before giving it all up for the aristocratic life of Monte Carlo. She made *The Swan,* in which she very adequately played a young princess opposite the incomparable Alec Guinness. And, finally, she made *High Society*.

I admit that *High Society* has a place in the hearts of millions of people. It created a kind of magic which made it literally swing into becoming a classic. But I have doubts about its ever being placed high on the list of "All-Time Greats." It is a joy to watch, and it was a marvelous idea to do a musical remake of the old *Philadelphia Story*. Frank Sinatra and Bing Crosby, playing sympathetic cronies, gave it a unique status. But it departed from the popular format of great musicals. The old MGM way was to string some script between the songs—which tell the real story. In *High Society* the people told the story, and the music just hung about. This made many of the songs, however good, incidental.

It is no great secret nowadays that Bing was crazy about Grace, and he always claimed *High Society* was his greatest film. Who am I to argue? But my feeling is that they were willing to compromise the old musical tradition to accommodate Grace Kelly, who was not overfamous for her ability to sing and dance.

The greatest song in the film is, of course, "Well, Did You Evah!" in which Frank and Bing cement their friendship at the bar. It would have been impossible for either of them to upstage the other, and neither tried. Funny enough, this is the only song in the whole film which wasn't written especially for it. It had first been performed on Broadway by Betty Grable and Charles Walters, and the director of the movie happened to be the same Charles Walters. "Well, Did You Evah!" did it for me, and I suspect for Mr. Walters, too.

In the Clan days, under Sinatra's influence, we all tended to be One-Take Charleys, and we used to try to keep actual shooting time down to a minimum. Sinatra lost all the impetus if he had to hang around for take after take. Bing was very much the same. Both of them always knew their lines, turned up on time, did a good job, and wanted to get on with the next bit. Both found filming tedious when they played opposite someone who couldn't get it right the first time.

Of the two Frank was the more notorious; he has even been criticized for trying to shoot the rehearsals. I remember Bogey told him one day that if he put as much care into his movies as he did into his singing, he would be as great as Spencer Tracy, who, Bogey always maintained, was the greatest living American film actor. But having worked with Frank several times, I think his way succeeds very well for him. For instance, I was around when he was shooting *The Man With the Golden Arm*, an extremely controversial story about a drug addict. The drug withdrawal scene was by far the most potent in the movie, and the director, Otto Preminger, allotted a whole expensive week to shoot the single scene. Frank got there on the very first morning and said, "Come on, Ludwig. Get the cameras rolling. I know exactly how this thing's got to be played. Forget the rehearsals." Preminger risked it, and it became a classic scene, one of Sinatra's finest pieces of acting.

Bing was very much the same. I watched Billy Wilder direct Crosby on the set of *The Emperor Waltz*. They were shooting one simple line of script, and Bing was clearly getting annoyed. He had only to say to a little dog, "So they want me to go. Come along, little doggie," and the dog was supposed to run and jump into a bag Bing held open. The trouble was the dog would not move, whatever the inducement. By the eleventh take Bing was clearly getting distraught, and the rest of the film crew was catching his frustration. Wilder was rubbing sweat from the palms of his hands, something he rarely does outside a Turkish bath. On take fifteen, some of the old Bing magic had been worn down, and there was an edge to his voice. The dog still refused to move until Bing said, "Get your damned ass right in here." It shot across the stage, right into the bag, as the entire set broke into convulsive laughter. Wilder was wise enough to allow a break to get over it. By the time they reassembled everyone was relaxed again. Bing did those lines one more time—substituting a withering look for the offending words. That dog *moved*.

For movie buffs it is a historic snippet. It was the only time Bing swore while the cameras were rolling. I like to think that some cutting-room Joe kept that little classic and, when he wants to cheer himself up, brings it out and runs it through the projector.

So it was natural that when Bing Crosby and Frank Sinatra got together to sing "Well, Did You Evah!" they weren't going to hang around all day, and Walters was shrewd enough to realize it. They made one take. Everybody recognized that impromptu sparkle and spontaneity right away. It established the mood for the whole movie, and I firmly believe that it was because of that one song that the film became a classic. The immortal words sounded: "Print it."

It was the last movie Grace Kelly ever made.

Show business is a sentimental affair, even if a lot of it is *schmaltz*. We do care about our peers, especially if we ourselves have been through many of the same problems. The night in the Copacabana when Grace Kelly won the Oscar, I wanted Judy to win. Now it seemed the last great prize had been snatched away from her.

The Judy Garland story has been told many times already, and she was a legend long before she died. Her legacy—the amazing scope of her life and times which embraced every field of the entertainment world—will ensure that the story is told many times more. I don't want to start feeding that legend. I knew the lady, and I can still hear that infectious, throaty giggle. When Judy died, Liza Minnelli, whom I'd cared for as a child, gave me her mother's dancing shoes. They are among my most cherished possessions. Judy Garland wasn't a legend to me.

She was a warm, affectionate, generous, witty, and totally dedicated human being. History will assess her one day when her incredible contribution to the industry is shown.

In the old days, when she was in her heyday and Liza was a tot, we had some of the greatest fun evenings I can remember. Liza was never a precocious child, considering her upbringing. We often used to go to Judy's house when Liza was a kid, and she was always looking out of the window when we arrived. She used to call me Uncle Sammy. When they are ten or twelve years old, kids seem to gravitate toward me. Maybe it's because I'm so small. But also I've got this soft spot for kids, and I tend to gravitate toward them as well. Liza was no different. We always played games like hide-and-seek together, and even when she was four years old, you could feel that vast energy coming out of her.

She had the same face with the turned-up nose, and she was always unmistakably the child of Judy and Vincente. Judy used to joke that they weren't going to invite me to the house anymore because Liza always wanted to stay up to hear her Uncle Sammy singing. In those days we used to give ourselves a private cabaret in the living room. Judy used to sing, then I'd do a turn, and maybe we'd tap-dance around the furniture a bit. Whoever was there would do a turn. We had so much fun you wouldn't believe it. Frank would skip around the patio, singing his latest hit. David Niven would tell a new anecdote, and Bogey would just be Bogey. Bogey never needed to do a star turn. He was cabaret just sitting there.

While all this was going on, Liza would be creeping around upstairs, peeking through the banister. One day I asked Judy if I could bring her down to join us. Judy said, "I don't want to spoil her. I told her to go to bed. But I guess it'll be all right if you go get her."

So I crept upstairs, put her in a robe, and brought her down for the fun and games. Sammy Cahn was singing some parodies at the time, and Liza was completely engrossed as she sat on my knee.

She sat there for about an hour, fascinated by everything that was going on. Then she couldn't contain herself. She had to sing. She got up in the most natural way, when everyone else had done his turn, and gave us a version of the latest hit of the day. It was totally natural and spontaneous, and despite the star-studded audience, she stole the show. I forget all the people who were there, but if they'd put the show on in Las Vegas, it would have cost a million bucks.

I remember turning to Judy at the end of it and saying, "With friends like this and talent like that, that girl has just got to be a star."

Judy was thoughtful for a moment. Then she said, "She'll either be a star, or she'll turn her back on the whole damned mess and get a nice husband and a safe job. You know what we've done, Sammy? We've thrown her right into the middle of the Atlantic Ocean, and she's either going to swim or drown."

By this time Liza was tired, and I took her up to bed. She nuzzled close to me and kissed everyone good-night. As I tucked her in, I remember saying to her, "You're going to learn how to swim, little girl. I just know you can swim that Atlantic." Liza had no idea what I was talking about.

Nowadays she remembers those times, and we have remained close. I really do feel like an uncle to that girl. I was best man at her wedding to Jack Haley, Jr. After all, they were two of my best buddies. This also made me eligible to be the main shoulder to cry on when they were breaking up. That's what uncles are for.

All marriage breakups are messy, but I like to think theirs was a lot less messy than most. At least they managed to remain friends. They both are such sensible, nice people that I am sure it would have been that way without Altovise and me. But it was good to know we were close enough to both of them to share the troubles, and that may well have helped.

We continue to see both of them separately and, in fact, are in a way their personal telephone link because they always ask after each other.

Naturally enough, with a big rapport going for us, Liza and I enjoy ourselves immensely if we ever get together for a jam session. The public loves it as much as we do. Liza might be playing Vegas, and I'll suddenly walk out of the wings and ask, "How much longer you gonna be, lady?"

She doesn't need to answer me. The audience does it for her. Our chemistry ignites immediately and spreads to the audience.

Generally, when the audience goes into a theater for their hundred minutes of escapism, they see the plot in terms of what is happening to the stars. The public has already built up a mental picture of who they are and what to expect of them. Judy played any number of different roles, yet in the end the audience saw her only as Judy Garland, almost as if she were a fictional character in her own right.

This, of course, is the stuff of legends, and it was by no means unique to Judy. But the fact that over the years a spate of novels improvising on her life came out proved she was even more of a fictional character than most. I am not trying to add to the legend, but I am trying to justify my feelings of disappointment all those years ago. Her track record was really formidable. She made thirty-five films grossing $100 million, yet when she died, Sinatra had to give the family $10,000 to pay for the funeral. At forty-seven she had had five husbands, three major mental and physical breakdowns, and at least half a dozen comebacks. She was in vaudeville almost before she could walk and had an overbearing mother who was determined to push her daughter into stardom. She was taken into the MGM school, but at first no one knew what to do with her. She made a sort of test shot for MGM called *Every Sunday* with Deanna Durbin. The MGM mogul, Louis B. Mayer, woke up one morning to find Deanna's option had lapsed, and she had signed up with Universal. He hit the roof and roared, "We'll make an even bigger star out of the Garland girl." So Judy's career was launched in a fit of pique.

She made all those "Come on kids—let's put on a show" movies with Mickey Rooney, and Mayer knew he had a potential star when she stole *Broadway Melody of 1938*. She was starting one film the day after she finished the last.

Previously Mayer had been so taken with "Zing Went the Strings of My Heart" when he heard Judy auditioning that he had built the film *Listen Darling* around it. She kept it in her repertoire right to the end. The following year, when the studio couldn't get Shirley Temple for *The Wizard of Oz*, Judy played Dorothy and became an overnight sensation. Despite all the hard times later on, people always associated her with the little girl on the "yellow brick road." She got a special juvenile award from the Academy that year. It was the first and last time they recognized her.

Judy told me later that everyone had backed into that film, never knowing it would become a legend. Judy was actually third choice and treated it as just another job. Mayer was rooting for Shirley Temple, annually head of the popularity charts and owned by Darryl F. Zanuck, but he and Zanuck had a row at a party one night, and Zanuck shouted, "Go screw yourself. . . . You'll never get my little girl."

After a long argument Mayer stormed out of the room, ranting, "I'll do it without you. Who needs that little bitch anyway?" But the next day he was looking around desperately. The vehicle had

been built for Shirley. The first choice they came up with was
Virginia Weidler, who played the smily little kid in all the MGM
films, but she didn't do well on the tests. Then, almost as an
afterthought, someone tested Judy. The attitude was more or less:
"We might as well see what else we have hanging around the lot."
She got the part.

For the next seven years—until she met and married Vincente
Minnelli—she made smash hit after smash hit. Just look at the
history of MGM, and you will quickly see her vast contribution
to that studio. Her *Meet Me in St. Louis* helped MGM make
record profits in 1944, $14.5 million. She went on to such hits as
Easter Parade, in which with Fred Astaire she sang "We're a
Couple of Swells," another song which became associated with
her for the rest of her life.

When she took part in the MGM Silver Jubilee in 1949, Judy
was still riding high as one of its biggest money-making assets.
But it was also the year she began to crack up. The girl was simply worn out. She had never had a youth. She was working on
The Barkleys of Broadway but broke down several times, and
Ginger Rogers took over. Then she tried to come back with a
bounce in *In the Good Old Summertime,* the charming box-office
smash in which Buster Keaton made his last appearance for
MGM.

By the end of that year she had prerecorded the whole of *Annie
Get Your Gun* (only recently released as a record) before MGM
decided to replace her with Betty Hutton. The studio had bought
that show for an unprecedented $700,000 especially for Judy. The
crack-up came fast, and those of us who knew Judy could see it
happening. Mickey Rooney begged her one day, "Just slow down,
honey. You're burning yourself out. Take it easy. Take a year
off." It was the kind of thing we all were telling her. I guess we
were a little too late.

First the studio suspended her for not turning up on time.
Then she went into the hospital for a rest, with Mayer picking up
the tab. When she came out, she made her last film with MGM.
Summer Stock was a foretaste of her next nineteen years. She wore
herself and everyone else to a frazzle, alternating dizzily between
triumph and disaster. This picture was her swan song for MGM.
The studio which she had helped build into the biggest and best
of its kind dumped her, publicly calling her "unreliable, un-

predictable, temperamental, and costly." No one else would risk hiring her.

She was also washed up with Vincente. She took baby Liza with her to New York and, after her dazzling career, found herself completely alone. For the first time in her life she had no one to look after her, and she was also flat broke. She never did discover where all the money had gone. She yearned for affection and found it very quickly in Sid Luft, who took her under his wing. He nursed her slowly back to health and mended that bruised ego. He persuaded her to make a stage comeback, first in Europe, where she broke up the London Palladium. She sang "We're a Couple of Swells," and the place just fell to pieces. When she later sat on the side of the stage under a single spotlight and sang "Rainbow," the audience couldn't get enough.

At last Luft thought his wife was ready for a comeback in her real testing ground of New York. It was the first of many, and it coincided with the reopening of the refurbished Palace Theater as the nerve center of variety. No one will forget the evening of October 16, 1951, when the curtain went up for that glittering first-night audience. She didn't need the special effects of the "yellow brick road" to carry her over this rainbow. Smith and Dale, the original Sunshine Boys, courted them all in the first half. Then it was Judy's night. It was the all-time smash hit everyone wanted it to be—a complete sensation. The show was originally billed for four weeks, but they seemed to go so fast she was persuaded to do four months. This was a mistake. Judy was geting ovations all the way, and the Palace scooped $750,000, but the run was a couple of weeks too long. One night she had to be helped off the stage, suffering from exhaustion. When she came back, apparently revitalized a few nights later, it seemed like opening night all over again. The last show was probably better than them all.

After Judy had had a long rest and some other very successful concerts, Sid Luft was convinced she was ready for *A Star Is Born*. She was ready all right, but Hollywood did not seem able or willing to let her back into the fold. She eventually got over her disappointment and went back on the road.

She had a good character lead in *Judgment at Nuremberg* and was even nominated for Best Supporting Actress, but the award finally went to Rita Moreno for *West Side Story*. Then Judy departed on her historic final tour of America, which included Carnegie Hall. It was probably the night she became a living legend, though it's hard to pick a single night out of such a career. The recording of that show was the first double album to make more than $1 million.

After two more brief, unhappy marriages, to Mark Herron in Los Angeles and Mickey Deans in London, Judy died on June 22, 1969. Twenty thousand people waited in the rain outside a Manhattan funeral parlor—they knew that a hell of a lot of show business was lying there with her.

Right up to the very end she had been working, for Judy never gave up.

People always remember Judy's tears. In fact, she became so identified with, and good at, crying to order that the studios began to put salt water into every script. But how many people now remember that totally contagious laugh with which she could light up any society she found herself in? And usually she was laughing at herself. There were undoubtedly low times for Judy Garland, but I don't think they were much worse than for many other people in the entertainment business. Most of the time she was vibrant, hardworking, and bubbling over with affection. People began to build their own image of her, and they "saw" her as being a tragic person. It was *they* who began to put the emotion into her songs.

Both Judy Garland and Edith Piaf had to have mountains to climb. They were at their very best when fighting the biggest problems. When Piaf went onstage after hearing her lover had died, she took that grief out there with her. It seems a sad thing to say, but she was never better. Judy was the same. She played it all out front. I don't mean to say that she was dishonest; she just couldn't hide it. The rawness made both of them seem terribly vulnerable, yet actually they were very strong. You can tell that by the *power* of the emotion coming from them. In turn, we as an audience tend to glamorize the sad-clown angle—the happy face hiding the broken heart. The performer has a general tendency to "play" the sympathy his way. We all know that a great artist bleeds from time to time, some more than others. But the really great performers, some of whom have undergone terrible personal tragedies, rarely bring their sadness onto the stage.

Neither Judy nor Piaf could hide the ache, and consequently

it became part of the act and a major part of the legend. The funny thing is that both of them were such entertaining giants that it is ridiculous to think of them merely as poignant women. They had so much more in them than that. Judy sometimes played for sympathy, but in reality she had the balls of a lion and became a brilliant cabaret artist with fantastic audience rapport. And when she did play for sympathy, you can bet your life someone had told her to do so. There are many people on the fringes who like to try to make a contribution by giving advice. If you are influenced by them, they will manipulate your true image. Judy was manipulated by everyone, even though her basic honesty always shone through. The people around her saw her as the audience saw her, and they tried to create that image of her. It is *we* who create the auras.

I know a dozen people who could have sung "Over the Rainbow" just as well as Judy. But we began to identify it so much with her personality that she became the only person allowed to sing it. I have found very much the same thing with some of my songs, especially those written by Anthony Newley and Leslie Bricusse. When I sing "What Kind of Fool Am I?" the audience reads all sorts of things into it. They've formed their image of me before they come in, and that song seems to give them things they can associate that image with. I don't ask them for that; it just happens. Tony Newley tells me they don't read half as much into it when *he* sings it, and the lyric probably has a lot more to do with Tony than with me. It is the same with "Bojangles." People have made that song what it is because of what they have read into it. It is indefinable, but it is a very great part of what staying power in show business is all about.

Rapport with an audience is an essential factor for success. Many people consider themselves successful only if they get standing ovations. They are very flattering, but Judy was craftsperson enough to know that the best kind of act never keeps an audience up high all the time. There have got to be lulls. She knew, and I know, that sometimes the least demonstrative audiences are the best. The key is to *be able* to get the ovations when you want them. No one will ever doubt that Judy was a past master at that game. It's very much like a boxing match; you feel them out in the first couple of rounds, get in a couple of sneaky shots, parry awhile, then POW, hit them with everything you've got.

The commitments we all make are nothing to do with the contracts; they are with the public. You can't lie to them because sooner or later they find you out. Everyone has low periods, but if you haven't got the natural resilience to bounce back, you might as well reserve your place in the toilet because that's where you're heading.

The absolute ideal, which in a funny way Judy often managed to attain, is to hang on to the pendulum and move on a continuing counterbalance: to be able to evaluate coolly, swing on the highs, deal with the lows, but never stop the pendulum from moving. Most of the time you'll find you're heading for the middle, and it is then that you are probably at your best. Some entertainers get panicky when it's not all highs, but no entertainer was made like that. Judy had got that pretty well worked out in the last decade of her life. She got there just a little before I did.

Liza Minnelli, like her mom, is learning the same lessons in the same way, the hard way. I know she'll survive her bad times because I know what she's made of. She has the resilience to come back. Altovise and I have had to nurse her several times when she was down. Sometimes she'd turn up in the early hours of the morning with some new catastrophe or other, just as her mom did many years before. But she gets the pendulum swinging, and like us all, she's a hard one to keep down. Like her mother, she knows how to bounce back and back, and back.

We shouldn't always remember the Judy Garland who tried to commit suicide. That was a small part of her. We have to remember all the great highs she had as well. I finally got over that night in the Copacabana. Now I just like to remember all the laughs we had. And I know one damned thing: Oscar or not, the way she sang "The Man That Got Away" will live as long as anything else Hollywood ever produced. In fifty years' time, when the Academy Awards celebrate their centenary, I for one know that song will still be haunting them.

Chapter 8

The Duke and History

Since the beginning movies have recorded, and altered, history at will. Hollywood always happily changed the facts to fit an acceptable story. Yet the social problems of the thirties were reflected in the glut of gangster movies; musicals paid tribute to the golden age of Broadway; in the forties action pictures became the main means of propaganda during the war. Above all, America's official history has become legend through countless westerns. Throughout much of it, John Wayne strode with his six-foot-six frame to become one of the great American heroes. He shot up the bad guys, conquered the West, won the Second World War on most of its fronts, policed our gangsters, walloped our heroines, and kept the cattle moving. What would America have done without him?

John Wayne was to westerns, of course, what Errol Flynn was to the swashbuckling era, Cary Grant is to light comedy, and Christopher Lee will always be to the phantom genre: the Very Best. He had his own stamp of character and personality which was instantly recognizable, continually attractive, and, more than anything else, much larger than life. He rarely needed more than the lightest touch in direction. His death left a huge void in the movies. There may be a few superstars around, but Wayne was completely distinctive and, as with all the truly legendary actors, he made it all look so easy. He was one of perhaps ten actors in the history of motion pictures who were literally big enough for Hollywood. It never daunted him. He played the entire industry his way.

Wayne managed to brand a massive *D* for Duke on the very hide of the Hollywood western. He epitomized the way people see the early West—big, brave, and brash. Not only did he make an awful lot of cowboy films—leaving us a rich legacy—but he made the very best of them as well. *Stagecoach* gave us the definitive western, a film which left an indelible mark on movie history. But in *Red River* he went on to make the finest cowboy picture ever conceived. The brilliance of these two films remains as a monument to Wayne. He didn't need to do another thing.

When I got the chance to ask the Duke about *Red River,* all he said was: "Yes, I guess it was a good film. But I was able to play it like an excellent hand of poker. You got the cards so you just play them with all the confidence. I had the cards in that film. We all did. Monty Clift was great. He didn't know how to ride, and he couldn't tell one end of a pistol from the other. But he acted his butt off, and we all chipped in and helped him. We didn't exactly cover up for him, but we sure made it so he looked good. Now *Stagecoach* was a different matter. In that film I really had to act."

Years after I had first seen these films, I began to rent his huge converted minesweeper, the *Wild Goose,* for what was then $1,000 a day, a bargain price because it could sleep a regiment. I'm still kind of proud of the fact that every time we turned up at the dock, he was always there to pipe us aboard. Everything on the boat seemed to be incredibly large; it needed only John Wayne to add to the dimensions. He'd yell, "Hiya, Sammy, come on board," as if he were doing a marine movie. When we got inside, he'd personally check everything and pour everyone a drink. No detail was too small. He'd pound the steaks to make sure they were tender, run his finger along the curtain rod to find dust, and take a large drink to make sure the crew hadn't watered the liquor. He was the ideal host, and I'm pretty sure when he went to sea himself, he was the ideal captain. When he was sure everything was shipshape, he'd give us one of those salutes that only Wayne could execute and send us on our way.

Naturally I had met him several times over the years, long before I first hired the *Wild Goose*. He had been up to the house a couple of times, and we had been invited over to his place for various parties and meals. He was always a very regular guy with me. Early on he learned of my fascination and obsession with cowboy movies, and one day, backstage someplace, he came into the dressing room and presented me with the hat he had worn in *Stagecoach*. It was a very touching gesture, which I will appreciate for the rest of my life. He said something like: "I didn't even let my kids ever touch this stetson. It was very dear to me. But I guess you'll be able to find a home for it, knowing you and your love of westerns." It was an emotional moment for both of us when I took it from him. It had very great sentimental value for him. John Ford, who directed *Stagecoach,* had been his closest friend—far more than a movie acquaintance, a really close buddy. Wayne and Ford had been friends for as long as either of them could remember. Jack Ford was the greatest influence on Wayne's life. They'd sit for hours together fishing, and maybe every now and then they'd say a word or two and then get back to the fishing. Their friendship started when Ford was filming *Men Without Women* for Fox Studios. There was a point when some actors had to dive over the side of a boat into very heavy swells. They wouldn't do it because they said the seas were too heavy. Ford had to get the shot that day, and he suddenly yelled, "John?" It was a question, but Wayne didn't hesitate. After the crew picked him up, the rest were so ashamed they jumped to order. Ford simply said, "Thanks, John," but it was the beginning of a long friendship.

While he was still at college, Wayne got a job carrying scenery for Jack Ford, and in fact, Ford kept him humping scenery for a long time, but John Wayne was learning all he could about the movies. It was Raoul Walsh who gave him his first break, in the most ambitious western ever attempted, *The Big Trail*. The film turned out to be a failure, but Walsh had recognized Wayne's potential.

Wayne then hung around for several years, playing bit parts. He made several pictures which were box-office poison before Fox dropped him. Columbia eventually picked him up, but Harry Cohn, who was then the boss, took an instant and unshakable dislike to him. He unfairly accused Wayne of "fooling around with my girls" and threw him out of the studio. On top of this Cohn got on the phone and told everyone that Wayne was an alcoholic. An amused Jack Warner heard the story and decided to try Wayne out, if only to annoy Cohn. Warner put him in a series of low-budget quickie westerns which started off as Bs but soon won Wayne a following. He left to join a studio called Republic, where, after five years in the wilderness, Ford found him again when he was casting *Stagecoach*.

The rest is history. *Stagecoach* was the film which cemented their friendship and both their reputations. It was a very important film for them and for Hollywood. Wayne was the last to see the dying Ford; they had a slug of brandy together. That hat was a symbol of the whole era and of their friendship. I naturally treasure it very much indeed.

A lot has been made of John Wayne's right-wing politics, and maybe this view of him is justified. The public saw him as the all-American Conservative with a capital *C*. He certainly took a stand over his dislike of the Communists, and frankly I don't blame him for it. He was the archetypical patriot, and I never saw anything bad in that. But conservative is not racist, and where I was concerned, the Duke was the kindest, nicest guy in town, a real gentleman. Eyebrows were raised when it was learned we'd socialized and it was rumored we were pals. The talk certainly didn't mean a thing to me, and I'm sure it meant nothing to Wayne either. He was bigger than that.

I knew nothing but respect and kindness from him. We may have stood for different things, but within reason this should not affect personal friendships. I know Wayne felt exactly the same way. He may have been considered a reactionary, but that never made him prejudiced. He was just as aware of man's abuse of his fellowman as I am.

Wayne never made a film which lost money, and more than a dozen of them were record money-makers. He worked with some of the best and some of the most difficult costars in the business. He completely won over such directors as Ford, Howard Hawks, and Michael Curtiz. He had some memorable moments in movies, and privately I've heard some accolades from people who worked with him which would have made his ears burn if he had heard them.

He was stereotyped as the supertough guy who would rather use his fists than waste time on a verbal argument. His screen reputation rubbed off on him and people who worked with him for the first time were awed and a little intimidated. I like the story Mark Rydell told me about when he first directed Wayne in *The Cowboys* in 1972. Rydell is a new-wave director—and brilliant. He does his homework, loves his work, and is a professional director in every sense of the word. The story is about an aging rancher who is forced to take eleven youngsters with him on a cattle drive. When they put the whole package together, Rydell was concerned that he and Wayne might start fighting. They were poles apart in everything. Mark was the intelligent street kid from New York, a superhip cat, a groovy now person. He had just finished shooting *The Fox* when he was offered *The Cowboys*. He was of two minds whether he could go through with it. He saw Wayne only as the superestablishment figure who would be stubborn and probably rude.

Mark remembers he got to the set on the first day ready to establish his will from the beginning. "I was determined that Wayne should toe the line," he said. "If it meant a big breakup on the first day, then that's the way it had to be."

They had a script conference, and Wayne asked Mark why the hero had to die. Mark loaded his guns ready for a fight. "Well, Mr. Wayne . . ."

"Call me Duke."

"Well, Duke," he said, keeping his cool, "the whole point of the film is the turnaround with the kids going after the bad guy themselves. This couldn't happen unless the hero dies."

"Good," said the Duke. "I wanted to know whether you were getting the same message out of it as I was. Because if we were on a different track and had the guy dying for different reasons, it might not have made sense to the audience."

Mark soon learned what most directors found out about Wayne. He didn't like to die on screen unless there was a very good reason for it. Mark had made his point, and the Duke had agreed with him. Before the morning was out, Wayne got up and said, "OK, let's roll."

There never was an argument. Wayne played it exactly as he was told to. Mark told me, "I have never been more surprised or pleasantly impressed. Wayne was the ultimate professional. Once he realized we were both in the same key, he became completely cooperative. He was the easiest person to direct because he played the character he knew he could do best—John Wayne. I had far too many preconceived ideas about the guy, and it was a great surprise to find him so charming both on and off the set."

It was exactly the same with Katy Hepburn when Universal made *Rooster Cogburn*. Everybody was convinced there would be a huge battle of wills between these supergiants of the screen. The world's largest ego problem became Topic No. 1 in Hollywood. The only people who were not absolutely fascinated by the prospect were Wayne and Katy themselves. They immediately recognized they both were true pros, and they got on like a house afire. Wayne did have a strong personality, but he very rarely tried to impose his will on anyone. With fellow professionals he could be an angel.

When Hal Wallis first thought of casting Wayne and Hepburn together, it was from a devilish sense of humor. But the more he thought about it, the more he felt, Why not? Only someone with Wallis's vast reputation—after all, he had made 400 films, including *Casablanca*, which among them had pulled in 32 Oscars and 126 Academy Award nominations—would have been taken seriously when he came up with this idea.

However, once they started shooting, the director, Stu Millar, told me he knew they all would have a lot of fun together. One day Kate had to do several takes and was beginning to lose her cool. Wayne went over and put his arm around her comfortingly. When they'd finally done the shot, he picked her up in a huge bear hug and gave her a smacking kiss. Kate was as tough as he was, and he liked to say that when he watched her work, she reminded him of himself.

On locations up in Oregon, Kate had a lot of difficulty riding a horse. In fact, she admitted she couldn't ride a hobbyhorse. To get through some of the scenes, Millar hired the best stunt girl in the business. Kate watched her ride for a while and decided to do it all herself. "She doesn't sit on the saddle as straight as I do," she said, and, as Wayne observed later, "she got up on that horse and gave it hell." Both of them came off the set raving about the other and agreed they should have met as costars twenty-five years before.

The Shootist, which Wayne made soon afterward with Betty Bacall, was a very courageous film for him to do, considering he himself had only just escaped death from cancer. He gave the role of the dying gunman his own mark of courage and dignity, and Betty found herself, just like Kate, dumbfounded by his sheer professionalism.

But the Duke's favorite leading lady was always Maureen O'Hara. They both were big and blustery and made for each other on screen. In *McLintock,* when he dragged her through the pig manure, they had to do half a dozen takes while Maureen got furious. She took it all in good spirit, of course, but she was fed up because the whole scene had originally been a mistake. She and Wayne were larking around when he gave her a playful kick and she went sprawling in the muck. The director, Andrew V. Mc-Lagen, loved it. "We've gotta use it," he said. "Let's do it again."

Wayne and I once talked about making a movie together. We both realized it would have to be a special vehicle. It depended on the script. He also asked me to do a part in *The Alamo,* which he directed in 1960. It was a project very close to his heart, and on the set there were several of my pals, including Laurence Harvey. The Duke wanted me to play a slave who helped one of the wives out of the Alamo, supposedly the only ones to escape. While I desperately wanted to work with Wayne, several aspects of the idea didn't attract me. I was into making fun movies at the time, and I felt too young for the part. I saw my movie breakthrough coming with the Clan pictures rather than playing a small part in a very big Wayne film. However, I was going to do it just for the experience, but in the end it clashed with the filming of *Sergeants Three.*

I always fancied myself as an old-style western gunslinger, and I spent years in Hollywood trying to get people to cast me in such a role. The studios didn't think that a black cowboy was plausible. They hadn't read their history books. After the emancipation of the slaves the West was covered with black cowboys. Film historians also forget that there were entire black regiments in the Civil War. In fact, the "All-American Cowboy" is the biggest myth of all. Nearly everyone in the West during the nineteenth century was an immigrant. The studio heads hit the roof when someone suggested Errol Flynn should play in a cowboy film. "How can an Irishman play a cowboy?" Yet the West was opened up by people from just about every European nation. Billy the Kid's first legitimate job was for an Englishman. It was the same for the blacks, who built most of the railroads in this country. A movie which acknowledges this has yet to be made.

In my youth Hollywood was not so much dependent on as completely indebted to the cowboy film. It was the staple diet of the nation's movie houses. At one point any studio that had financial trouble made a western and got out of it. These days even the fortunes of television rely heavily on the western, not just by creating their own series but by endlessly showing cowboy movies. America and a very large part of the rest of the world respond to this familiarity with the kind of affection given a comfortable old shoe.

Times have changed, and the public now demands something more from its heroes. But in the old traditional western the men were strong and aggressive, and the women weak and passive. Parents were firm and loving, and the children respectful. The old hero was a strong man who stood aloof against weak social groups—as in *Shane* and *The Far Country*.

The classic plot had the lone gunfighter who was self-sufficient enough to survive against all the obstacles. His violence was accepted by the community because they needed him. It was part of the American dream of making it good in your own way. *Dodge City* and *Bend of the River* are other typical examples.

It may have been corny and a complete distortion of history, but I can't help yearning for the old-style western, like *Jesse James* with Henry Fonda. It also had Tyrone Power and Randolph Scott, and the viewpoint was that James was really just a mixed-up kid who went wrong. I don't know, or care, whether that was the real story of Jesse James, but the film gripped me, and that is how I like to think of it. I don't like people trying to mess it up with "realistic" arguments. It was 1939 when they made the movie, and Hollywood was at its romantic best.

I remember sitting in the movies, knowing Jesse is going to get shot because it was history and inevitable. But the film managed to build us all up to a false sense of security. He has given up crime and returned to his wife, and they have begun to recon-struct their lives together. It is a real "Home Sweet Home" situation of married domestic bliss, but we know there is some-one out there trying to gun him down. At that moment he decides to take his gun off forever—and the whole audience is shouting, "Put it on again!"

He had to go, to get shot down, misguided or not. It's one of the moments in movies where I wish the moviemakers had really corrupted history and allowed him to live on. I can still see the way Ty Power fell on the seat. You could hear the crunch of the wood as the chair cracked. Few people realize it wasn't a prop chair; that crack was for real.

It was guys like Gary Cooper who really conquered the West. Cooper was born in the saddle. In fact, he always felt a bit lost when he didn't have a horse around. He became the world's great-est expert at jumping on and off a steed, and when he had to shoot a scene indoors, he didn't know what to do with his legs. Most actors didn't know what to do with their hands, but Cooper had huge, thin, gangly legs, and he always felt awkward. It gave him quite a complex, and sometimes they'd have to do thirty takes because he got so fidgety. They finally worked it out by allowing Gary to do all the inside shots while standing behind a sofa so no one could see his legs.

The other kind of western, which appeared during the sixties, was about the professional mercenary who fought only for money, never for morals. These new heroes disdained society, which they saw as dull, bigoted, and corrupt. In films like *The Wild Bunch, Rio Bravo,* and *The Professionals,* an elite group of self-reliant individuals pitted their wits against the rest. These are "profes-sional" westerns, and the most typical example is *Butch Cassidy and the Sundance Kid.*

Today the western has almost disappeared from our screens, and those that *are* made are often confusing. Clint Eastwood hung up his six-shooter for a Magnum, and along with him, the old western died. Producers started making "realistic" stories of the West, and the old-fashioned mythical cowboys finally bit the dust.

Clint Eastwood is a very old and dear friend of mine, and I can boast that I taught him how to draw a gun. I have something of an obsession about collecting guns and am proud of my permanent display in Beverly Hills. Years ago, when Clint was just an unknown actor getting an occasional bit part, he was always hanging around my dressing room. I got to like him a lot mainly because he'd seen every cowboy film ever made about ten million times, and we had a great mutual interest. We reenacted some of the great movies together, and this was when I outfitted him with some classic six-shooters and showed him how to draw them. I'd go out and do the show, and when I came back, I'd find Clint standing there in front of the mirror, still trying to get it right.

Obviously I took a very great interest when Clint started to make a name for himself in the *Rawhide* TV series. He was at the house frequently, and I could never keep him out of the room which houses my gun collection. He was still an up-and-coming actor in those days, and he enjoyed the chance to laze around the swimming pool. There were times when we knew he was hungry, and we'd feed him as much as we could. As soon as he made *A Fistful of Dollars,* of course, we didn't need to feed him anymore. But he still used to drop by.

I wish I could say the same of Steve McQueen. He was very much in the same position in the fifties, and he was always coming to see us. Unfortunately, we never see him anymore.

Clint, of course, now has his own collection of guns, and believe me, it is every bit as impressive as mine. If we get together for an afternoon, the women go off and do their own thing because they know damned well we're going to talk guns all day.

Clint is still an enigma in Hollywood, and I believe, like a lot of other people, he has not yet shown his full potential. He gives the impression he does not take himself very seriously, but that is a mistake. Clint is one of the guys who work very hard at what they are doing. His films may not have much significance, but they are extremely good entertainment.

Both Clint and Burt Reynolds know their audiences. Burt realizes there are millions of middle-of-the-road people out there who don't want messages; they want entertainment. Clint says, "I like to play the line and not wander too far. If a guy has come out of a bad day in the mines and wants to see a good shoot-'em-up, that's great by me." Burt does the raised-eyebrow routine and has become the Cary Grant of his generation. People buy him when they want sheer entertainment and relaxation. He does a throwaway movie like *Smokey and the Bandit,* and it makes $50 million in its first run. Yet Burt is also capable of brilliant acting, as he demonstrated in *Deliverance*. With respect for the others in the film, Burt walked away with it—doing a serious version of what he does so well in comedy. I'll never know why he didn't get nominated for an Oscar because it was a great screen performance.

Clint began to establish himself as Rowdy Yates in *Rawhide*, but it wasn't until 1964 that he got his big break by going to Italy. He did the first film for $15,000 because he saw the opportunity to establish his own brand of character. *A Fistful of Dollars* was based on a Japanese film called *Yojimbo* which Clint had admired. The Italians had been desperate to get Steve Reeves to play the Eastwood part. Steve had been going strong in all the Italian spears-and-sandals epics. Sergio Leone, the director, saw him in *Hercules* and ran after him, waving dollar bills all over the place. Steve turned it down because, ironically, he was a western movie buff. He said he had too much respect for them and didn't think the Italians could make a decent cowboy picture. After Leone saw a few episodes of *Rawhide* on Italian TV, he wired Clint with an offer. Soon Clint became synonymous with the iron-man, cool-as-ice western killer, and he was always careful to use props which eventually became his gimmicks. You see a cigar, a hat, and a poncho these days, and it is as recognizable as Sherlock Holmes's hat. Yet he also used himself to establish the image. He developed a profile, a coolness, and he used his eyes instead of words. He became the ultimate in machismo in much the same way, and with many of the same gimmicks, as Monroe epitomized ultimate femininity.

Between *Dirty Harry* and *A Fistful of Dollars* you will find the real Clint Eastwood. He was the tough loner who went his own way and owed no man a thing. In life he has an incredible ability to come and go from a situation without anyone's noticing. After years of knowing him I realized I had never seen him come into a room or leave it. Suddenly you look up, and Clint is there. Then you look around to tell him something, and he's gone.

He made the spaghetti westerns for virtually nothing so he and his wife could eat. But he remembered the hard times when he got back and made some of the best deals a motion-picture actor has ever achieved. He struck while he was the hottest property in town. It never went to his head. He just said to himself, as we all do, "How long's it gonna last?" Every movie actor knows he can

Keeping Frank covered on the set of *Robin and the Seven Hoods*.

With Dean, Peter Lawford, and Frank outside our dressing rooms at Warner's.

Frank and Mia Farrow.

On NBC with Jerry Lewis and Diahann Carroll.

Laurence and Pauline Harvey with Peter Lawford.

Dominguin and Ava Gardner in Reno as she waited out her divorce from Frank Sinatra.

John Kennedy and Judy Garland.

On the road with JFK and Adlai Stevenson. Stuart Symington in the
background.

Campaigning with Bobby Kennedy.

Bobby Kennedy.

With President Johnson at a Democratic party fund-raising event.

With President Nixon.

Nixon borrows my camera to take my picture.

Making faces with Steve Blouner, Judy Garland, and Joan Collins.

With Princess Grace and Jack Benny after the annual Red Cross Ball in Monte Carlo.

Some of the wedding party after Liza's marriage to Jack Haley, Jr.: Liza and Jack on the right, Altovise second from left.

make three smash hit pictures and be the greatest thing in the world. The fourth goes into the toilet, and by the fifth he's yesterday's news. That is the constant threat nagging away as soon as the success starts. Clint built a fantastic foundation for his future life as a safeguard against this. Consequently he will never know those hard times again.

He not only took care of every aspect of his future in a business sense but also invented the character that he knew he could play successfully. Then he didn't go around auctioning himself off to the highest bidder, although he could have; he waited until he found the right package. He was meticulous about the kind of character the public wanted from him. He was instinctive about it, and luckily he was completely right. Every now and then he will do a non-Clint Eastwood role and act up a storm. But he knows that is indulgence on his part. He soon goes back to the roles the public expects from him. There are tremendous temptations for an actor to go on stretching himself into new areas. But when it comes down to it, the public has already built up its image of him. Just as audiences don't want me to come onstage and sing like Bob Dylan, when they go to see Clint, they want to see the man they know as Dirty Harry.

Clint lives in Carmel, which is as far removed from the Beverly Hills atmosphere as you can possibly get inside California. Up there he's got a beautiful house and a restaurant called the Hog's Breath. He walks around in his Levi's all afternoon, and no one bugs him. We once went up to stay with him for two weeks. I rented two houses, and we got a bunch of people together. It was a terrific gas. Clint is the ultimate outdoorsman and a nut about ecology. Consequently his place in Carmel is an ecologist's dream place. The water is fresh in the streams, and the trees are all beautifully looked after. Now, when we go up there, Clint and I just sit down and smile at each other. Neither of us ever needed to say, "Well, here we are, we made it."

In fact, Clint has spent most of his working life trying not to be famous. He enjoyed the game of getting there and was sensible enough to know what to do when he arrived, but he has never enjoyed fame in the same way that most of us like to revel in it. He is one of the shyest men I have ever met. He can't stand drawing attention to himself. He likes to get lost in crowds, yet he doesn't even take chances with that. If he goes to a football game, he wears all sorts of disguises, including a false mustache, false eyebrows, glasses, and a panama hat.

Now Clint has his own corporation, and there's no one in the industry who can put anything over on him. He knows the business upside down, and he always delivers. He is just about the only actor/producer who always finishes under budget and ahead of schedule. He knows where every cent is going and studies all the contracts—right down to the extras. He also knows where everyone should be at any given time.

The company is called Malpaso, by the way, which is Clint's little joke. The word means "bad step" in Spanish. It goes back to when all his advisers told him it would be death to get tangled up in low-budget spaghetti westerns. He kept hearing the word *malpaso,* yet when he came back loaded and famous, he decided it was the best step he had ever taken. *Malpaso* became his lucky word.

Eastwood epitomized the sixties hero. In the seventies, with such things as Vietnam, Watergate, inflation, unemployment, and the energy crisis, people seemed to want different heroes—guys who don't treat authority as a bit of a nuisance but as an evil force. With the changed thinking it was logical that Clint Eastwood should get rid of his poncho and put on Dirty Harry's jacket. Films like *The Ox-Bow Incident* and *One-Eyed Jacks* are outdated today for purely sociological reasons. One man against the system used to be part of the popular myth. Now the whole of society challenging the system seems to be prevalent.

The situation is very much the same with that other great piece of Americana—the gangster movie. Fashion has changed abruptly, and the old-style gangster would be laughed at if he appeared in a film about modern society. What would Cagney have done with the part if he played the Godfather (which he was asked to do)? Would he have looked absurd in *The French Connection?* I'm afraid he might.

It says something for Cagney's immense talent that forty years later people like myself are still doing impersonations of the man which are instantly recognizable. (Can you imagine doing an impression of Robert Redford?) We help perpetuate the memory of Cagney as the irrepressible gangster. Cagney always thought of himself as a variety performer. That's why he went to Hollywood in the first place. But they could see those craggy looks only in character parts, and he had to make all those gangster movies before anyone allowed him to show his other talents as a song-and-dance man.

Because I remember him in the variety halls, know every line of every film he ever made, and have spent a good deal of my working life impersonating him, I feel justified in putting myself forward as a Cagney expert. In the old days the troupers watched his advance into superstardom with a mixture of incredulity, scorn, admiration, jealousy, and, eventually, downright awe. As a kid I saw him from both sides. I knew him as one of our own—a song-and-dance man. But I also quickly recognized his brilliance as a movie star.

His mother was Irish, and his father Swedish, and he grew up in the tough way in the slums of New York. Most of his street pals ended up in prison, and he always said it was his mother—with her Irish temper and a strong right arm—who kept him and his brothers on the straight and narrow. They loved her, but they were scared as hell of making her angry. Years later, when he played hoodlums in tough areas of New York, he was acting against a background entirely familiar to his childhood. He was tough, and picking a fight with Cagney was extremely inadvisable. He got his apelike arms from lifting crates in a warehouse. He was almost deformed before he'd admit the work was too heavy for him.

There is no doubt he was the biggest star of his kind in his day, but he was as surprised as anyone could be when he woke up to find himself a heart throb. Most of the films we now consider classics started off as B movies which Cagney accepted merely to keep himself gainfully employed. He didn't come into his own in Hollywood until it let him do *Yankee Doodle Dandy*. He loved and cherished that film. It was always his favorite. Cagney was sometimes difficult to work with not because he wasn't entirely professional but because he didn't take any crap. The studios never impressed him, nor did the money. The big company bosses left him cold. As soon as he became box office, they had to put up with this seeming chip on his shoulder. But they found themselves working with a completely different James Cagney when he did *Yankee*. He gave everything he had to that film, and the industry rightly rewarded him with an Oscar.

He had, it is true, enjoyed making *Footlight Parade* with Busby

Berkeley, way back in the "gangster" days, but it never gave full vent to his talents. All the guys who had known him in the old days winked at each other when he made his last musical, *The Seven Little Foys;* it put Cagney back on the road.

The gangster movies, as we know them, started when Edward G. Robinson said, "All right, you guys—I'm the boss here, see?"— a phrase which was repeated around the nation for the next decade or two—and films like *Little Caesar* dominated my youth. Cagney had, in fact, been around for three or four movies like *Doorway to Hell* and *Sinner's Holiday* before he made *Public Enemy* and became a recognized name. He went on to make the great classic gangster movies and, rightly or wrongly, will always be remembered, even cherished, for them. There is no doubt Cagney was the greatest star of his type in his day, although George Raft and Edward G. Robinson were in the same stable.

In those days the censors hadn't got around to putting pressure on the companies, and it was highly fashionable to tell these stories from the gangster's point of view. Cagney made *Angels With Dirty Faces* for Michael Curtiz and established one of the great acting-directing partnerships. At the end of the picture you still don't really know whether he was a coward or not. Nor did Cagney ever actually say, "You dirty rat," but in *Angels* and, later, *The Roaring Twenties,* he said many similar things, and they immediately entered the language.

He made *The Roaring Twenties* and *White Heat*—another film with an immortal ending—with Raoul Walsh, and the two of them made another brilliant team. Walsh never overdid it and was a first-class director for many years. Somewhere in all films he made, during the last third of his Hollywood reign, you will hear the line "I'm going to get out of here faster than I left my first wife." Scriptwriters were perplexed when this line suddenly kept popping up in their work. When I once asked him why—because it rarely has anything to do with the rest of the story—Raoul said, "It's my trademark. I put the line in all my films. You see, my first wife took me to the cleaners, and I still have to pay her alimony. Now I know she goes to see all my films, just to check on me and make sure I'm still working hard for her. So I get a great kick when I think of her sitting there hearing that same line every goddamned time."

While Cagney was still riding high in Hollywood, there were a lot of other tough guys around. John Garfield, for instance, started a whole trend almost on his own. When he played *We Were Strangers* with Pedro Armendariz and Gilbert Roland, it continued the realistic era of thirties movies but reflected the malcontent society of the postwar era. Warner Brothers had shrewdly recognized the potential and made it a new vogue. It was a direct result of the Second World War. Men were coming back from Europe and Asia tough, hard, and disillusioned. They wanted films which reflected that mood: the little guy who couldn't make it against the system. Garfield almost invented the period. He'd been a good cat in war movies, but he became a movie gangster because of the social conditions and because people had got used to killing in the war.

Richard Widmark was another actor who, almost by mistake, started a new trend when he played Tommy Udo in *Kiss of Death*. The role still burns in the memory, not just the actual performance, but the way the whole piece was constructed around the two leading actors. Widmark played a ruthless psychopathic killer on a train to the penitentiary with Victor Mature. Widmark's wild maniacal giggle at the end of every sentence chilled the whole nation. It was the beginning of a long era when actors were allowed to take dramatic roles seriously. They never lost contact with reality and brought real people to believable locations, almost as a dramatized documentary.

Widmark quickly followed up *Kiss of Death* with *Road House,* in which he played a sadistic and crooked nightclub owner, very much in the same mold. But Zanuck was clever enough to realize the role could be overplayed. It would lose its impetus and value if Widmark relied totally on his giggle. So Zanuck switched him to a series of hero war epics and westerns.

Much of the hard truth about the war was not told in the movies; much, much more was exaggerated. But this was not necessarily wrong. America was in a fervor of patriotism at the time, and the entire war effort had emphasized this.

They brought blacks into these war films only as light relief. We were most likely to be seen as servants opening the door to a homecoming officer in a rich white home, oceans away from the action. In fact, it wasn't until the Korean War—in films like *Pork Chop Hill*—that Hollywood even admitted we had any significant black forces. By then they had to. Our contribution, as in Vietnam, was too colossal to ignore. But during the Second World War itself I don't remember any hue and cry about being ignored from blacks themselves; we just accepted it without thinking. The movie industry as a whole, although it would be the first to deny it, always had a hard undercurrent of racism, especially during the war years.

I'll give you a dollar, for instance, for every handsome Japanese soldier seen in any American-made war movie. Yet the Nazis were always spit-and-polish, square-jawed fellows with glistening monocles. Even the really evil ones were beautifully turned out. The first thing I noticed when I got to Tokyo was just how many good-looking Japanese there were. There were also some very sophisticated and honorable Japanese fighting in the war. But on film the officers were always played as stereotypes by guys like Sessue Hayakawa. They all wore pebble glasses and raped the white nurses, and you never saw a healthy-looking Japanese.

Britain was no better. When the Nazis were bombing the hell out of them in 1942, they released *Mrs. Miniver,* in which a German pilot was even better-looking than the British actors.

Racism is based on a fear of the unknown. The British always understood the Germans and even had a sneaking regard for them, but they never tried to understand the Japanese. It wasn't until *Bridge on the River Kwai* that they even admitted a Japanese could have a sense of honor.

By then we Americans had poured so much cash into Japan we had to start finding out about the people, so we got all those films like *Teahouse of the August Moon,* in which the Orientals were seen as lovable little devils after all.

The producers almost blew *Tora! Tora! Tora!* when they kept trying to swing audience sympathy toward the Americans. Both directors, and I knew Dick Fleischer, who directed the American side of the film so well, had to fight like hell to stick with the original concept: to tell a story from both sides.

In 1951 *Go for Broke* told the story of Van Johnson commanding a special United States squad of Japanese Americans. It was the first-ever indication from Hollywood that the Japanese Americans had played any part in the war.

In this the Japanese were luckier than the blacks. The story of the black Ninety-second Air Division and the Red Ball Express was not told for two decades. Until the early seventies the only

thing ever heard of the black contribution to the war effort was
that we made excellent galley boys. Black war heroes were not
noticed when they got home. The black community itself had to
find them and tell the stories, and even that didn't happen until
the mid-fifties.

The stereotyped Pacific war film has become a standard joke.
Five marines are going to land on some island. The tough
sergeant, who really has a heart of gold, is yelling at them, and
they're all cracking jokes to show they're not really scared. Then
the young boy—a tough kid from Brooklyn—shows a picture of his
girl, and you know for sure he is going to be the first to get hit.

When John Wayne died in *Sands of Iwo Jima,* it was a tremendous shock because normally the Duke didn't die in films. He, at
least, always came through. When the sniper got him, I can remember everyone in the theater went, "Jesus . . . look what's
happened. . . ." The producers almost changed the ending, but
to his everlasting credit, Duke wouldn't let them. He said, "Let
him die. Nobody's safe in this war. Not even me."

Gradually Wayne's wish to tell it like it was began to infiltrate
the thinking of the producers, and attitudes began to change. War
had altered the way people thought about things. Children had
waved good-bye to their moms and come back veteran soldiers.
It was difficult to pull the wool over their eyes; they'd seen it all.
So when Carl Foreman did *The Victors,* every guy who had been
anywhere near the war immediately recognized it as the truth.
There was nothing pretty about that film. There was no propaganda, just the mud, the slush, and the death. There were no
heroes, just people trying to survive in circumstances beyond their
control, waiting for the next bullet or shell, and hoping to get
the hell out of there.

Most cats did what they had to do, often out of fear or a simple
desperation to live. I remember asking Audie Murphy how he
really got on that tank in *To Hell and Back,* which told his own
story as the most decorated American soldier in the Second World
War. He told me he had done it in real life because he thought
they were certain to kill him. He was as scared as hell and didn't
understand what was happening. "It seemed the only way out of
the situation at the time," he said.

Audie, of course, had also been decorated by most of the Allies,
and all his heroics were well chronicled. He told me that to re-

create them on film was an eerie experience. The producers cut many of them out of the movie because, they said, people wouldn't believe them. The film has its unique place in history, yet Audie knew it didn't tell the whole truth. That's why, when he had the chance earlier, he had leaped at *The Red Badge of Courage,* which was an interesting choice for him.

This story of a Civil War coward failed because it confused people. They knew and loved Audie Murphy as the war hero, fighting his guts out. They didn't accept what Audie knew personally: A lot of "brave" actions were motivated by pure fear in the face of the enemy. The people who understood *Red Badge* loved and cherished it, but they were few and far between. It didn't agree with the mood of the time, which was all for people like General MacArthur. They wanted blood-and-guts glamour, and this message was too near the real truth.

Later on Darryl F. Zanuck, at Fox, was another producer who wanted to show just how desperate real war was. When he was shooting *The Longest Day,* he kept stopping the action because not enough people were dying. He'd yell, "I didn't see anyone falling down. Shoot it again. This is war. Guys get killed."

It was the Vietnam War which finally drove the message home. America couldn't have gone through the whole Vietnam experience and come away to show John Wayne leading his men up the beaches. This was a completely different war in which we all became disillusioned. Instead, they started making sensitive war movies, turning the cycle back to *All Quiet on the Western Front.* It was odd because just after Vietnam you couldn't mention the war without everyone's running a mile. Yet as soon as people showed you *could* make a sensitive picture about war, everyone started making them. So Hollywood, as ever, strode on.

Chapter 9
Magic Moments

I know an awful lot of people who are film buffs. I should. Like the gunfighters of old, there's many a man who has tried to take my title away from me. But I've never met one who could tell me how or why he got hooked on movies. Somewhere along the line we all just drifted into buffdom, individually and without any conscious planning, because of some deep-rooted, probably romantic fascination.

You can take as many college courses on film production and techniques as you like, but they will not necessarily give you that special gut feeling when you see a little familiar movement which you have loved and admired a hundred times before. Film buffs are essentially amateurs, most of them on the fringes of movie-making. They are there because they once had that great emotional reaction touching their very souls, probably when they were very young and impressionable, and so deep it stayed with them for the rest of their lives. Anyway, that is about as near as I ever got to describing my irrepressible desire to spend all my spare time watching films.

It would be difficult to name the most ardent movie buff in the world. Mel Tormé has a great claim to the title. He lives and breathes movies, and I have yet to stump him when we play the "movie game." But Jack Haley, Jr., and I would certainly be on the short list. We both have photographic memories, and out of the 10,000 movies going the rounds I reckon we could hold our own on 90 percent of them. We can spend whole days gassing about our favorite magic moments. Buddy Rich and Elvis Presley could always give me a run for my money, but it was Jack Haley, of course, who conceived, inspired, produced, and edited the great nostalgic hit *That's Entertainment* for MGM. He spent years in a huge labor of love, sitting in darkened rooms with fifty years of MGM musicals hitting the screen. There was so much fine footage he felt almost criminal when he had to cut a lot of it out. Even so, he ended up with about eight hours, and he had to make two films.

By Beverly Hills standards Jack's house is not exactly big. But so he could work at home, many times all night, he decided to build a projection room. This took over about half the living area. He told me one day he didn't give a damn about losing all that space. His idea of heaven was to live in a movie house.

I share his sentiments. Way back, when I was a snot-nosed kid, it was just about my greatest ambition. Now I have many hundreds of films in my library, and I get a tremendous amount of pleasure out of my little screening room, but I do have one remaining ambition. Jack has promised to help me fulfill it, and since he is the best editor in the business, I shall be grateful when we both can find the time.

I want to run just about every great film ever made and pluck out the highlights, to get all the magic moments and put them into anthologies under various film types: all the great dance sequences, the magnificent sword fights, the car chases, gangster shoot-outs, and so on. It's a great ambition.

The only other man I know who has ever done this kind of thing properly—and he did it on 16 mm film—was the late Arthur Jacobson. He had every major musical number copied until the day he died. He eventually recorded some fifteen big reels of 16 mm, a complete history of Hollywood musicals. He had a lot of other sequences which he liked, among them some magical gangster pieces, especially many classic shots of James Cagney.

One of the great joys in my life was to visit his projection room and sit for hours on end watching magic musical moments. Even the most fanatic movie buff can forget certain shots which may have gone out of circulation. You sit there and keep saying to yourself, "Jesus, I remember that one." Then so much more comes flooding back.

The only trouble with having someone like Jack help you out on a major movie project is that you can never get rid of him. Once he finds the projection room, he loses weeks. Among his many talents as an editor he combines the instincts of a native Hollywood historian with the love and care of a true movie buff. He will spend days finding little isolated bits of film which, for various reasons, mean something to him. He may be half asleep; then suddenly he'll leap up in the air and say, "That's it. Run it back. I've found it." He'll get really excited. He'll have the frame numbers logged and get a clip. He can locate a few moments of pure movie magic in a mile of celluloid. It is uncanny how he can zoom in on something. He'll have an inkling at the back of his head, a vague memory of a movie he saw when he was a kid: a little obscure shot in a film or a scene where something spontaneous happens. He'll always track it down.

In a lifetime of looking he has discovered some truly marvelous pieces of film, almost by accident. Most of them were long-forgotten by the public, and many of them are unique because of some production abnormality. A shot in *That's Entertainment* is a good example.

Jack rushed up to our house one day dancing with excitement. "Sammy, you've got to see this. You're going to *die* when you get this piece. I've found an ad-lib dance sequence. You won't believe it." Then he played the movie game on me. This can get into the most vicious, loudmouthed, heated, and aggressive game ever invented. Jack and I have often found ourselves at the point of shooting each other's kneecaps off, testing each other out on the most insignificant piece of movie nonsense.

"You'll never get this one," he shouted triumphantly.

"Try me," I said with a nasty squint to the eye.

"An ad-lib two-minute tap dance piece between Fred Astaire and Eleanor Powell."

My mind shot through the musicals like a computer. There

were only two with Astaire and Powell. If she were tap dancing, she'd have a short dress on. It had to be *Broadway Melody*. I sped through the numbers. I made my guess—and I was right.

Jack looked crestfallen for only a second. He was too pleased with his find to get angry with me. "You got it. C'mon, let me show it to you. It's a gas."

We sped to the projection room, and Jack threaded the clip through.

He knew this clip was completely ad-lib because of a technical point. Normally when dancers work out a tap dance sequence, they do it step by step and then put every tap on a separate sound track. It is the same with a singing piece; you will very rarely find a "live" performance on film.

Jack was still excited as he loaded the film and started running it. I immediately recognized the ad-lib, which lasted for about two minutes without a cut. Then, suddenly, on the cut, the film went back to the sound track. For every two minutes like this Jack had watched between 300 and 400 hours of film. He knew it was all there. All he had to do was run it through the projector and find it.

It was actually because of his great romance with movies that he fell in love with Liza Minnelli, who was also a very great friend of ours. They had seen each other casually for some time, often in our company. But when he was going through a load of old movies at MGM, he put together some of Judy Garland's really magic moments. Out of interest and politeness he invited Liza down to the studio to look them over. She went down there, feeling pleasantly curious.

The first thing she saw was Judy's original screen test, and she burst into tears. She and Jack were sitting in a huge empty 800-seat theater, and Liza was howling the place down. Jack had to stop the show and comfort her. They fell in love soon after. In a funny way Judy had brought them together.

Building a film collection is a big part of being a real movie buff, but I have been lucky because I was also allowed to become one of the great set visitors. I always have my camera swinging around my neck, and no one has yet stopped me visiting a working unit. I just turn up, often uninvited, and have consequently seen hundreds of films being made. This is a huge advantage if you are a student of film. Years later you can watch a shot, and you know exactly how it was made. You've seen the tensions build up over a certain scene, and you know why a director did it that way because you were there.

When Billy Wilder saw me coming, he used to yell, "OK, you guys, Sammy's here with his camera. Let's have your best profile."

Otto Preminger would jest with me: "Hah, you still a frustrated actor, Sammy? Come and see how it is really done."

During some very tense moments on set there were a few times when I felt I should make myself unobtrusive, but not often. The film world knows how crazy I am about movies, and mostly it seems happy to accommodate my great interest.

Everyone has different favorite moments in films. There are the all-time classic shots which everyone recognizes as definitive. But many people remember their own little scenes with special affection: maybe just a feel they had for a certain few words, or something they related to, or an idea which moves them in a particular way. I suppose I have about a thousand favorite moments in movies, and I'll play a film through and through just to get to those little bits.

Now and again I'll pull a movie out that I haven't seen for a few years and rediscover some of those old scenes. That's my idea of heaven.

Videos, of course, are going to be gigantic in the future because they answer so many practical needs. You all can be sitting around having dinner, and someone will say, "Hey, you remember that bit in *Hud* when Paul Newman comes through the door. . . ?" All you have to do is pull the film out of the file, and you can show the actual scene within minutes. I can see the day when I'll be able to take most of Hollywood with me in the back of the car. It will relieve my business people. Right now, to keep myself amused, it takes a planeload or two to keep my collection on the road.

Some people, like the film historian Leslie Halliwell, have made a career out of loving movies, and a very profitable one, too. But most buffs remain strict amateurs with a burning, but incidental, interest. I woke up one day realizing movies were a drug. I had withdrawal symptoms because I couldn't get to a film. I knew then I would have to take my own along. Now a very large slice of Hollywood goes with me in a suitcase, and I never get into a position where those withdrawal symptoms can come back.

The movies dominated my early life. When I entered a movie house, I went into an escapist world of glamorous adventure or spine-chilling torment. But I was never bored. To me the movies were very like what the sea must have represented to European kids a few centuries ago. Out there was all the swashbuckling adventure you felt you were missing in real life at home. I never wanted to go to sea, but I spent my youth dying to be a cowboy.

The movies were everything to me. They were magic, another world, fantasy, escapism. They took us all away from the humdrum of real life into some glorious Aladdin's cave of adventure. It was the Depression, and we all had hard times, but those movies just came rattling out of the big studios. All the guys were larger than life, and the women seemed dressed to the nines in billion-dollar bills. Some of them were romantic, many of them dramatic, or they could take you along on some wild and carefree adventure. All of them gave a believable realism to fantasy. And fantasy became hard currency when things got bad. I didn't realize it at the time, but I was the classic embryo movie buff.

In those days we were *dedicated* filmgoers. Not just the movie buffs, for the term had not even been invented then. Everyone went to the movies at least once a week, as a matter of joyous routine. Many people went twice. I don't just mean a few, I mean millions. They became dedicated to their favorite stars in a very personal way. It was enough to say that a new Gable or Harlow picture was playing at the movies to send everyone scurrying downtown regardless of the title or the subject matter. It was fun in the neighborhood theaters, which were cozy and intimate. But if you could afford it, the greatest pleasure in life was to get to the big movie palaces in town, many of them newly built, which offered the height of luxury. You could sink into the huge, plush seats as the lights went down, and you could relax in the beautiful mysteries about to unfold. We were a soft touch in those days. We needed that escapism. We needed heroes. The film stars seemed to be the only people miraculously untouched by the breadlines or the shock waves when the banks closed. Somehow you could never imagine Robert Taylor or Leslie Howard going hungry.

Night after night I stood in the wings and watched an agile twenty-year-old called Gary Cooper strap on his gun or Myrna Loy flickering those irresistible eyelids as "talkies" suddenly became the rage. All of a sudden any guy who could read lines on a stage found the instant lure of a growing Hollywood, and actors were arriving by the trainload. A young but, even then, craggy-faced actor called Humphrey Bogart arrived with a battered suit-case. It wasn't until I was a teenager that his immense talents were fully recognized by the studios.

But he came in the wake of Claudette Colbert, Ann Harding, and Barbara Stanwyck, who electrified the screen with magnificent femininity. Claudette became an instant goddess as soon as her first film was released. The real sign of puberty in a youth of my day was when he first fell seriously in love with Miss Colbert.

I think back now to films she made like *The Egg and I* with Fred MacMurray in 1947. Seeing Miss Colbert as a delightful city girl struggling to help out on a chicken farm struck a chord in the whole nation, and we fell, and stayed, hopelessly in love with her.

Her looks seemed almost indestructible. She was always a highly gracious lady, in both tragic and comic roles, and she had a warmth which made you feel protective. But she could also play the spectacular heroine, as she did in such epics as the original *Cleopatra* and *Sign of the Cross*.

Even in these films she was a "little lady," but she managed to pack so much sheer dynamite into that tiny body that you never really thought of her as small. She was one of the first ladies to take a nude bath in a movie—*Cleopatra*. The whole nation watched as she undressed, but the moviemakers covered it all by only showing her ankles. We all know now that she must have been wearing something, but the rumor soon got around town that she was entirely naked. We rushed to that movie hoping to catch a single glimpse of the forbidden thigh. Of course, we saw absolutely nothing, but the allure was there, the huge turn-on. I spent a great deal more time and effort trying to catch a glimpse of her boobs than I ever did watching Linda Lovelace in *Deep Throat*. At the time, of course, I did not realize that there were fifty people on the set watching her. Somehow or other it was nice to believe, as we all did, that someone had got this private shot of her having a bath.

We guys didn't have it all our own way, of course. The armies of star-struck women who flocked in the millions to the movie houses were held spellbound by Rudy Vallee, Paul Muni, Walter Huston, and Fredric March.

What a wealth of delight there was for a star-struck kid in the thirties, who still had no idea about the harsh, often cruel, and desolate real world outside. I had eyes only for Marlene Dietrich, purring her seductive way through *Blue Angel*. Joan Crawford seemed to descend from heaven itself, and Garbo had only to walk into a cardboard room to send shivers of delight down a million spines. Spencer Tracy, John Wayne, and Clark Gable were then all handsome young upstarts, who subsequently managed to stay around for three more decades. It was the time when James Cagney, Edward G. Robinson, and George Raft were "running" America. Even at that stage I could impersonate them all.

In all those years only Garbo failed to move me as much as the others. She seemed so remote and cold compared to Colbert or Harlow. I had the chance to meet her once, in a Paris restaurant where we were both dining; I have no idea whether she knew who I was, but she was unmistakably Garbo. I thought about it for a while and decided to leave her undisturbed. Maybe it was the legend talking, but she really did look as if she wanted to be alone. I decided to respect her wishes.

Her retirement from movies has always remained a mystery. Either there was some deep, personal moment in her life when she felt she couldn't go on, or it was purely professional. There is a running argument that the magic and mystique which had been built around her were in fact so inhibiting she had to release herself from them. She has never been tempted to return. She was offered the world to play the Helen Hayes part of the grand matriarch in *Anastasia*. She would have been absolutely marvelous in that role, one of the great comebacks of all time. I don't think she even answered the letters.

Fashions in films changed with each decade, and along with the fashions, stars came and went. Only a few survived the whole Hollywood saga. In the old days, for instance, *Network* would have been played by Leslie Howard, Bette Davis, and Bill Holden, who was still around when it was actually made in the seventies. Gable and Lombard would have played the parts inherited by Burton and Taylor, and so on. Over five decades I have watched it all with deep fascination.

When I was eight years old, the film industry was already in trouble for the first of many years. The huge conglomerate called MGM—which already had a past of fabulous proportions—managed to deal with the crisis by putting virtually every one of its stars in *Grand Hotel*. It was one of the few studios which made money in 1933. The screen dripped with beautiful women. Crawford, Harlow, Garbo, and Norma Shearer were all the rage, but not even they could upstage Cagney when he pushed the grapefruit into Mae Clarke's face. It was also the year of *King Kong*, a film which I never fully understood until I was years older. I doubt very much if the people who made that film realized the full social and racial significance of that immortal tale. But it reflected much of the thinking of that era and eventually became a classic for that reason.

One of the great parts of the old Hollywood system when I was a kid was the B movie. This not only gave people a good three hours' entertainment for their hard cash but also worked as a sort of glorified training school for possible future stars and a place for the pensioned-off. But many Bs were unexpected hits. Both *Casablanca* and *Viva Zapata,* two all-time classics, were first conceived of as Bs. *Andy Hardy* and *Dr. Kildare* began as obscure B movie characters who suddenly found a place in the national heart.

Hardworking actresses like Dorothy Lamour got their breaks while toiling night and day in primitive conditions on B movies. As long ago as 1935 Paramount signed her to make a typical B called *The Jungle Princess*. The returns were immediately spectacular and led to a host of starring roles before she found, almost by chance, Hope and Crosby in the *Road* films which were to ensure her everlasting fame.

The last thing we wanted then was any form of realism. We went to the movies to see stars. I didn't want to witness Hedy Lamarr walking down the street in a pair of jeans. I wanted her in her full glamour and glory as an untouchable, yet sensuous woman. You had to see them as larger than life, and to a great extent the successful ones always were.

Algiers became a classic because Hedy and Charles Boyer took every woman away from her kitchen sink and transported her into a dreamworld. All women saw themselves actually falling in love with Boyer, and there wasn't a woman alive at the time who wouldn't have gone with him to the Casbah.

Hedy, by the way, had made a highly controversial film, *Ecstasy,* just before she teamed up with Boyer. It got a very limited release because Hedy could be seen, for several minutes, running through a wood entirely naked. It was outrageous for the time and caused quite a stir. When she later married Fritz Mandl, all his pals taunted him about the scene. People used to stop him in bars and say they thought his wife's pubic hair was very attractive. It drove the guy half crazy, and he spent his entire fortune—some $2 million—buying up every print of the film he could find. He burned them all in a huge ceremonial pyre. He went broke, but he firmly believed he had at last got Hedy Lamarr for himself. Unfortunately some shrewd guy had made a copy of the film before selling out to Fritz. Various copies were made from this master, and the film is now a collector's item.

These days shots of Hedy Lamarr running through a wood in the nude, full frontal or not, don't exactly drive one crazy with lust. I like to remember her as I saw her, the ultimate in sophisticated glamour.

Poor Hedy was heavily criticized for such scenes, and so were any other actresses who might take a chance, both on or off the screen. Generally speaking, the big actors could get away with anything. They had saving graces whatever part they had to play on the screen, and if they got caught boozing in a brothel, the committees of decency seemed to be able to turn away their moralistic eyes.

The stars tried very hard to build up wholesome images of themselves. Gable was always having his photograph taken while he was hunting. Robert Taylor liked to be seen riding horses. They loved to be viewed as tough, manly, outdoor types. Consequently, if they got drunk and womanized, the public indulged them with "Boys will be boys." But the women had to remain pure and glamorous. Even into the sixties a woman star's contract had a morals clause in it, and she could be fired if she spent a night with a guy. The only time women were allowed to be seen getting drunk was when they visited Bogey. It was generally accepted that you couldn't survive in Bogey's company without a glass in your hand.

The great thing about all this was that it actually worked. The top glamour queens became public property in a very personal way. They were almost members of the family, and one felt the need to protect them as if they were kid sisters. I never wanted to think of Bette Davis or Joan Crawford in some sleazy hotel room. Their screen purity became a reality for movie buffs who would have been shocked if they had turned up in some sordid drama. We all remember them, and their great scenes, as if it were yesterday. I often look at some of the modern films and wonder if the new stars will be remembered in twenty years' time.

Many of the people who began making films in those early days had been on the road with us. Our family didn't know much about worldly affairs, but we could tell you which variety act was playing which downtown saloon in every hick village in the United States. Our grapevine kept us alive. We were showmen and entertainers who depended on one another and merged into a complete community in the backwaters of America. They were great, but hard, sometimes merciless times, in which the affinity between performers was sometimes all we could rely on.

Mickey Rooney was the key box-office figure of my youth. His father, Joe Yule, was a burlesque comic whom we were always bumping into in some town or another. Mickey Rooney was born on the road and had show business deeply ingrained in every pore of his body. We were also around when the O'Connor family proudly announced the birth of their son, Donald. And the grapevine kept us tuned to the activities of the Gumm Sisters, one of whom was that great bundle of talent Judy Garland.

In my youth I saw that the transition from variety halls to celluloid could happen very easily if you had the energy and the talent. But more than this, their films became important to me because the people were part of the family. We knew them. We knew their backgrounds and the hard times their kinfolks had been through. We were rooting for them.

Out of the whole MGM school of young talent Mickey Rooney, later to become a great pal who helped me tremendously just when I needed it, became one of the most diverse screen entertainers ever known. To switch from the *Andy Hardy* series into a dramatic performance in *Boys' Town,* to swing in the Judy Garland musicals, and then to go back to being Andy Hardy—that kid just had to have talent.

O'Connor invented the role of the kid who had to get smacked down before he could get up and win. He didn't need the people in vaudeville going for him; he got the whole nation rooting.

Once he had found the formula, he did it virtually every time. It became as predictable as a Perry Mason script, but as with the TV lawyer, it always worked.

So, throughout the thirties, Hollywood strode on. A little girl called Shirley Temple started a new cult, just before I discovered Errol Flynn in *Captain Blood* and I thought perhaps being a pirate might be better fun than being a cowboy. By the time I was ten the industry had become a completely integral part of American life. Chaplin finished the silent era with *Modern Times,* and 220 million people paid for seats in 100,000 movie houses. Variety artists were still in demand, but mainly as between-shows acts in movie houses. The Will Mastin Trio could still find work, but the writing was on the wall. The grapevine began to disintegrate as more and more of our strange nomadic community were forced off the stage. But nothing could stop my enthusiasm for the infinite magic movies continued to bring me.

In every dressing room in the land performers were saying movies were a passing fad and that the people would flock back to the vaudeville halls as soon as the novelty wore off. At this time of disillusion, hope was their only weapon. But this "passing fad" suddenly exploded into one of the most glorious periods in movie history. *Gone With the Wind* burst into the world. In my thirteenth year such greats as *Stagecoach, Gunga Din, Wuthering Heights,* and *The Hunchback of Notre Dame* coincided with the arrival of Ingrid Bergman in *Intermezzo* and Marlene Dietrich in *Destry Rides Again.* Bette Davis alone had four gigantic hits in a row. There was no stopping this massive onslaught called the motion picture industry.

Chapter 10

Great Movies...

Whenever a couple of movie buffs get together, sooner or later the Great Game begins. It can last all night and normally ends with the two of them trying to decapitate each other. The game is simple: What are the ten greatest movies ever made?

The selection of the top ten is a highly personal matter upon which no two buffs to my knowledge have ever agreed. There are so many hundreds of great moments in films that it is often difficult to know where to begin. With only ten on the list do you reject *Viva Zapata* or *The Hustler*? Do you select by categories, like swashbucklers, westerns or musicals, or do you take note of the Academy Awards, which virtually ignore musicals? The question is so difficult to answer that I even spend weeks arguing with myself. There are currently some 10,000 films in circulation or available to TV. There are many thousands more in various archives. I know almost every magic shot worthy of remembering in all of them. In selecting the best ten, you have to be entirely brutal in cutting out everything which is not absolutely the best. So, to this day, I still fight battles between *The Hustler* and *Zapata*.

I know that when the director, Robert Rossen, saw the final print of *The Hustler*, he told Paul Newman he could now die in peace. He knew, and Paul knew, he had made his finest movie. It was a small-budget black-and-white film about pool halls. It seemed to have nothing going for it, except the word of mouth which packed them in while the industry was still blinking. It was George C. Scott's first major role, Jackie Gleason had made only a few movies, Piper Laurie hadn't done one for six years, and Newman was the only box-office name. Yet you can go around America today and still find a million guys trying to play Paul Newman at the pool table.

Rossen had previously directed *All the King's Men* with Brod Crawford and Joanne Dru, and the film had been covered in awards. But that was a blockbuster subject with a brilliant script and a wonderful cast. It would have been difficult to louse it up. But a game of pool, a minority game played essentially by working-class drifters, didn't have a chance—until people saw the movie.

I rate *Anchors Aweigh* as my favorite musical. The story—two sailors home on leave setting their sights on Miss Kathryn Grayson—is almost incidental. The 140 minutes of sheer magic lie in the song-and-dance routines. When the film emerged, it contributed greatly to MGM's record profits of $175 million for the year. Sinatra had come a long way since his original MGM appearance in 1942, when he was uncredited in *Ship Ahoy*. Gene Kelly did all the choreography, which included his famous dance with Jerry, the cartoon mouse. Jerry, incidentally, had also been used in *Dangerous When Wet* with Esther Williams. The MGM executives had been scratching their brains out trying to find new ways of shooting Esther in the water. They had done it all, and it looked as if she would have to put her clothes on and take the next Greyhound bus out of Hollywood. Then some guy rushed in and said, "I've got it. Let's get Esther to give Tom and Jerry a swimming lesson." And Esther went back to the locker room.

The Crimson Pirate was the great classic of its kind. Burt Lancaster, a former successful trapeze artist, was in tremendous shape, and no one will ever be able to swing through the rigging as he could. When the film was made in 1952, Robert Siodmak directed, and Eva Bartok and a young—but even then villainous—Chris Lee costarred.

In the drab early fifties *The Crimson Pirate* became an immediate hit as a pure escapist movie and started a trend which was later developed by such people as Cornel Wilde, billed as the male Maureen O'Hara. Maureen had an established name when Cornel first hit the headlines. In fact, with her he had made one of his best films, *The Homestretch*, and one of his worst, *At Sword's Point*, a picture so awful it seemed for a time his career might be over. He was rescued only when he played a French aerial artist in *The Greatest Show on Earth*. Wilde was never a great swashbuckler, but he was one of the shrewdest. In the early seventies he had his own production company, and with such films as *Shark's Treasure*, he handled everything—direction, main lead, packaging, and marketing. It made about $7 million, and almost all of it went into Cornel's own pocket.

Maureen O'Hara was at her best playing opposite Douglas Fairbanks, Jr., Errol Flynn, or Tyrone Power in the swashbucklers. She could hold her own with them all. She had a great comedic gift which gave the buccaneers a lighthearted sense of fun, and she always played the fiery tigress who had to be tamed.

Ronald Colman began his great days as a swashbuckler, especially in such top-of-the-list classics as *The Prisoner of Zenda*. He was already famous as a buccaneer when the talkies came along and Hollywood woke up to realize he was about the only actor around who could speak perfect English. Selznick loved him and adored his style. He was the ideal choice for *Lost Horizon*—one of the successful films of 1937—because he really did spend most of his life trying to find Shangri-la.

Both Selznick and the director, John Cromwell, chose a brilliant cast for *Zenda* and managed to play them against one another like a finely tuned orchestra. Apart from the lavish costumes and the fairy-tale plot, the potpourri of characters made it the classic of the thirties.

Even Raymond Massey, who had a fairly minor role, excelled in this drama of mistaken identity. Anyone who knows the films of the era found it highly amusing when Raymond ended up as the kindly and indulgent Dr. Gillespie in the *Dr. Kildare* TV series. Raymond Massey had gone through his "desert period" in the fifties, when, in *David and Bathsheba, The Desert Song,* and *Omar Khayyam,* he was never out of a turban. But as far back as the original *Scarlet Pimpernel* in 1934, the public and the studios had sensed his photogenic quality as a villain. With Basil Rathbone, Massey's particular sense of evil made him one of the most slippery characters of the thirties.

David Niven began his climb to fame with *Zenda,* when Ronnie Colman persuaded Selznick he was the only man to play Fritz von Tarlenheim. Niven jumped at the chance, but he quickly had a fight with the director. Both Cromwell and Selznick had a preconceived idea of how they wanted the film to be made and how each of the characters should interact. Niven wanted to play his role as comedy. Cromwell let him try it his way, then fired him. However, when he and Selznick saw the rushes, Cromwell hurriedly brought him back and apologized. He admitted, "I was wrong. It's exactly how it should be played."

Stewart Granger was one of the most brilliant swashbucklers of the fifties. His 1952 *Prisoner of Zenda* came hard on the heels of the brilliant *Scaramouche,* a remake of a Rex Ingram script from the silent era. In *Scaramouche,* Mel Ferrer plays such a dastardly and evil man that everyone roots for Stewart Granger almost from the first few minutes. Ferrer keeps the upper hand throughout. After he has killed Stewart's brother in an unfair duel, Granger seeks revenge and makes himself into one of the world's finest swordsmen. The final scene, in which the two fight all over a theater—upstairs, downstairs, along the balconies, onstage, and in the foyer—is probably the most perfectly constructed sword fight ever filmed. It lasts some fifteen minutes, yet it took months to shoot.

Errol Flynn was the most famous or infamous swashbuckler of them all. When he died, it became fashionable to say Flynn's bad reputation considerably outstripped his fame and his fame outstripped his talent. I think that's far too harsh. Few actors gave me so much everlasting enjoyment. Any man who could do *Captain Blood* and *The Charge of the Light Brigade* would have a place in my heart. In addition, he went on to make such classics as *The Prince and the Pauper, The Adventures of Robin Hood,* and *The Sea Hawk.* I'd fight anyone who denied him his rightful place in movie history, and I have a constant fight with myself when selecting which of these five should go into the top ten. All these films were made between 1935 and 1940, when I was between nine and thirteen—the most impressionable age of my movie life. That counts when I make up my list. And with the exception of *The Prince*, they all were directed by Michael Curtiz.

In all five Errol was the definitive swashbuckler, and I don't want to see a remake of anything he ever did. His *Captain Blood*, with Olivia de Havilland and Basil Rathbone, was the first of his fast-action swashbucklers, and it shot him immediately into the hearts of the public. It was wonderful, escapist stuff performed by a born maestro. He had come to Hollywood on a whim from Tasmania, where he was born, via Australia, where he had gone to make a fortune and ended up as a film extra, and London, where he whetted his appetite for movie work. Hollywood finally nurtured him into a star.

Curtiz knew how to handle him, and when they made *The Charge of the Light Brigade* in 1936, even a cynical Jack Warner, who had signed him in London, realized he was onto something hot. Warner could never stand Flynn—he was often at odds with his top stars—but he happily acknowledged Flynn's sheer animal excitement. With Olivia de Havilland again costarring and backed up by a superb Niven, he thundered and crashed through the most lavish production of the year.

In 1937 Warner cast him superbly in *The Prince and the Pauper*, and the next year came *The Adventures of Robin Hood*, which dominated my youth. I've seen it hundreds of times, and you can tell from watching the movie that the cast must have had a great deal of fun making it. Flynn quickly wins the hand of Olivia de Havilland, foils Claude Rains as the evil prince, and continually duels with the wicked Rathbone. The whole thing was packaged beautifully in color. I don't want to see *Robin Hood* done any other way. I don't care what the real history was or whether Hood ever existed at all. In my camp they should never fool around with Flynn's version.

He was still going strong in 1940, when they cast him at his dashing best in the high-seas adventure *The Sea Hawk*, again with Claude Rains. But this time that lively old devil of the swashbucklers Gilbert Roland was around to add to the piracy, romance, adventure, and epic swordplay. Gilbert was one of the great character actors, and the fact that he became completely stereotyped never hurt him.

The other marvelous period pieces were the great romantic stories epitomized by such screen lovers as Charles Boyer. He was in more than fifty elegant extravaganzas, including *Algiers*, in which he is supposed to have asked Hedy Lamarr to "come wiz me to the Casbah," a line which was actually made up by an imaginative press office. Hedy was one of a handful of delectable females who succumbed to Boyer's lady-killing image. He also wooed Greta Garbo, Jean Harlow, Ingrid Bergman, Rita Hayworth, and Marlene Dietrich among several others. Women swooned when they heard his name. Charles Boyer did not so much swashbuckle his way through all those romantic period films as ooze and warble with pained sincerity. Some people took him as a lightweight, but he worked almost harder than anyone else to perfect his craft.

Many of the great films of the time were made with established partnerships such as Gable and Harlow or Astaire and Rogers. Boyer was able to lead with them all, and when he appeared on screen, there has never been such uncontrollable and open weeping. He was equally brilliant with Irene Dunne, Claudette Colbert, or Loretta Young. He gave each role a sense of passion or tragedy which would have entire continents pulling out their handkerchiefs. Boyer left his indelible mark on a whole era. Moviemakers are welcome to try remakes of his films, but they will never get away with it.

For movie buffs remakes are themselves an interesting study in Hollywood history. Once the studio had found a winning story formula, they dressed it up in a thousand different ways and told it over and over again. Then, after a period of ten or fifteen years, when they had other stars in the stable and a new generation of filmgoers, they would package the story as a remake. The remakes were rarely as good as the originals and were a constant source of annoyance to movie buffs.

At last, in the eighties, the industry is getting wise. *The Thirty-Nine Steps* is a perfect example. The original Hitchcock classic starred Robert Donat and Madeleine Carroll. Hitchcock gave it wonderful overtones of high comedy and romance and kept the audience gripping their seats throughout the whole movie. Based on John Buchan's best-selling spy yarn, it helped introduce Hitchcock to a very successful Hollywood reign. To the older generation of the public Donat *is* Richard Hannay.

A quarter of a century later—in 1959—Ralph Thomas, an English director, decided it was time to do a remake. He cast Kenneth More and Taina Elg in the top roles and had a lot of support from the British film industry. The mistake he made was to look at the Hitchcock original over and over again, until, in the end, he felt he could hardly improve the movie in any way—despite twenty-five years' technology. Consequently he shot the film almost frame by frame as Hitchcock had done.

Twenty years later, in 1979, the British felt it was time to bring the classic out again. This time none of them even looked at the Hitchcock film. They cast Robert Powell as the new Hannay. Since he played Jesus in Lew Grade's *Jesus of Nazareth,* Powell is generally regarded as the best British find since Dirk Bogarde. He made a perfect Hannay. He almost turned the movie into a fast-moving romp; it travels at such a pace that it leaves you breathless, and it was made on a budget which would be regarded as petty cash in America. But the most important thing about this remake is that it is a completely original film, intended for a completely new audience, and it was quickly recognized as such.

Robin and Marian is another perfect example of this new thinking. As I have said, I would have killed anyone who had tried to outdo Errol Flynn. Yet who can argue with how this was done? Sean Connery is a disillusioned fifty-year-old Robin still trying to woo a middle-aged Marian, who has long since given him up for dead. There's Robert Shaw as a powerful and evil sheriff who fights Robin hand to hand and wins; a scruffy and warped Little John, played by Nicol Williamson; a roaring king (Richard Harris), who has finally come home to debauch himself. The whole thing is about a million miles away from the Flynn version.

Hollywood has probably taken more liberties with the Bible than with any other form of history. For Cecil B. De Mille, so long as it was epic, it need not even have been near the truth.

My favorite religious epic was *The Sign of the Cross* with Fredric March and Claudette Colbert. Years after I first saw it, I met Miss Colbert at Bogey's house. There was a whole bunch of people there, but she still stood out firmly as a star; it was almost as if she were the only one in the room. Claudette told me she had been shocked at some scenes in a film she had just seen. It included an explicit sex scene, although this was twenty years ago and "explicit sex" still meant something else.

"I don't know exactly how much bolder they can get on the screen," she said, never guessing that two decades later *Deep Throat* would become family viewing. "But I sometimes forget how bold we thought we were in the old days. We really believed we were stretching it as far as it was possible to go."

We went on to discuss the milk bath in *Cleopatra* as an example, and I told her the scene had electrified my entire neighborhood. She smiled and said, "That's exactly what I mean. We thought at the time that was the ultimate in risqué naughtiness."

We both had a laugh about Cecil B. De Mille, who was always getting diplomas from the Legion of Decency, yet in reality was quite interested in sex. He gave a public image of puritanism and godliness, yet on the set he used to urge the cameramen to get closer shots of someone's tits. He was the master of the innocent crotch shot. He never made it obvious, but it was there when you looked for it. The breasts would be just barely decent, and De Mille loved it when they flopped out by mistake. He would drive the costume girls crazy by saying, "I've got to have those knockers bigger. Hey, I can't see those knockers. Tighten that outfit up at once."

Claudette told me she used to laugh her head off every time De Mille got another "decency" diploma.

De Mille, of course, was a legend in his lifetime, a complete but powerful eccentric who was treated as a god by most of his underlings. His eccentricity was on a par with Howard Hughes's, although De Mille was anything but a recluse. If he invited people to dinner, the manservant laid out a special dinner dress of colored Russian blouses and slacks. All the guests' attire was identical. De Mille would appear in the same garb, but it was jet black. He carried a revolver because he was scared of rattlesnakes—even at the dinner table. When he was really pleased with someone, he would give him or her a fifty-cent piece of the Virginia Dare issue. He bestowed it almost like a Congressional Medal of Honor, and people believed it to be of rare value. Long after his death someone, out of pure interest, had one valued; it was worth less than $1.

The best story about his bestowal of this great "honor" came when he was shooting *Unconquered* with Gary Cooper and Paulette Goddard in 1947. It was a gargantuan cowboys and Indians film of almost ludicrous proportions, but it was one hell of a lot of fun. One day they had to film a battle scene with the Indians storming a blockade. They couldn't get it right, and on take twenty-one a De Mille underling told the boss that if they went into overtime, the bill would go up by some $50,000. There were minutes to go, and De Mille realized that come what may, this had to be the master take. He watched in horror as he saw that a burning arrow had set fire to the drumsticks of a little drummer boy perched on a hill. He was just about to call, "Cut!" when he noticed the kid was refusing to move—despite the fact that his white gloves were beginning to singe. He ordered the cameras to zoom in on the boy's hands and got the only golden shot in the film. When he eventually did say, "Cut," men were running toward the kid with buckets of water, and as he plunged his burning gloves into the pail, De Mille ran over to him, offering the coveted fifty-cent piece. The kid became a hero on the lot, but he never realized he had saved them a cool $50,000.

During the remake of *The Ten Commandments* De Mille demonstrated his talent for single-minded ingenuity in bending human nature to his own ends. By now he could do almost anything he wanted in Hollywood, without question, and frequently did. People recognized his genius for the big epic and for getting "impossible" things done. He would never take no for an answer. During *The Ten Commandments* a costly regiment of U.S. field artillery was provided to play the fleeing Hebrews. The colonel in charge refused to allow his men to charge on horses down a dangerously steep escarpment. De Mille had a problem. He had to get the shot, yet here was a professional army of soldiers saying it was impossible. With that he ordered his daughter to mount a horse and ride down the bank; she did it immediately with a small smile and a "yes, Daddy." A red-faced colonel then ordered his 300 chariot drivers to follow, the cameras started rolling, and De Mille sat back with a satisfied grin on his face. As the colonel and his men reached the hill, the whole scene became sheer chaos. Most of the chariots capsized, and many of the others rolled and tangled in a huge melee of confusion. De Mille sat there, using up miles of film, never admitting to the embarrassed colonel that his daughter was one of the most accomplished child riders in the United States at that time.

Many of the great old classics had the period tag, but so did some of the worst films ever made. In the early fifties, for instance, Alan Ladd made a whole string of those horrible movies, like *The Black Knight*, with completely unbelievable scripts. Bryan Forbes was brought in one day when they "ran out of words." He used to spend all night writing some fresh pages which they would film the next day. No one knew how the story would end, and Ladd was running around, saying things like: "This Christianity—can anyone join?"

One night they left Ladd on top of a burning castle and had to find a way for him to escape. Forbes had him jump from the smoking ruins into the conventional haycart, then leap onto a horse, and away to safety. Alan had script approval, and his wife was acting for him. He did everything she told him. She went crazy when she saw the scene and threatened Ladd would fly home unless it was changed.

"You can't have Alan stealing a horse," she said. "It wouldn't please the Boy Scouts of America."

They stood around all night, trying to think up ways Alan could escape without offending the Boy Scouts, Bryan got behind the typewriter.

Ladd jumps into the haycart, and there's a soldier standing by, holding a horse. "Is that the horse I ordered?" he asks.

"Yes, sire," barks the soldier as Alan Ladd rides away.

Mrs. Ladd thought about it for a moment and said, as they mopped their brows, "I'll buy that."

It was the kind of film which spanned 500 years of history in three minutes and got every historical detail wrong. When someone pointed this out to the producer, he said, "So what? They won't know the difference in Little Rock, and that's where it'll make the money."

King Richard and the Crusaders was another of the all-time bum movies—despite the formidable star lineup. The sheer weight of names made it a fair box-office success in 1954. Rex Harrison, George Sanders, Larry Harvey, and Robert Douglas vied for the favors of Virginia Mayo. Movie buffs love to run the film through simply to hear Virginia's line to her cousin King Richard, "War, war, war. That's all you ever think about, Dicky Plantagenet."

Even John Wayne fell for one of these movie disasters when he played Genghis Khan in *The Conqueror* with Susan Hayward. The laughable script mainly has Wayne grunting loudly at his reluctant bride. Howard Hughes loved the film so much he spent $6 million buying up every copy so that only he could enjoy it. That's why it never appears on TV. If it is ever released from Hughes's estate you will be able to hear Wayne saying to Susan Hayward, "You're beautiful in your wrath."

Despite the mountains of truly bad films, generally speaking, I think we can be immensely proud of directing achievement in America. We did not produce a David Lean, but we found a Fred Zinnemann instead. America could never have invented a Ken Russell, but then England could never have produced a Mark Hellinger. Only guys like Mel Brooks could have been born on either side of the Atlantic. Roman Polanski could have come from anywhere in the world. Anyone who could make a film with the sensitivity of *Knife in the Water*, the kinky zaniness of *Cul-de-Sac*, the madness of *Repulsion*, and the sheer humor of *The Fearless Vampire Killers* needn't have been invented by any particular ethnic background. *The Fearless Vampire Killers* stood as the great ghoulish takeoff, until Mel Brooks did the takeoff of the takeoff.

Stanley Kramer surrounds himself with the most professional people and takes every precaution before he starts filming. He is the safest of directors. I love what he stands for in many ways, but I've always considered him a pedestrian director who never needed to do more than point the cameras. When you are making films like *The Defiant Ones* and *Guess Who's Coming to Dinner*, with that caliber of story and stars, you don't need to do much directing.

Judgment at Nuremberg was probably his best single achievement as a director because he moved the camera all the time. Until then he had always been competent and very adequate but without much inspiration. When he took a stage play and put it on the screen, it remained a stage play which had been filmed. He could never master the movement of the camera. After all, *motion* is what a motion picture is all about.

Hitchcock mastered it, as he did in *Rear Window*. Sidney Lumet did it brilliantly in *Twelve Angry Men*. He took the camera over the shoulder, followed heads around, closed up on moving lips, got a camera on a 360-degree turn all around a single table. Each of the ninety-five minutes moved in a static atmosphere. It was done so skillfully that the audience was riveted on a whole kaleidoscope of action which was confined to a small room.

William Friedkin did the same thing with *The Boys in the Band* in 1970. The whole weird thing was done in a single room. It was about the cheapest set built for any major film. The interplay about the homosexual's birthday party, in which hidden thoughts and feelings were suddenly and sadly brought into the open, was never static. It lasted 120 minutes, but the whole apartment was alive with constant action.

Chapter 11

...and Great Actors

It's a Hollywood truism—only the joker in the pack becomes an overnight sensation—whether it's a film or a star. There is always a *Rocky* out there somewhere and a Sylvester Stallone to shake up the establishment, but they are extremely rare.

The unlikely surprise is what makes Hollywood fun. But, like the joker, it turns up only when someone drops it into the pack almost by mistake. *Grease* was shelved as a no-hoper until the low-budget *Saturday Night Fever* suddenly took off and John Travolta became an overnight international idol. It amazed everyone, not the least its producers and distributors, who saw it as a college movie. Someone bothered to slip it into a sneak preview to see whether it should join *Grease* on the shelf. Before the following weekend the industry was rushing out Travolta merchandise.

Ninety-nine percent of the time movies are created with a pretty clear idea of their potential market. "Overnight sensations" in the acting profession are exceptionally rare. Actors may well find a right vehicle at the right time which can lift them suddenly into the heights of fame, but I would bet my bottom dollar that most of them spent a long time paying their dues.

Take Walter Matthau in *The Odd Couple*. People raved about his performance, and it seemed as if he had just arrived in town. But they had forgotten how long that guy had been around before he got his just recognition. He even played a heavy in *King Creole* alongside Elvis Presley in 1958. By then he was almost into his forties, and I can't think how he must have felt playing junk like that. He knew what he had in him; he'd proved it time and again. You can imagine him looking at this young kid Presley picking up a million or two and saying to himself, "How long must I go on doing this shit?"

I knew him vaguely, and he was always saying, "I'm going back to Broadway. There's nothing here for me." But as soon as he packed his bags, another offer came along, and he stayed.

He told me that throughout the times when he had to play awful parts just to stay alive he had this special feeling. Even in 1964, when he played in *Goodbye Charlie* with Tony Curtis, he felt that such dreadful crap couldn't go on forever. And it didn't. When *The Odd Couple* came along, it was time for the world to give him a break. I was around when he got nominated for an Academy Award, and I was MCing part of the show. I met Walter backstage just before the ceremony started, and I said, "You ready to pick up your piece of gold, Walt?" To my surprise he bet me a hundred bucks he wouldn't win. I was happy to take him on, although he must have been the first nominee in Oscar's history to have bet against himself.

After the show it didn't take him long to find me and claim his C-note. Apparently he'd had bets all over town and came away with a small fortune. The betting was typical of Walt Matthau. He knew he was up against some heavyweights that year, and he was always a realistic and down-to-earth actor. But if he had won, he would not have resented paying up.

Walter has always been a superb actor who just happens to be able to play comedy brilliantly as well. He did twenty-five Broadway productions before he headed west to try his luck with the movies. Now he calls his acting in films retirement acting. He told me once, "It's so easy I consider myself retired."

Many fine actors fail to bridge those middle years. Either they see themselves as glamorous romantic stars and can't take middle age, or they haven't got the real deep-down talent to give.

I get angry when I pick up a movie book that says, for example,

"Fredric March started to decline in his thirties." What does it mean? He was still making pictures when he was sixty, very good ones at that. But people remember him in his golden age, and on the day he stopped being the great romantic leading man they called it a decline.

I was hosting a *Tonight* show recently when James Mason was one of my guests. I asked him about this very thing. How did he manage to face not being the handsome young buck anymore and having to look for other kinds of parts? He said he had been able to bridge the gap with a single film—*Lolita*. It was the perfect transition, of course, a part almost tailor-made for an actor who needed to change his entire appeal.

He told me, "I knew the time was coming when it would be absurd for me to go on playing romantic leads. I made the decision to find something else which was interesting to do, and luckily *Lolita* came along."

We all have faced it. I realized one day that middle-aged tap dancers were vaguely absurd if they didn't have any other talents. So I tried to diversify long before it became necessary to do so. For all of us it depended entirely on how much we were willing to gamble and how much we had invested in future audiences.

It was very much the same with Kirk Douglas. He came back out of the blue rather suddenly in *The Fury* in 1978, and everyone behaved as if he had just been rediscovered. Yet he'd been making pictures constantly for thirty years. Kirk had consistently worked far below his real market value. His record is formidable. He's made more than fifty pictures, some of them all-time money-makers. *Champion*, for instance, which he did for Mark Robson in 1949, was one of the greatest fight-game pictures ever made, the story of the unscrupulous boxer who fights his way to the top and finds the gangsters are tougher than he is. Before doing *Detective Story*, he worked on the beat with the Forty-seventh Precinct in New York for a month to get the feel and atmosphere of a policeman's life in the city at night.

He also made some definitive westerns like *Last Train from Gun Hill* and *Man Without a Star*. Mind you, Kirk is haunted by *The Big Trees* every time it comes up on TV, which seems to be about once a month. He loathes himself in that film. He would willingly burn every copy. I don't blame him, and we laugh about it every time we meet.

But the distinctive feature about Kirk (and about that whole generation of actors) is that he is consistent. He can play a western, a romantic lead, and a detective story and then go on to do something like *Spartacus*. You can always rely on his performance. On top of this he could play Van Gogh in *Lust for Life* and really blow everyone's mind with a serious acting *tour de force*.

Burt Lancaster was in the same mold. He always had the dynamics working for him. He invested himself all the way from *The Crimson Pirate* to *Airport*, and along the way he left some truly fine performances in such films as *Elmer Gantry, Sweet Smell of Success, Trapeze*, and *From Here to Eternity*. He knew all the tricks. But he could also breeze something special into a role which was unmistakably vintage Lancaster. It is this breezing in which marks the great movie actors.

When, for instance, John Sturges first saw the script for *The People Against O'Hara,* he knew he didn't have much of a film. The story was weak, and the whole thing was a bit turgid. But Sturges also knew that if he could get Spencer Tracy for the lead, he would be home free. He realized what all good directors knew about Spence—they could rely on him to give the part that something special which would make it an important movie. Spence, through sheer hard work, character, personality, talent, and know-how, made it a vehicle which began to work for him. He upgraded a minor part into a major performance, and the public immediately recognized it.

Tracy was one of the few actors who could more or less pick what he wanted to do. Generally, under the studio system, the actor did what he was told and faced suspension if he turned down a part.

Nowadays, of course, the superstars have turned themselves into individual corporations, and it is easier for them to pick and choose. A lot of actors, Bogart included, *had* to make toilet movies, and their reputations suffered for it. But Tracy was able to be choosy and consequently made very few bad films, and even with those he often took the vehicle up with him.

This ability to uplift mundane scripts is the mark of the reliable actor. Ray Milland did this in *The Lost Weekend*. The film was a complete surprise. For years Ray had spent his movie life walking through comedies, giving them an added sparkle and a consistent performance, but hardly setting the world on fire. Then he turned around and played an alcoholic with a host of personal problems. When they offered Milland the part, he moved into Bellevue Hospital in New York to see at first hand what life as an alcoholic was like. However, when everyone started screaming and spewing and more drunks were being brought in all the time, Milland panicked and ran out of the building at 3:00 A.M. Some cop saw him in his nightclothes and arrested him. It took him two hours to explain his way out.

In the forties and fifties a new star network was born and flourished. The new stars became famous mainly for playing themselves: guys like Robert Mitchum and Gregory Peck, who had enough talent and character to keep going through various fashions and across several decades.

Peck was incredible. He could play all the masterful gunfighter bits and then spring *To Kill a Mockingbird* on us. He was big and lanky and manly, yet he was no natural athlete. When he was making *Arabesque* with Sophia Loren, he had to chase and catch her, but she ran faster than he did, and he ended up on his knees.

He was a man of integrity, and somehow it shone through for the public in all his films despite his real-life mishaps. He was also a "human" man, much given to emotion, and this always came across, even when he was playing ice-cool roles such as *The Gunfighter*. During *To Kill a Mockingbird* he was defending Brock Peters, the great black actor, against a charge of rape. Brock told me that at one point Greg had to question him brutally. Peters was so convincing in his own defense that he had all the crew and extras crying their eyes out. This began to affect Gregory Peck, who found a huge lump growing in his throat. As Brock's voice cracked with emotion, Peck just couldn't look him in the eye, knowing he was about to break down. When he got the Oscar for the role, he said, "It was the toughest moment in my career. I won the Oscar for fighting back the tears."

Peck's first important role came in *The Keys of the Kingdom* way back in 1944. Thirty-five years later he was still around in *The Boys From Brazil*. All his life filmmakers have wanted him to do a carbon copy of his last success. After he made *The Gunfighter*, they fell over themselves to offer him *High Noon*. He refused. As soon as he did *The Guns of Navarone*, he got a dozen offers from producers to rescue or damage guns in a hundred even more inaccessible places.

Interestingly he also produced *The Trial of the Catonsville Nine*, the story of the priest Daniel Berrigan, who was tried in 1968 for demanding action against the Vietnam War. Peck had seen the play in Los Angeles and stayed on to talk about it with the cast. He was impressed and put up most of the $400,000 needed for production and distribution. He lost every penny; it was a total disaster. Despite his own feelings about the subject, Peck told everyone after he had seen the film, "I couldn't sit through it again. Frankly it was a self-righteous bore." Peck brought that kind of honesty to all his roles.

Robert Mitchum was a different kind of man and a different kind of actor. He has spanned the decades, but he was never forced to bridge the gap. He paid his dues over many years, playing comic-strip characters, and at first, when the fashions changed, Mitchum looked dead. His old style became unbankable. However, *Ryan's Daughter* came along, and Mitchum played Mitchum. Everyone suddenly remembered he could act. When David Lean directed him, he told everyone, "Mitchum has always been a misdirected but gifted actor. He is the master of stillness. Other actors act. Mitchum is."

Brando dominated the first half of the fifties, and Marilyn Monroe took off from *The Seven-Year Itch* to dominate the last half of the decade. But it was James Dean, with only three films, who left his indelible mark between those two. I have the jacket Dean wore in *Rebel Without a Cause* stored safely in my house in Beverly Hills. He gave it to me, and I often take it out and remember that sad, desolate youth whom, in one way or another, we all abused. It is not a morbid ritual, but one of total respect and retrospective love. James Dean was more than a phenomenon or even a legend. He was far more than a cinematic genius who could act his balls off. He was simply the greatest screen experience of all time. The fact that he was cut off in his prime is unfortunate but irrelevant. The three films he left us with stand as their own monument. He remains indestructible.

Lee Strasberg became famous because he tutored Marlon Brando; he became a legend when it was learned he had also inspired James Dean. He put the final touches to his remarkable genius with Al Pacino. In between, his Actors' Studio in New York trained some 400 people who now cover the entire spectrum of American show business. *The Godfather* was cast with generations of Method actors. But if Lee Strasberg had done nothing but coach Brando and Dean, his contribution to motion pictures would remain immense.

Because of Lee, Brando was able to establish a "nervous" cinema full of violence and passion. Then Dean created a "mood" cinema full of raw and pulsating emotion. He accomplished only three roles, but he ruined the careers of a hundred other aspiring actors who tried to follow him.

My own deep regret is that when Dean was hanging around town, I didn't take more notice of him. He would sit alone in the corner at some Hollywood party, looking depressed and sulky. If someone approached him, he would look up and say, "I want to act," and then slump back into his own world. Hollywood hardly touched him as a person. It is to our eternal shame as a community that we passed him off as a bit of a slob. He *was* difficult to talk to, but we should have tried harder. He was desperately trying to say something, and none of us bothered to listen—to the point where he gave up trying. I remember him now, crouched in a corner, looking unsociable, and I was thinking to myself, So what, kid? Everyone wants to act in this town. I did befriend him, after a fashion, and he came up to the house several times. But I must confess I didn't try very hard.

Like Marilyn, he went on to touch us all in a peculiar way. Both of them had beamed into the antennas of the times. We didn't recognize it then, but we all were going through a very confused period, both in and out of the movie industry. We wanted someone who could show us the way out. Jimmy knew the answers, and he began to tell us. Unfortunately, until he was gone, only his contemporaries—the kids of the world—bothered to listen. Dean knew all about the confusion of youth. He said it all in *Rebel Without a Cause*. But by the time the message came across it was too late. Jimmy Dean didn't do anything on screen which wasn't pure magic. When I think of some of those scenes, I still get goosebumps. I had to sit through *Rebel* five times before I could watch the bit where he appeals to his dad, "Give me something, Dad. For once in your life stick up for me." Every time he said it I had to turn my head away because it was so raw and emotional. I kept feeling, Oh, my God, he's going to get hurt. All his wounds are open. Someone's going to gun him down.

Dean could put things into any situation in a way that no one else could. His little-boy walk became a classic all on its own. He could never have cultivated that innate vulnerability. It was born in him. He made everyone feel he had to rush up and protect him. Yet like Brando, he was an instinctive actor who could pull a part to pieces and reconstruct it in a way that was unique. Nick Ray, who directed *Rebel*, told me that huge pieces of the film were pure improvisation by Dean. The final version of some scenes would be written the day before. Jimmy would read it and throw it away. Ray said, "He had an instinct about how certain things should be done, and he was always right. He was so inventive, and regularly he would add new dimensions and a whole perspective to a scene which had only a few lines of dialogue. Surprisingly, he also had a unique and catching sense of humor which would come across as an undercurrent to the main theme. Even though the general message of the movie was invariably heavy, he could sprinkle an air of wit beneath the surface which would make him, and his performance, entirely endearing." Nick admitted to me later that when Dean was on the set, he felt impotent as a director. "I wasn't really necessary," he said. "After years of doing it I could never have dreamed up some of Dean's simplest improvisations."

Dean had such a gut feeling for each part he played that he touched not only the Bel Air circuit of professionals who could recognize special talent instantly but the people of downtown Akron, Ohio, at the Saturday-night picture show. He possessed intangibles on screen which lifted his acting from craft to art. He never used a gimmick to induce tension. I don't argue against gimmicks. Indeed, whole movies have been constructed successfully around them. But the most priceless film art occurs when something happens on screen direct from the gut.

I suffer from knowing that there were forty people on the set when Dean was trying to get down to the basic truth of the situation. I'm always aware that just behind the camera there's a guy chewing sandwiches and reading *Variety*, and another man doing the racing form, waiting to adjust the lights, and a girl wheeling the trolley over just before the coffee break. While the forty-odd people who make up the typical film set all are involved with their own piece of action, Dean was bursting his guts to keep the intensity and truth even after a dozen takes.

On film you can never build the momentum you can achieve

onstage. You have to do it shot by shot, sometimes in all manner of sequences. Dean's genius was that like a handful of others, including Al Pacino, he could switch it on whenever the camera was ready for him.

When Brando came along, he changed our conception of movie acting. I believe he is out there on a separate planet all his own. There's the whole of Hollywood—the studios, the industry, the financiers, all the actors and actresses, the rigmarole of show business, the pimps, the con men, the lawyers and psychiatrists, and the audiences who make it all possible. And then there is Brando. Like most stars, he has made toilet pictures, and there was a time when it seemed he couldn't do a thing right. But he dominated the fifties and has come into his own again in the seventies and eighties as a living legend who goes from strength to strength. When Brando decides to do something big, he knocks you out.

During his brilliant Elia Kazan period he was one of the most dedicated actors who ever lived. He made Broadway sizzle with his performance in *A Streetcar Named Desire*, and when Kazan brought him to the film role, the two of them electrified the screen.

In *Viva Zapata* he brought his mimetic ability to perfection. In *Streetcar* you could smell him as the sweaty Pole. Now he was a Mexican. I think you could put up any scene in *Zapata* and call it definitive Brando. Never again would he reach the same degree of brilliance he achieved with Kazan. Kazan controlled him—not in a paternal way, but as if he had his fists around the performance, letting out a little bit at a time. You knew his fists were controlling, molding a great and elemental power. He manipulated Brando without throttling him. It would never have worked unless Brando had had a great respect for Kazan.

Elia Kazan told me later the secret of dealing with Brando. "I would never criticize him directly if something was wrong. I would tell him, 'It just ain't going right, Marlon. There's something missing. Let's go and discuss it.' Marlon is such a brilliant, natural actor that he was intuitive about a part, and even if a scene looked good to me, I could feel when he was uncomfortable. So we'd go off and chew the fat for a while until we found the problem. There always was one when Brando felt uncomfortable. We would never actually experiment, but by the time we got back to the set we knew exactly how it was going to be done. When I thought Brando was happy with it, I didn't need to see the rushes before I knew we'd shot something special."

Kazan was always constructive with Brando, and Marlon knew it. If Kazan said he wanted Marlon to put a cigarette down in a certain way, Brando knew instinctively that it was right. This great working relationship was the key to their mutual brilliance. I have been on many sets when the director was not in control of the actors or their performances. When everyone knew something was wrong, the director would say, "Well, do whatever you want to do. Try it out several ways, and see what comes out best." Kazan was never like that. He had a sixth sense about the best way to do anything on screen. He never made things obvious. He let the power seep out and be recognized for what it was.

Brando never lets you down slowly. He takes you as far as he can go, and then he springs another one on you, as in *One-Eyed Jacks* when he overpowers Slim Pickens and you're rooting for him. Then he gives Pickens a final, dreadful kick, and you can hear the bones breaking. That is why he is always so disturbing as an actor.

Jacks was conceived because *Viva Zapata* had cost so little and made so much. The difference was that by now Brando was spreading his wings, not only as an actor but in understanding his own bankability. He took this low-budget black-and-white cowboy film by the collar and made it his way. He commandeered half the Paramount lot, scouted the most lavish locations, threw the schedules out the window, and displayed a flamboyant disregard for all of the studio's wishes, including its meticulously planned budget. Luckily the film was an overnight success and easily made its money back, so when Brando hijacked *Mutiny on the Bounty* halfway through and decided to do the same thing, MGM at first decided to let him have his way. It was a sad mistake, and the film nearly bankrupted the huge studio.

Brando has played some of the most potent beating scenes in movie history, and in *One-Eyed Jacks* he indulged his interest in sadomasochism to the fullest. On any level the film showed Brando's mind was a little warped by the theories of violence and pain. The whipping scene is one of the most brutal ever seen legally on a screen. His recovery, in which his raw whipped back is the central feature, is an exercise in self-indulgence. This is bad enough. Yet after the whipping, when Karl Malden's rifle butt smashes Marlon's right hand, the scene changed from being terribly uncomfortable to being downright disturbing.

In *Reflections in a Golden Eye*, in which he plays a homosexual army officer opposite Liz Taylor, the most potent scene is when Liz slashes him across the face with a riding crop. All the way back to his first film, *The Men*, the scene stealers occur when he is trying to defeat a deformity. In *Zapata* he ends up torn to pieces as a broken, bloody corpse in the village square. One of the strongest scenes in *Waterfront* is at the end when he defies a beating to lead the men back to work. In *The Wild One* he was smashed down violently by the townspeople.

No one has ever got a straight answer from Marlon when he is asked about the somewhat bizarre nature of some of his roles. In the early days, when newsmen tried to interview him, he delighted in being so obscene they were unable to print a word. Hollywood columnists can recall interviews in which Brando spent half an hour describing how he had just abused a teenage girl using butter. Years later, when Brando made *Last Tango in Paris*, they went to their notes and really began wondering!

In *The Missouri Breaks* he decided to play one scene in drag. When all the journalists flocked in to take pictures, he made grandiose statements about his homosexuality. During one interview he went into details of several of his "affairs." He winked at the rest of the cast and said, "Let them think I'm in love with Jack Nicholson. Who gives a shit?"

The Missouri Breaks holds a major key to Marlon's personality. He used to love saying he was a geek—nickname of the vaudeville tramps who used to bite the heads off chickens for the shock value and get paid with a bottle of cheap wine. "I'm no different," he'd say. "They just pay me more." As a direct result of this, he ad-libbed some of the film's strongest parts, including a bit where he actually does bite the head off a frog. One evening the scene called for Brando to wake up a sleeping member of the gang. The guy was lying back, snoring loudly. Brando held everything up and sent someone to find some locusts. He crept up to the guy and dropped the locusts into his open mouth. The scene had to be shot a dozen times, and the guy's mouth was swollen to hell by the end of the evening. It was a typical example of Brando's extending his personality beyond the script and giving a scene just that much more. The whole thing was warped. But it worked.

In the seventies Brando finally came into his own as a fully mature actor and began to extend the legend into its third magnificent decade. Personally I don't rate *Last Tango* very highly, but there is no doubt of its significance in Hollywood. In *The Godfather* he met another director who knew his measure. Francis Ford Coppola knew how to control Brando and remained firmly in charge. The whole film had that special low-key violence in which the mood often seemed more menacing than the gunfire. It was a natural for Brando. By then his "screw you" philosophy toward the motion-picture industry had become a celebrated way of life.

In many ways I don't blame Marlon for this attitude. The more he despises the industry, the more it tries to court him. There have been very few actors in the history of Hollywood who were *that* big. He now takes the money and runs, and in some ways, good luck to him. But each time I pick *Viva Zapata* out of the library and run it through, I can't help feeling it is rather a shame. Marlon is one of a kind, and his God-given talent is so special that if he just breathes on screen, it is worth watching. It is not that he owes us a thing. But with brilliance like that he owes something to himself. It is almost as if he doesn't understand the hugeness of his own art and wants to blame it all on something else. That's a shame because Marlon could achieve almost anything he wanted.

I have some very pleasant memories of being on the set with Brando when Chaplin made *A Countess from Hong Kong* costarring Sophia Loren. This film was, of course, directed by Charlie as a labor of love. During a break in the shooting I went with Brando to Sophia's trailer for drinks. Marlon was in a frivolous mood, and for more than an hour we cracked jokes. Sophia was in top form and was playing hostess for all it was worth.

Brando is famous for taking his screen image onto the street at the end of a day's shooting. I'm sure, if it had been the set of *The Missouri Breaks*, we would have found a very different Brando. As it was, he was playing a comedy and had become completely enchanted by the diminutive Chaplin. I think we all got a little high before someone came along and said Chaplin was waiting for Brando. We ambled across, and Marlon asked if I had met the "little man." I had, but there was no reason why he should remember me. "He's everything they ever said he was," Marlon said. "If they could make a film of him directing this movie, it would be an all-time classic."

When Marlon reintroduced me to the pint-sized legend, he immediately admonished him. "You don't have to introduce me to Sammy." Then he turned to me. "I remember you well. You move well, young man, you should do a lot more pantomime."

"Thank you, sir. Being a dancer helps."

"Yes, of course, but you are a natural clown. I've always wanted to tell you that."

Throughout this conversation Brando was ambling around with a big grin on his face. He had become almost beatific about his performance. There were no bad moods or pouting, just apparent elation. Marlon has never behaved better on a set, and I'm sure it is because he recognized that he was working with the Master.

Chaplin broke off the conversation by saying, "We have a little unfinished business to attend to. Come and sit over here and watch, Sammy."

The scene was a little piece of humor Chaplin had dreamed up years before but had never found the right vehicle to carry it out. It was a short shot of Brando during a press conference on a boat. Sophia is hiding in his cabin when the press guys burst in for an interview. Brando is left holding her underpants. The comedic situation is created by how Brando gets rid of the panties. He pretends they are a handkerchief and tries to put them back in his pocket. It is a classic piece of mime comedy. They rehearsed it two or three times, and Brando was clearly uncomfortable. He couldn't quite master the fumbling way in which he had to get rid of them. After long rehearsals and several takes Chaplin said, "Do it this way, Marlon."

Charlie Chaplin then held the pants, looked at them with horror, and put them into his pocket in one single movement, which had to be the only way that scene could be played. The set broke into immediate and spontaneous applause, and that included a bemused and fascinated Brando. We all felt eminently privileged to have seen the Master at work. Brando showed his immense talent for impersonation. After a few more rehearsals he did it exactly as Chaplin had shown him. He mastered an act which was entirely Chaplinesque. I think that little clip is a screen gem, and I never tire of looking at it.

I had once done a small Chaplin cameo with Nat King Cole, and it had gone over very well. But the Master deserved something really special. I got all the buddies together, and we talked it over. We decided the only way it would work magically was if I broke into the routine without any preamble or announcement. The key to the act was to keep it completely unexpected. We tried to make the whole effect spontaneous, but we actually worked very hard on it before we gave Chaplin back to the public.

We were playing Miami, and the only difficulty was getting the props. We scoured the whole town, looking for a Chaplin outfit. We found bits here and there, and I finally got everything together except the famous cane, the hallmark of the Tramp. I was going crazy until one of the guys had one flown in from New York. It arrived only a few minutes before I went onstage.

I went through my normal act as we smuggled the cane and hat into the theater. I had also taken an artificial carnation from the hotel room and remembered it only after I got onstage. I had one hell of a time getting the flower from the wings and hiding it in the piano without the audience's seeing. Finally, I signaled the band that I was ready. The props seemed to come out of nowhere, and I just turned around and began a long Chaplin routine. The delay in the applause was about three seconds as the audience adjusted. Then they blew their minds. Over the next few minutes I got to know more about Charlie Chaplin than I had ever realized. Being Chaplin's ghost destroyed that audience not only because everything Chaplin had done was inherently funny and superbly simple but because of the immediate and overwhelming love everyone had for the little man. You could feel it just radiating out of the audience— a strange but wholly definable affection.

I subsequently put the act through a self-editing process until I had exactly the correct combination of humor, pathos, dignity, and clowning. I still do it every now and then, and some people feel it is the best part of the show. I normally perform it right after "Bojangles," and in a curious way the old dancer sets the scene perfectly. I had always yearned to do something in the act which would say to people, "We're all fools, man. We're buffoons and little tramps. Let's kick the ass off pomposity and come down to earth." Playing Chaplin was the answer. I never say a word, but the audience picks up all the messages: "We mustn't forget the first little guy who showed us the way. He was a little bit of all of us, a small man who got kicked around, but survived to fight back. Charlie leveled the score for everyone, and I shall die loving him."

Jerry Lewis was one of the first real pals I had in Hollywood, and when he saw my Chaplin piece, he came backstage crying his eyes out. "How can you do it to me, Sammy?" he said. "You've brought the Master back." Jerry was Chaplin's number one fan; he idolized him, and the act had really moved him. He gave me some advice on certain parts, and I listened intently because Jerry is the ultimate professional. He knows theater, and his advice was sound. Partly because Jerry urged me, Chaplin has stayed with me to this day.

Jerry, of course, had his fair share of problems as an entertainer, but probably not a lot more than most of us who have survived. He knew himself, and he knew his business, both stagecraft and filmmaking. After all, he was good enough to teach film directing at UCLA for several years. His knowledge was priceless, and people were running over each other to get into his course. He has also directed me, and I have nothing but respect for his methods. When I was in London in 1957, Jerry was also there, making *The Delicate Delinquent*—his first movie after his split with Dean Martin. Years later it showed up on TV, and everyone around me was saying, "Did you see Jerry in that movie? Wasn't he great?" It was as if he had been discovered all over again. The film was packed with classic gems. Jerry has now got a fabulous act, and he still packs them in. He works just as much as he wants to, which is not very much. He knows he has to be content with what he's got. We both found that when we were not looking for it—and not out there scrounging for it—something wonderful nearly always turned up.

A dozen or so guys have given the public the benefit of their "inside" knowledge on why Jerry and Dean Martin broke up. Many people said it was professional jealousy. I know both guys intimately, and I can tell you that the bitching about them played a big part in splitting them up. "Hollywood pressure" is a special disease called bitching, and I've seen it destroy a lot of people. There is no denying they got hurt by it. But both were immense pros, and they always had respect for each other. When I meet one of them nowadays, he's bound to ask about his old partner. They keep in touch. When Sinatra put them together again in a telethon, it was the big emotional thing of that year. It was also great for all the mutual pals who had known some of their bitter times together.

Jerry's only real problem is still that people would never let him grow up. When he tried to do something more than the zany bit, they got confused and wanted their old Jerry Lewis back. He woke up one day and found he was middle-aged and felt completely absurd playing the crazy teenager. He was always very big in Europe. Even today, when he walks down the street in Paris, they throw flowers in his path. I followed him onstage during my first Royal Command Performance (probably one of the most difficult entertainment media ever invented because the world's greatest entertainers follow one another with only ten minutes or so in which to do their act). Jerry got ovations at first, but then he started singing straight, without a joke in sight, and the place broke up in confusion. At the end of his nine minutes he walked offstage to muted applause. I walked on, brought him back, and mimicked him. He immediately fell into the old routine again. We only had a minute or two, but as soon as they saw the zany Lewis, the audience screamed. Jerry was able immediately to restore all that great affection and showed that he was still the best. It's just a shame no one would ever let him do anything else.

His kind of crazy humor has always been around in different guises. What the Marx Brothers did once is being repeated by Mel Brooks, a delightful guy. He was years before his time, but suddenly the mood caught up, and everyone raved about him. He emerged just at the right point for American movies. What he did in *Blazing Saddles* was tell the jokes we had been using over the years, especially on such things as black cowboys. He put them all into a single narrative and called them satire. His *Young Frankenstein* was even better at this.

It was up to Woody Allen, however, to wrap up the zaniness of seventies humor. He is the Chaplin of his time and creates his own special and vulnerable world. Along with Jules Feiffer

and James Thurber he has given us a slice of social commentary
—and put a sting in the tail. Woody Allen has taken the more
neurotic and psychological times of today and done a Chaplin
with them.

Humor comes in many guises, and the stand-up comics or the
zany clowns don't rule the roost. Some true comedians rarely
need to say a humorous word. Bogart had a streak of humor
which made films like *The African Queen*—a war adventure yarn
—into a comedy. Bill Holden has a light touch with comedic
parts, and guys like Tony Curtis are masters of comedy when
they want to be. But the greatest of them all is Cary Grant,
who is a funny man in real life and who completely mastered
light comedy.

Cary carefully invested in his career and did all the right
things at the right time. He started off as a lightweight pretty
boy when it was fashionable to be one, and he is going stronger
than ever. He never seemed to have to bridge the gap which
haunts so many actors. We all got older with him. He could play
the light heavy superbly, as he did in *Suspicion,* or light comedy,
as in *Arsenic and Old Lace.* In that film, when he opened the
cupboard and found the body, he did just about everything
conceivable that a comic can do. Frank Capra, who directed it
in 1944, told me he just kept the cameras running as Cary began
inventing. It was completely impromptu, and Cary played it all
for laughs. It was a great example of Cary's self-editing. Yet he
never overplayed a part. Unlike so many actors who clutter
comedy up, he knew exactly when to stop and keep it simple.
Only a few of the greats—like Bogey, Gable, and Spence—were
able to do it. They could strip the part down to its essentials,
play with it, and build on it without any gimmicks until it came
out as their own invention. This kind of self-editing is a trial-
and-error affair which develops only with experience and instinct.
No one could ever teach them how to do it. Cary always had it.

A greater combination of personalities than Cary and Audrey
Hepburn could not be invented. They were made for each other.
No actress is ever more comfortable than when she is with Grant,
but equally no actor is better than when he is playing with
Audrey. Bill Holden attests to that. He played with her in that

delightful little comedy *Paris When It Sizzles*. They sizzled themselves. They fried that simple little film into a soufflé of talent
and affection. It was the same in the film *Sabrina*—Holden has
rarely been better. But with Cary Grant, it was something else
again. He and Audrey managed to bring out the essence in
each other.

Cary Grant had got his first break when he played Pinkerton
in *Madame Butterfly* at Paramount. He was walking around,
looking dazzling in his naval uniform, when Mae West swept
by with Paramount executive Emanuel Cohen. "Who's he?"
Mae asked. Cohen had to find out. "I want him for my next
lead," she added. Paramount had outbid everyone else in Hollywood to buy Mae West for *She Done Him Wrong*—the screen
version of *Diamond Lil*. It was the first of two films she eventually
made with Cary. *I'm No Angel* was no classic, but the two films
established Cary Grant as a star.

David Niven is, of course, another of the great survivors who
bridged the same gap without blinking an eye. He has a less
subtle comedic sense than Cary, but it always works for him.
David is the kind of guy you would meet in Paris and he'd
say, "Got to dash, old chap, I'm going to Rome for some tea." And
he would be off with a flourish. That kind of offhand modern
buccaneering was almost invented by Niven.

Spencer Tracy and Katharine Hepburn became another of
the great comedy teams with such films as *Adam's Rib*. Again
they were made for each other, and it always worked. Katy
was like Cary Grant in terms of light comedy. It was always
so subtle. A comedic sense like that is a gift from God. Shirley
MacLaine had it in such films as *The Apartment* and *The
Trouble with Harry*—lighthearted and never obvious, but humor
ripples through. Marilyn Monroe, of course, only found her
true forte when she played her classic light-comedy roles in
The Seven-Year Itch and *Some Like It Hot*.

Anyway, there are all these films and all these wonderful actors
—plus a few hundred more—and each of them has a little something which makes it entirely unique. Trying to weigh them all
to decide which are the greatest of them will continue to keep
me awake at night probably for as long as I live. It's the kind
of pleasurable nightmare we buffs masochistically impose upon
ourselves.

For now, though, my "Ten Best" list would have to include these all-time favorites:

1. *The Informer*
2. *The Charge of the Light Brigade*
3. *Stagecoach*
4. *Casablanca*
5. *Anchors Aweigh*
6. *Red River*
7. *A Star Is Born*
8. *Psycho*
9. *The Hustler*
10. *Dracula* (with Peter Cushing and Christopher Lee)

I might even cheat one day and extend the list to the "Top Twenty." That way I can have both *Viva Zapata* and *The Hustler*. But that might spoil a lot of the fun.

Chapter 12

Sexy Films
and Sexy Ladies

If Louella Parsons—the former journalistic scourge of Hollywood who could make or break a star with a single caustic comment—were around today, she would find herself virtually unemployable. Louella thrived on the naughty nighttime antics of the studio-system stars. As all the women had stringent morality clauses written into their contracts, a sniff of scandal would have the studio bosses ranting and raving for their suspensions. The naughtiness went on, of course, but the trick was not to let Louella, and the half dozen others of her kind, find out about it.

Nowadays most of the superstars, like Robert Redford, Charles Bronson, Paul Newman, and Clint Eastwood, are happily, even boringly married, and they tend to keep their private lives very, very private. But the real reason Louella would be obsolete today is that our outlook on morals has completely changed. Stars like Warren Beatty and Burt Reynolds actually flourish against a background of scandals playing Superstud. They flaunt themselves as lovers on and off screen, and no one holds it against them. In fact, sometimes it's hard to stifle a yawn.

I'd also like to see how someone such as Louella would have dealt with Vanessa Redgrave or Jane Fonda.

But gossip writing did have its heyday, and right up to the sixties a note of scorn or a breath of scandal in one of the columns could have very serious repercussions. It gave Louella almost unprecedented power. She could tolerate the fact that half the world was killing the other in a gigantic world war. But show so much as a nipple, and she believed America would be completely corrupted. In these permissive and promiscuous days, when you've got to be Roman Polanski before you raise an eyebrow, Louella would have choked on her own self-righteousness. When *Deep Throat* did the rounds, I could almost feel the earth reverberate as Miss Parsons turned in her grave.

I make no bones about the fact that when they started making explicit sex films, I became an immediate and avid collector. There was no lack of people of both sexes to flock to see my collection, and I gave the premiere of *Deep Throat* in several countries. I am anything but prudish in these matters, and I loved the day they threw out the etchings and put everything onto celluloid.

Naturally, as the world's most constant set visitor, it wasn't long before I was finding ways of getting into the porno studios. But I was in for a big surprise. Within five minutes of being on the set I felt I was watching a remake of *Charlie's Angels*. For openers there were twenty or thirty people there, all behaving as if it were just another movie. To them it probably was, but to me this seemed weird. There was absolutely nothing sensuous about what was going on. At the supposed moment of orgasm, which was often simulated, the director yelled, "Hold it. Hold it right there. Get in closer, camera number two. . . . OK, one more time. . . ." The couple resumed in a completely mechanical way until the director said, "Cut," and the guy put on a robe and the lady went off to the toilet and everyone else stood around, drinking Cokes, waiting for the next scene. What a turnoff!

But the significance of *Deep Throat* in terms of the taboos it shot down in the history of movies is huge. It was the first time you could take your wife to the neighborhood movie to see explicit sex scenes. It liberalized the law by taking X-rated movies out of the sordid stag-movie houses into the local drive-in.

It was wonderful in the sense that a guy could take his girl-friend and even his secretary without pulling up the coat collar. Now we are blasé about such things, so *Deep Throat* has proved its point. Someone had to be first across the line, and Linda Lovelace got there.

I first met Linda in Miami with her first husband, and she has remained a good pal ever since. So has Georgina Spelvin, who did *The Devil in Miss Jones* and is probably the best actress in X movies at this time. Marilyn Chambers and her husband, Chuck, have been close pals for a long time and we've even considered working on a film together. Some of today's sex queens are good-looking, hardworking professional actresses who treat the new medium seriously as a way of life. The reality of the sex film couldn't be farther away from the orgy scene. The girls work a hard nine-to-six day and go home to their husbands when the shooting stops.

Deep Throat opened the door, but *Inside Jennifer Wells* and *The Autobiography of a Flea* broadened the scope because they were well-filmed productions. In the old days porno moviemakers used to play the camera on a couple in a seedy Mexican hotel room. Now they spend a month getting the shots exactly right. This is good for the industry because one day we shall have some really high-class, artistic sex films. They can only get better. If it hadn't been for *Deep Throat*, I doubt whether we would have accepted *Last Tango*. Many things can now be broached on screen which have nothing directly to do with the sex act but were taboo before.

People who act in sex films have a special kind of ego because they are not allowed any props except those endowed by nature. Many good actors of my acquaintance have turned down sex films because they were not too well equipped. As fully clothed sex symbols they were not about to ruin anyone's illusions. Men who wear wigs don't like anyone seeing their bald heads. Women with wrinkles on their breasts don't burn their bras. There are a few superstuds running around who would be laughingstocks if they played a sex scene. When it was very chic to be into sex movies, a few of these guys went into hiding.

Everything finds its own level. In the early seventies you couldn't get through ten seconds of conversation at any Hollywood gathering without referring to the latest X film. Guys would stand in corners at parties all night talking about the significance of every shot in *Deep Throat*. It was fashionable to know the actresses and invite them to the house. Nowadays you couldn't raise a yawn if you talked about the latest sex movie. Consequently only the very best of them will survive, and the future looks good.

Linda moves through life seemingly unaware that her name has become a byword for a certain kind of movie. She is very happily married and lives a quiet domestic life. I don't think she's ambitious, more than wanting to keep working at something or other. Marilyn Chambers, on the other hand, used sex films as a launching pad to her career, and I'm sure we shall see her often in the future. She has already broadened her scope and grown into a different kind of entertainer. She's done several legitimate shows, and I think she could do very well in variety. To this day, when you see her in the street, she looks like just another good-looking actress. The simple truth is that none of the porno stars looks any different. I know one happily married couple, the husband of which directs X films while she plays second lead. He can spend all day directing her though very explicit sex scenes, but they still go home and have a great ball in bed that night. The neighbors see her going to the local supermarket or him pottering around the garden, and they have simply no idea what either of them does.

Most of the sex films were lightweight, but good sex themes have been around for a long time. They may not have had close-ups of the sex act, but they managed to examine many sexual subjects without causing offense. Take a film like *The Fox,* directed by Mark Rydell with Sandy Dennis and Anne Heywood. It was probably one of the most sensual pictures ever made about one of the most touchy subjects of the late sixties, the story of two women who develop an intimate relationship which is split apart by a rough soldier.

Rydell dealt with nudity, masturbation, and lesbianism long before they became Bel Air cocktail party subjects and managed to offend no one. *The Fox* is an incredibly sensitive film. Then Mark turned around a couple of years later and did *The Cowboys* with John Wayne, a raunchy, tough he-man film very different from *The Fox*. That is the mark of a great director.

People tend to forget these days that the old-fashioned casting couch was once a real part of Hollywood and was certainly more suspect, and immoral, as an institution than any of today's sex films. During the days when promiscuity was risky but rife, the casting couch was a formidable but wholly acepted part of a young actress's budding career. Nowadays, of course, all you have to say to a chick is: "Hey, you want to hang out tonight?" and she either says yes and turns you on or takes a raincheck. People don't have to chase each other around these days. We've got to the point where the girl probably asks the guy to go grooving, and certainly nearly all the most accomplished and successful casting directors these days are women. So, if they were still operating in the old-fashioned way, it would be quite a different ball game.

Despite this, very little is new in Hollywood. Fashions just change, and the rules are bent. Jean Harlow, for instance, never wore a bra. Part of the great fun of watching 1920s movies was trying to spot the nipples under the satin gowns. Nowadays the whole thing is done much better and certainly more forcefully, and maybe we take everything farther in a literal sexual sense; but no one invented naughty movies. They've been around since the first negative was developed.

In America we covered sex over for a very long time because the right-wingers had a complex about titties. We could murder the Indians, enjoy the gang wars of Chicago, and cheat people, but the only time you could find a bare titty in a film was in an African tribal documentary. For thirty years or so there were committees making sure the nation didn't get corrupted by a lady's left breast.

That's why the shots which survive are like rare postage stamps. Some directors, such as De Mille, could slip one in which escaped the committee's scrutiny, and Jean Harlow often managed to get away with it, especially in the twenties before the committees got into full gear. Right up to the sixties directors were still using every trick in the book to let you know things were going a little farther than the screen kiss. Actual sex was taboo, so they gave us illusions of passion to let us know the exact moment of orgasm. The oldest cliché—famous in *From Here to Eternity*—was waves crashing on a beach. But how many times can you remember the great screen kiss dissolving to . . . a window with the curtains fluttering in the wind . . . two cigarettes burning on an ashtray

. . . the phonograph record going clump, clump, clump, un-attended . . . or, most Freudian of all, the great fireworks display with rockets shooting off in every direction?

In the sixties, however, British and European directors began to break down the taboos. *Room at the Top* seems curiously dated today but was explosive material then. Julie Christie was openly promiscuous in films like *Darling*, and Rita Tushingham had a black baby while living in an attic with a homosexual in *A Taste of Honey*. It took nearly a decade for Hollywood to catch up, but when it did, typically American, it went overboard and became sexually explicit to the full degree.

It had taken a very long time for *Darling* to come along, and it was brilliantly directed by John Schlesinger. Julie *was* a darling, and the whole thing worked. Promiscuity doesn't suit every actress, of course, and for some of them it is bad news. The public would never accept Doris Day as a whore, even though she admits that she has gone through times in her life which were anything but "pure." The public bought her fresh screen image, and that's how they like her. Julie Andrews is another brilliant actress who has begged for meatier parts. The producers just won't let her. She has been typecast into her own goodness.

That girl can act. I have worked with her several times, and she has so much more to offer than her image. She has a wonderful gypsy sense of humor which affects everyone around her. In life she is also far more sensuous than her screen image allows. She is always the complete lady, and she is extremely professional, but after three minutes with her onstage you know that lots is going on beneath the Andrews image. She lets it out every now and then. She'll give a little look halfway through a number, and you know it's not all cream cakes for tea. A flick of her eyebrows can be a real turn on. PPPZZZAAA . . . it all comes out.

Her husband, Blake Edwards, is a buddy, and he, of course, knows Julie's potential more than anyone else. When I once did the *Julie Andrews Show*, Julie came onstage and jived around in a way that would have made Thoroughly Modern Millie faint. One day, if they ever do allow her a thoroughly sensual part, you will see what a brilliant actress and sexy person she can be.

Glenda Jackson, on the other hand, has been typecast in the opposite mold. She would dearly love to play a nice, sweet, genteel lady whom her mother likes to invite to tea with the vicar. This is one of the ironies of show business. Glenda, who is a brilliant actress but something of a neuter in terms of sex appeal, gets all the meaty, sexy parts. Julie, who has Sex Appeal with capital letters, was kept on as a perpetual virgin until *10*. There is nothing Glenda cannot do on stage or screen except look really sensual, yet when there's a controversial raunchy sex scene going, she is almost automatically cast.

Vanessa Redgrave is the perfect balance between these two ladies. She can do almost anything, and she can look very sexy if she wants to. She can play it all ways. Her track record as an actress is unparalleled. For its time, the most sensuous movie of the decade was *Blow-Up*. She didn't play the glamour puss but developed the intelligent attractiveness few men can resist.

She is the kind of woman every man would be pleased to tell his wife he has had an affair with. Any man would love to run away with her for a week. It would never last with Vanessa, but you'd never forget it.

Vanessa, and a few other actresses like Faye Dunaway, bring quality into their pictures because they care passionately about their work. There is nothing cheap about them. I don't think they will be remembered in the same way, or with the same kind of reverence, as Claudette Colbert, but that is not because of their lack of talent. It is because they don't have the vehicles.

Because I love Vanessa so much as an actress, I am sorry when she blows up publicly on political issues as she did when she won the Oscar for *Julia*. We all know there are things wrong with the world, but the Academy Awards show is not the place to start shouting about them. Jane Fonda is just as socially aware as Vanessa, but she stood there and put it on the line when she said, "There are a lot of things I would like to say, but this is neither the time nor the place. Thank you very much." The town loved her for it. Jane and I have supported many political issues together. We have also had fallings out over a few, and I certainly don't agree with some of her more extreme political feelings. But on that Academy Awards night I walked over and said, "I am very proud of being in the same business as you. You are a very special lady."

She said, "Thanks, Sammy, we both know where we are coming from," and we left it at that. The next day she was back at her protests just as hard as ever. But she had allowed Hollywood to have its night.

She also has exactly the right ingredients as a person and an actress, and it shows across the exciting spectrum of her career. She mastered some of the really explosive roles, as, for example, in *Klute*, but she was also able to play the sweet, comedic girl next door and some other highly sensitive parts. She could switch from playing the hooker to being the cool intellectual. Many actresses spend all their lives trying to find a film like *They Shoot Horses, Don't They?*, yet this was the same actress who did *Cat Ballou*. Nowadays Jane is applauded by everyone, but it is only a few years since her very name was poison. I can still remember people saying, "She'll never get another job. She's a Red, and she's dead." Even the people who stood by her did it quietly. Hollywood's built-in McCarthyism gave her a hard time for several years. Yet she had the talent and the courage to hang on, and suddenly she became the queen of the lot again. That's Tinseltown for you.

Hollywood once luxuriated in great lady "fun" stars who mastered lighthearted comedy. Carole Lombard always had it, and every now and then Bette Davis would show the laughter in her character. Bette could do anything, of course; she would walk through light comedies for breakfast. Take a film like *The Bride Came C.O.D.* with Cagney. The script was dreadful, but those two sizzled it into a brilliant comedy. At that stage in her career it was hilarious to see the great Bette Davis fall on her ass, and she played it for all it was worth.

These days there are very few women stars who have a genuine comedic sense. Jane Fonda has a natural bent, and Barbra Streisand was very funny when she did her nightclub act, "talking bad" on purpose. She managed to corner the Jewish humor market and translate it to the screen.

But there is no one around today like Kay Kendall, whose innate sense of humor permeated everything she did. Even when she was dying in dramatic circumstances, she remained funny. She was the female Rex Harrison, forever sophisticated and amusing. Knowing her was a great pleasure and always a lot of fun. In *Genevieve* she just about played herself. She *was* the kind of dame who might get drunk and play the trumpet, yet never lose her dignity. When she completed *Once More With Feeling*, her last film, she was acknowledged as the closest thing Britain ever had to Carole Lombard. She could get her stockings in a twist, as the British say, straighten them out, and be glamorous throughout. Then she'd walk right out of that shot into a beautiful love scene.

Kay had a huge zest for life. Even when she knew it was just a matter of time, she never stopped being that bubbly, gay person. She would do anything to make someone feel good or give them a laugh. Rex Harrison's *My Fair Lady* and my own *Mr. Wonderful* were playing at the same time in New York one Christmas. She decided we should have our Christmas parties together. She booked Danny's, and all the *Mr. Wonderful* kids came dressed to the nines. The *My Fair Lady* crowd turned up in Levi's and slacks. For the first twenty minutes the two groups stared at each other, but then Kay kicked off her shoes, and the party began. She suddenly brought everyone together in a flourish of activity. It was unique.

Her romance with Rex Harrison was a real one. There was so much happy affection between them. It surprised a lot of people who had known Rex over a number of years because his caring for her really showed. He was known as a highly reserved Englishman apparently trained never to show his emotions. But the combination of his marriage to Kay and the huge success of *My Fair Lady* made Rex's stay in New York one of the happiest times of his life. He was absolutely ecstatic both onstage and at home. At the party we had a little dance group, and Rex and Kay started singing Christmas carols. In no time at all the whole joint was swinging. Rex, of course, had no singing voice.

When Rex came to America to play Professor Higgins, he presented the producers with a big problem. He was perfectly cast as the professor, but when they came to the songs, they found he had a musical range of only one and a half notes, and a whole battery of musicians and writers couldn't do a thing with him. In the end they were happy when they found he could talk on pitch and chat his way through the songs. It worked; in fact, many people feel it even improved the show. But Rex wasn't careering around, looking for more musicals, even after the huge success of the show.

While talking about great broads on the screen, we mustn't leave out Sarah Miles, who has talents which have never been

Singing with Liza.

Liza and Altovise.

Duke lent me his good luck piece—the hat—which appeared in more movies than I was ever to make.

Examining guns with Clint Eastwood.

With Brigitte Bardot.

With Marilyn Monroe and Milton Greene.

With Martin Luther King, Jr., in my dressing room at Carnegie Hall.

Edward G. Robinson came to the closing night of *Mr. Wonderful*.

Entertaining close to the fighting in Da Nang in 1972. I hope Charlie enjoyed the show.

Doing my cowboy act at Da Nang.

My roast at the Friars with Jack Benny.

Playing golf with Sidney Poitier on Long Island. Sean Connery made up the threesome.

With Altovise.

In my dressing room at Las Vegas with my kids, *left to right*: Mark,
Tracey, and Geoff.

In England at the White Elephant with the Pimms cup they always have ready.

fully exploited on film and a sensual quality which is immediately recognizable to both men and women.

Janet Suzman can also do anything she wants as an actress. If a director needs a seedy little sex scene, she turns it into a work of art. If he wants a classical act, she can walk through it. The industry couldn't invent enough roles for that woman. She is probably the most multitalented actress alive today. The British film industry, in the doldrums at the best of times, simply hasn't been able to deal with her potential. I would rather spend ten minutes in her gracious company than a weekend with every glamour queen in the world. She is dynamic, concerned, keenly intelligent, vibrant, extremely sensual, and brilliant. It seems that when she breathes, she can breathe the whole world in and out. She is the kind of woman you'd like to meet on a desert island. If you did, you'd throw away the SOS flares.

The feminist movement and the sex-film syndrome are almost totally opposed to each other. Yet they both are vibrant influences on the immediate future of films. On the one hand, the X movies are cashing in on the old-fashioned exploitation of the female; on the other, the feminists are fighting to establish themselves in their own right as individuals who should not be exploited because of their sex. It is an interesting time for Hollywood and one of the reasons why the movie industry remains fascinating. The difference, of course, is that the sex movies are a passing fad but the feminist movement is changing the whole basis of Hollywood thinking.

The movement is beginning to affect the essence of sex and sensuality in movies. It may seem subtle at first sight, but there has been a huge pushing toward a new kind of relationship. Lois Chiles, for instance, refused to play a typical James Bond chattel in *Moonraker*, and the producer agreed to rewrite the script. The roles of the women haven't exactly been reversed yet, but scripts are far more aware of women's place in modern society.

When Marlon Brando played the homecoming war veteran in *The Men* in 1950, his wife bore the brunt of his troubles. Brando was aggressive, truculent, and abrasive. Poor Teresa Wright had to provide all the love and caring which helped him back in to society.

In *Coming Home* Jon Voight is in an almost identical situation. But three decades later he is an altogether softer character who

is not afraid to express his complete need for the woman in his
life. She's not the paid lackey but an integral part of his rehabilitation.

Actresses like Claudia Cardinale in Rome are being even more
frank in their grab for influence. Claudia has just finished making a film in which the only guys around the set were laborers.
The director, Sofia Scandurra, said, "For once the men around
here will find themselves the victims of their biological condi-
tion, regardless of their talent." This is a long way from the time
when an actress was happy, even grateful, to get any work she
could find and would act like hell on the set, however demanding the role. In the interim women in Hollywood found themselves going through a bleak period.

Shirley MacLaine, for instance, turned down scripts for four
years because she thought they were ridiculous from a woman's
point of view. Then along came *The Turning Point,* an apt
name, and Shirley threw herself into it. It is blatantly a "woman's
picture," and it gathered eleven Oscar nominations. It was a massive part for Shirley to play, and she needed a great deal of
courage to tackle it. But she knew the vehicle was right, and
she proved it.

Films like that become classics out of the blue. We didn't hear
much about *Julia* or *The Turning Point* until the first returns
came in and, to the amazement of the whole industry, people
were flocking in. Shirley became bankable again overnight, and
now she's inundated with new scripts. She told me she gets about
two scripts a day which she calls *"Charlie's Angels* Incarnate."
There are probably 5,000 scripts floating about Hollywood right
now in which four women rip off a bank. You can imagine someone sitting down and saying, "Let's write a caper picture and get
Shirley, Jane, Vanessa, and Diane Keaton together." This is typical of Hollywood thinking. It has recognized the bankability,
and now it wants to cash in on it by rewriting *Butch Cassidy* for
women. No one in Hollywood seems to know what to do with
adult males and females on the screen together. No one can find
the ultimate modern love story, and when someone does, it will
probably spring at us from nowhere. Then there'll be 10,000
"modern love stories" floating around, and the ball game will
go on. It was always the same, and it is the reason why some great

films never became classics. They became dated too quickly because of all the imitations.

I often wonder, had she lived, how Marilyn Monroe would have fared in these days of sexual freedom and the feminist movement. I seriously feel that she might have come into her own as a character actress. One of the games movie buffs play is that they cast her, in her fifties, in some of the films now making the rounds. Would they *ever* have let her escape from the dumb-blonde image? When buffs get together, it is a question that can provide days of conversation.

After Marilyn died, a number of guys came out of the woodwork claiming all sorts of things about her. We all know she found a basic enjoyment and inner security when she made love. But she was no whore. Of course, she was unhappy and often insecure. But I never once thought of her as tragic. She was an extremely caring and sensitive person who was easily bruised. Sometimes it seemed as she were walking around with all her nerves exposed. She was always vulnerable, to both love and abuse, and had incredible sensitivity to other people's views and emotions. She would become very involved in loving animals and even such things as plants and trees. She had the most endearing way of convincing even the most insignificant of men that he was the only guy in the world. There was a lovely story of the William Morris agent who happened to be very small. When they slept together, Marilyn puffed up his ego to the point of madness by whispering, "You're hurting me," in his ear. This was all a put-on, of course, but it was typical of MM's feeling for other people.

Marilyn was first noticed when she did a bit part in *Ladies of the Chorus*, a film she made for director Phil Karlson when she was still living at the YWCA. She seemed to be the original dumb blonde, a type of female enjoying a strange vogue at the time. Someone had suggested to Darryl F. Zanuck, "This broad could be the next Jean Harlow," and Zanuck's talent scouts recognized the same sense of comedy—touched with warmth and sympathy, a Harlow quality which could inspire love rather than pure lust. So Zanuck decided to try her out in *Ladies of the Chorus* but disagreed with his advisers. "Harlow could act," he bellowed. He refused to pick up Marilyn's six-month option, and she was out of a job, an action Zanuck regretted to his dying day, especially when he had to swallow his pride several times later and bring her back at exorbitant fees. He harbored a deep resentment that he had missed the boat, for the omnipotent Zanuck loved to bask in his genius for discovering potential superstars.

However, one of the people who *had* noticed her was Groucho Marx, and when he was casting *Love Happy*, he called her for an audition. Groucho was intrigued by her. Years later he told me he had made her walk up and down the studio for hours on end, just to watch her bottom. He couldn't take his eyes off those delectable curves. Groucho was happy to give her the part. The director, David Miller, asked Marilyn simply to walk on and off the set. But Groucho had other ideas. He wanted to spend a few days watching that bottom wiggle, so he specially wrote Marilyn some lines. MM was almost completely inexperienced at the time and muffed the lines several times. Groucho couldn't have been more pleased. He would pinch her ample rump and call for the scene to be done again. Marilyn told me later, "I didn't mind. Every time we did a take I was getting more experience. But I sure had a sore backside at the end of the day."

Marilyn had yet to make any real impression on filmgoers. But up in Bel Air the projection rooms began to buzz. In that tight little community, where in those days all the people that mattered had homes, they were playing Marilyn's shots over and over again. John Huston was one of them. It was during the days when John was very thick with the Holmby Hills Rat Pack, and he told us how he was intrigued by this new talent. Apparently he had called her to audition for *The Asphalt Jungle*. Before turning up late, Marilyn had spent her customary days getting ready. Her instructions from her agent had been: "Look as sexy as hell."

Insecure as always, Marilyn didn't recognize just how naturally sexy she was until long after she had become a household name. Consequently she turned up for the audition with her bra full of padding. Huston told Bogey, "I went right up to her, shoved my hand down her front, yanked all the padding out, and said, 'OK, now let's read for the part.'"

At this time her agent was Johnny Hyde, who, like most of the guys around Marilyn, was madly in love with her. This undoubtedly helped Marilyn's early career because Johnny was a

brilliant agent who pulled out every stop for her. MM was virtually untrained as an actress, but she had a special kind of talent
in front of the camera which was instantly recognized by the
people who mattered. She got the part in *The Asphalt Jungle*
and played Louis Calhern's concubine. It was not a large part,
but a new Calhern film made the rounds on the Bel Air circuit
immediately, and it was quickly agreed that Marilyn had stolen
the picture. The hills began buzzing with excitement, and Louis
quickly admitted, "We were always told we should never play
a scene with a child or a dog. I want to amend that to include
big tits."

Soon after, she made *All About Eve,* and the public began to
notice her. But more important, the Hollywood press fell instantly in love with her. She woke up to find that she was just
about the hottest property in town. Joseph Mankiewicz directed
the picture, which also starred Bette Davis and Anne Baxter.
For a nervous new actress, this was a formidable lineup of talent,
and Marilyn was a little in awe of them. It was here her real
insecurity in front of the camera was born.

Marilyn was naturally a prime target for the pen of Hedda
Hopper, a past master at cutting big stars down to size in her
daily Hollywood gossip column. The studios walked in fear of
her every word, and normally Hedda loved a sensitive soul like
Marilyn's, as she would stomp across exposed nerves with razor
blades between her toes. One day she went up to Marilyn at a
Hollywood party. She wore her most menacing look, and Johnny
Hyde was immediately nervous. It was a look Hedda reserved
for war. "Miss Monroe," she barked, "they tell me you drink
nothing but bullshots morning, noon, and night." Someone ex-
plained to a perplexed Marilyn that a bullshot was a mixture of
bouillon and vodka.

"What a perfectly terrible thing to do to good vodka," Marilyn
said in her most innocent little-girl voice. Hedda roared with
laughter, and Marilyn stayed a firm favorite in her camp for
several years.

With the press on her side and with a consistent interest
buzzing from Bel Air, Marilyn was poised for superstardom. But
many people now wonder whether the former Norma Jean was
ready for it. When she made *Clash by Night* with Fritz Lang,
she nearly drove the director crazy. She was already developing

her fear of the camera, and the larger her parts became, the more difficult she found them. In one small scene they had to do twenty-seven takes, and Fritz was tearing his hair out. He even gave her a cue card—unheard of on a professional movie set. This did not endear her to the rest of the cast, and her reputation for being difficult to work with began to spread around the studio commissaries.

Fritz told me, "Marilyn seemed scared of everything, and we all had to help her out, Barbara Stanwyck more than anyone. Paul Douglas, who costarred, got quite cross with Marilyn because he had such a warm regard for Barbara. When the press boys came in, they ignored Stanwyck and rushed over to take pictures of MM's tits; Paul got really steamed up about it. It didn't help the atmosphere of that film at all."

Marilyn had become a real experience to work with, especially for the directors. It was a challenge that most of them faced only once. Between her debut in 1949 and her death in 1962 she made nearly twenty films. During this time she worked with fourteen major directors including Otto Preminger, George Cukor, Joseph Mankiewicz, Howard Hawks, Henry Hathaway, and Laurence Olivier. Only two ever came back for a second helping. John Huston made *The Asphalt Jungle* with her in 1950, but he waited a full decade before he directed her again in the last film she ever made—*The Misfits*. Billy Wilder, however, was enchanted with her in *The Seven-Year Itch* in 1955. He came back only four years later to direct *Some Like It Hot,* probably Marilyn's best role and certainly the one in which *she* felt she had come to fruition as an actress.

Nearly all these people agree she was extremely difficult to work with not because she wasn't magic once the cameras started rolling, but because she traditionally caused such chaos on the set. Despite this, the top directors of the fifties were falling over themselves to try out their talents on this unique cinematic experience. For she did things on film which inspired admiration, even from the most grudging directors. She could fill a screen in a way which was entirely special to her. By saying this, I am not gauchely referring to her ample and famous breasts, although they naturally made a large contribution to her visual image. I am talking about her presence on celluloid. The greatest example of this came when she made *Gentlemen Prefer Blondes* with Jane Russell. At first the director, Howard Hawks, was not sure what the hell was going on with the blond star. He even turned to a subordinate and growled, "She's unfilmable." Later he changed his mind.

By this time Marilyn had become like a sister to me. I loved her, but it was almost purely spiritual. I tried to behave like a brother, and consequently I was often around with a spare shoulder for her to cry on. Janie Russell, on the other hand, was a great old drinking buddy of mine, and I adored her spitfire personality and her work as an actress. Janie was a "great broad" in every sense of the words. There was a magnificent difference between the two girls, and I was sure this magic concoction was going to work. Luckily I was filming on the same lot at the time, and naturally I spent a part of each day watching the film's progress. It was an experience I wouldn't have missed for anything in the world.

Janie Russell always gave the impression, in life and on film, that she might eat her man up for breakfast before finding the next one for lunch. She was all woman, yet you thought of her always as one of the boys. People instinctively handed her a beer in the can because they thought she'd never use a glass. She was the kind of girl who never had to spell anything out. A nod or a wink would write chapters.

On the set she had an aura which was completely her own. She was hardworking and extremely competent as an actress, but without ever saying a line, she seemed incredibly impudent. She'd put her hands on her hips and give Howard a single look before the cameras started rolling. The look said, and Hawks felt it, "OK, let's get this damned show on the road. Let's *go*. I've got to get home. I've got a footballer to feed before I make love to him." She was highly professional, and she didn't like hanging around. With slowpoke Marilyn on the same set everyone was a little nervous.

On this particular day I'd got there about midmorning to find everyone sitting around, waiting for MM. As usual, she was still pulling herself together. Countless people had gone up to try and hurry her up. It had been the same every morning. She'd start at nine to be ready by midday. Janie was chewing her nails, waiting to get going. I finally went up, as I often did, to try and encourage her. Marilyn didn't mind slouching around at home, but in public, especially on the screen, she had to look like a billion bucks. Even when she *was* looking like that, she would go on staring in the mirror. I'd be trying to make her move, and she'd be looking at herself from every angle.

"Do I look OK?" she'd say.

"Sure you do, Marilyn. You've never looked more beautiful."

"Do you really mean it. I mean really? Will they love me?"

"You know they always do, Marilyn. Let's go down to the set. You'll see, everyone will agree with me. You look gorgeous."

But she needed that reassurance over and over again. Sometimes she took a large slug of vodka; sometimes she didn't. It wasn't until much later that she came to depend on it.

On that day I finally walked her down to the set and could feel the great sigh of relief which went up as soon as they saw her. "You see," she told them, "I told you I'd make it all right."

Marilyn really *didn't* have any idea of the time she'd kept them waiting. She had to look her best, however long it took, and she somehow assumed that everyone else was doing the same thing.

Jane Russell is a large woman—literally and figuratively. On this particular morning, dressed in black tights, she looked even larger than usual. She is a big-boned woman, with wide shoulders for a gal and other natural attributes which are far from small. She was fuming. Marilyn was diminutive against her. Jane seemed to tower over her, and for a second it was a little eerie. Howard and several others were trying to get everything in place. They became seriously worried because Jane still seemed to tower over a crestfallen Marilyn. Someone suggested they put an extra prop on Marilyn's side of the set to "offset the space." Janie began to chuckle. Her temper had gone down as soon as the work was about to start. "You won't need that," she told Hawks. "As soon as the cameras start rolling, that space will fill up." Hawks decided to try it.

The next hour was uncanny. Marilyn was in the mood, and she grew in stature and *presence* until she towered over Janie. She filled the screen until Janie had become almost incidental.

It was because of Janie's carefree attitude toward Marilyn that that film stands as a monument to them both. Janie was magnificent about everything. She remained highly professional throughout the shooting, yet she tempered this with a sharp good humor and a complete acceptance of the fact that whatever she did, Marilyn, almost without trying, would outclass her.

Janie was a sexy lady, and she had half the men in the world hungering for her. Yet she never took this seriously. Day after day she kept the *Gentlemen Prefer Blondes* company in the best of spirits, cracking jokes at her own expense. She never once allowed herself to vie for position with Marilyn. She knew her own limitations. She was a damned fine, hardworking actress with a lot of guts and fabulous good looks. But she also recognized that MM was one of a kind.

Consequently Marilyn really enjoyed making the film. The two stars built up a huge rapport and eventually had a great deal of fun. Because Janie was such a gas, no rivalry or jealousy ever developed between them. Janie would come off the set and wink at me and say, "I'm wasting my time. There's going to be nothing on that screen but Marilyn. Boy, has she got what it takes."

Janie was right. Diminutive though she may have been at the dressing table, as soon as Marilyn Monroe heard the slight whir of a camera turning, she became a veritable giant.

After a couple of weak films, *Niagara* and *River of No Return*, MM bounced back in *The Seven-Year Itch* with Tom Ewell, a film which deserves its place as vintage Monroe. In it she fully developed her comedic genius. It was based on the old dumb-blonde innocence, but no one could do it like MM. She would look sweetly at everyone, as if to say, "Who me? Well, whaddya know? I'd never have guessed. Oh, dear, are my tits showing? Fancy that. Tell me, why has all the traffic stopped? They're looking at my tush, you say. What a crazy thing to do! Would you believe it?" At that she was gorgeous. She cultivated that baby-dumpling quality into an art form. She made it beautifully endearing because she was never vulgar. Everything had the same sweet finesse, and in this she did honestly portray much of the real-life Monroe. She was genuinely one of the sweetest creatures I have ever met. She couldn't fake anything. It was all there up front.

But by 1955 Marilyn Monroe had become completely frustrated as an actress. She desperately needed to find a vehicle which did more than expose her body, but she had become Fox's hottest sex symbol, and it wasn't going to let her muck up the formula by experimenting with more sophisticated roles even though she was ready for another dimension. Fox kept the reins on her until they almost choked her and invaded every aspect of her life. The studio not only dictated exactly what roles she could play with whom but went to very great lengths to control her private life as well. It wanted to know who she was with and where she was at all times, and this often made her distraught. Marilyn was like a bird that had to be free. If the tragedy was as big as the myth, then it was solely because of this.

When she was making *The Prince and the Showgirl* with Laurence Olivier, she was going through one of the most difficult periods of her life. She was having an affair with a close friend of mine. He was a photographer, and they were deeply in love. They met clandestinely, often at my house. She was always being followed there, and we had to get up to all sorts of intrigues to keep the affair secret. I used to pretend we were having a party, and Marilyn would arrive and leave at different times from my pal.

Once they were in the house, of course, they went off to the swimming pool, which had its own self-contained bungalow. She was particularly vulnerable at this time because she was genuinely scared of working with Olivier. Even though Larry was incredibly kind and patient with her, he was, after all, the great Laurence Olivier, and she was in awe of his reputation.

Larry claimed later that working with MM had added ten years to his life. Maybe it did, but I know she did not escape completely unscathed herself. It was during this picture that her terrible fear of the camera became fully developed, and this, along with the studio's dogging her every move, was what turned her on to booze and drugs. She was never into drugs in the big way many people say. She needed uppers and downers to keep going, but so did half of Hollywood. However, she did develop a complete dependence on vodka during this period. She couldn't face the sunlight, let alone the studio, without a long plug from the bottle.

Later we were making *Porgy and Bess* when Billy Wilder moved onto the same lot to start shooting *Some Like It Hot*. *Porgy* was taking much longer than anyone had expected, and we had already been filming for several weeks before Marilyn's film started. We were also still going long after her picture was in the can. But for eight weeks, when I wasn't on call for *Porgy*, I was over on the other set, watching the fireworks. People said a lot of cruel things about Marilyn during and after that film. Tony Curtis was particularly scathing, and Billy Wilder growled after a certain day's shooting, "I feel like going home and beating my wife."

Wilder believed that making two big handsome men dress up as women was cinematically impossible. In fact, the whole idea was very daring for its day. Wilder told me later, in the sixties, "I wish we could have saved it until now. It would have been a much bigger hit." As it was, Jack Lemmon, who is an all-out extrovert and clown, found the role stimulating. Tony Curtis was much more coy about dressing in drag.

Day after day I ran across the lot to see how things were going. Day after day the temperatures were rising under every collar except Marilyn's. Tony Curtis and Jack Lemmon were always good buddies, and Jack had to spend a long time cooling Tony down. It wasn't all Marilyn's fault. The two guys had to spend day after day on a boiling set in heavy women's clothes and makeup. Wilder was always a perfectionist who insisted on making dozens of takes. They would play a scene fifteen times, and Wilder would say, "Print number four and number nine."

They'd ask him, "What about the last six takes?"

Wilder would say, "I don't like them. Number four was perfect. But I like number nine as well." It did not endear him to a cast that had spent two hours making ten extra takes when Wilder already had the one he wanted in the can.

Tony took this especially badly. In fact, what with Wilder doing innumerable takes and Marilyn spending about ten hours getting ready, Tony was gradually going out of his mind. The film was a comedy, and these guys were finding it more and more difficult to be funny. We used to watch Tony stumbling around the set, grumbling like hell. Then he would go before the cameras and be the essence of good humor. But as soon as Wilder said, "Cut," Tony would charge off the set, turning the air a vivid blue with a torrent of swearwords.

At one point, when Tony had to kiss Marilyn, he turned around and mumbled to someone out of her hearing, "It was like kissing Hitler," indicating his mood at the time.

It didn't help poor Marilyn's standing on the set when Wilder told them all, "When Marilyn gets it right, that's the one we're going to use. The rest of you just better make sure it's the right one for you as well."

Wilder knew full well that Marilyn was trying hard but that she was "difficult and disorganized." In fact, Marilyn gave some classic performances. There were days when she was phenomenal, and even Tony grudgingly admitted it. Once she started really rolling and her inhibitions disappeared, she could be sensational. Because of this, Wilder was willing to put up with anything.

"When the metabolism is right," Billy told the company one day before Marilyn made her belated appearance, "she is the most marvelous thing in the world to direct. We are utterly dependent on her moods, but when she gets it right, there is no one to touch her—so please bear with us both."

On one particularly agonizing day Tony and Jack had to sit around for ten hours while Marilyn did a single take. They had their heavy makeup on, and they were getting very angry. Then Billy came over and said, "We can't fit you in today, boys. We'll see you at six A.M. with the same makeup on."

This was too much, even for Jack Lemmon. He jumped up and screamed, "You son of a bitch." No wonder all three men were very happy when that film was finally in the can.

After *Some Like It Hot*, Marilyn went into decline. She even began to lose her international clout at the box office. In 1960 she made *Let's Make Love* with Yves Montand, for George Cukor. It was another bubbly light comedy, but it certainly *wasn't* vintage Monroe. Finally, she made *The Misfits*, written by her husband, Arthur Miller. By then her life was pretty much dominated by depression, booze, and drugs, and she had only a year to live. John Huston, who directed, found her emotionally crippled, and she certainly gave Clark Gable a hard time. Clark thought it was the best script he had ever read, and he was eager to do the film. But he said a week before he died, "Working with Marilyn nearly gave me a heart attack. I have never been more happy when a film ended."

If the truth be known, Marilyn felt the same way.

Unlike Jimmy Dean, who never realized his own real potential, Marilyn became prematurely spent as an actress because she was never allowed the personal and artistic freedom she craved. She still hangs like a bat in the heads of the men who met her, and none of us will forget her. The legends and myths continue to be spun out. I can add nothing of significance. To me she was one of the sweetest creatures ever to have lived. And I can only thank her from the bottom of my heart for providing us movie buffs with a virtually endless topic of conversation.

Chapter 13

Black Cats

Being an entertainer has taken me to the fringes and into most aspects of our American way of life. It is one of the side benefits of the job, and I always appreciate hobnobbing with so many people from such varied backgrounds. The political world, for instance, fascinates me because it has a certain potency which I find irresistible. In show business we are as good as our last show, but politics seems somehow to go on forever.

I like to be around the handful of sincere senators who have good heads on their shoulders. If they know what they are doing, they can be extremely impressive. Kissinger was a powerhouse with an aura about him which gave him a strange attraction. The four Presidents I have known impressed me deeply.

Nowadays I've cooled down politically. I used to be very frustrated, angry, and impatient about what was going on. I wanted things to change fast. Maybe I was an optimist. You can heal such sores as violence politically, but it's difficult to change intolerance and bigotry by Washington decrees. I didn't feel I should keep quiet about my ideals. I used to shoot off my mouth about all sorts of things, both privately to anyone who would listen and

publicly on any platform I could find. These days I don't get involved with the great issues. It is time for some of the young ones
to take over. My generation of blacks has moved mountains, although many times it didn't seem like it. We've broken down
many taboos. Now it is up to the younger generation of all colors
and creeds to build on the foundations we have laid.

I no longer get up on platforms, but that doesn't mean I haven't
got definite views about most issues. I just don't spout my mouth
off anymore. If someone asks me what I think, I tell him as intel-
ligently and coherently as I can. But I've thrown the soapbox
away. Without any more excuses or explanations, I'm back in the
entertainment business.

In the early sixties, at the height of President Kennedy's influence, I took part in America's greatest march for black freedom
which brought 200,000 people to the streets of Washington. It
was a demonstration but, more than that, it was an exercise in
solidarity which was not trying to push the President into anything but to back him in the types of reforms and changes he had
in mind. We felt confident that for perhaps the first time, it was
really worth putting ourselves on the line. The march came just
about a hundred years after the Emancipation Proclamation, and
Kennedy said, "These recent months . . . have seen the decisive
recognition by a major part of our society that all our citizens are
entitled to full membership in the national community." It was
strange that a century after the proclamation itself, this kind of
thing still needed to be said. But it did, and it was, and we were
very happy to hear it.

Planeloads of stars came up. Charlton Heston was there, with
Paul Newman, Burt Lancaster, Marlon Brando, Lena Horne, Sidney Poitier, Bobby Darin, and Robert Ryan. The celebrities is-
sued their own statement, saying, "All forms of racial segregation
are injurious to the arts of the nation." It seems obvious now, but
then it was daring.

I had become involved in the whole Kennedy era because of
various things, including Sinatra's influence, and it was one of
the most confusing and dreadful days of my life when Jack Kennedy got that bullet. Naturally we canceled the show.

We also stopped the show when Dr. King was assassinated; it
just blew my mind that such a brilliant man could be so cruelly
wasted. When Robert Kennedy was shot, we were in London at

the Palladium doing *Golden Boy*. I heard about it several hours before anyone else in England. The man who ran my head office in Los Angeles had been in touch with the Kennedy family, and they were holding up the news of his death until all the members of the family had been told. I tried to keep the secret, but by curtain time, I knew I couldn't go on. It was only the second night in London, and the management pleaded with me to try to do it. Then the cast came and told me their careers would suffer if I didn't. They knew what I was thinking, but because hoofers are born with "the show must go on" syndrome, I did the first half, and I had tears streaming down my face the whole time. I could hardly hit the pitch, and my feet felt like lead. Eventually, during the intermission, I told them I was through for the night. I felt helpless. I asked the audience to pray for the senator and told them, "For once in my life my heart is not in this theater. It is somewhere in America, where one of our last dreams has just been murdered." I got muted, respectful applause, and I just walked off. I know that audience had paid its money to be entertained. But I had been Kennedy's friend, and if I had been false to that friendship, my entertainment value would be nil. They understood that.

When I think back to that night, I remember how angry and hopeless everything seemed. The Kennedy brothers and King had, among them, held not only the beginnings of the end of the black problem in America but also what seemed the answer to most of the world's other problems as well. They had been cruelly murdered by the bigots in our society, and it seemed the shits always got away with it. The guys who were wearing the authentic white hats were gunned down. And it suddenly seemed as if they had all died for nothing. The gun laws haven't changed because of them. Kids can still buy mail-order rifles. Violence remains all over the place. Peace has gone out of fashion. If their deaths had meant something, it might have been possible to come to terms with them. But it looked as if the sickness had come full circle and the world had gone crazy. I had recently been in Robert's company every day during the New York campaign. I, and everyone else around him at the time, had a tremendous feeling that great things were about to happen. We had a vision of a wonderful America which would be marvelous for everyone to live in, regardless of color or creed. We had caught his enthusiasm and we were all going forward together. It may have been naïve, but at the time it seemed very real. The violence of the deaths of his brother and of Martin Luther King suddenly seemed diminished as we strode on to better things. The advances of the black man in American society seemed imminent. We were on the Kennedy bandwagon again, and it looked and felt good.

Then, suddenly, we were sitting in the dressing room and heard that the guy, and all his dreams, had been wasted, and everything was back to square one. For me, the bitterest message of all was that I felt that 80 percent of all Americans were behind that final bullet—not just the bigots but the huge percentage who never gave a damn what happened. In many ways they were just as responsible.

Politics in Hollywood was always very much a two-sided affair. You've got the liberals, and you've got the conservatives, and both of them are deeply and genuinely involved with what they are doing. The liberals continually put their careers on the line when they back unpopular causes. But they seem to be winning through. Nowadays there is a huge liberal influence spreading over most of the country, and much of it is coming out of Hollywood. It certainly wasn't always like that. In the old days, during the studio system, all politics was taboo.

There is no doubt there were a lot of communists in the arts during the twenties and thirties. This came to a head during the McCarthy witch-hunt era, which upset everyone. No one liked what McCarthy was doing, but at the same time there were a lot of people around who were trying to upset America when the country was down and bleeding.

In the past two decades even the right wing has realized that people with humanitarian or liberal views are not necessarily Reds. "Extremists" gradually became the norm because it was no longer considered extreme to have liberal views. Conservatives are not as rigidly right-wing as they were in the forties. Both sides are swinging toward the middle. The typical Republican of today would have been considered a liberal before.

For me the two-party democratic system is dynamite because it continually gives us a chance to change our political viewpoints. I don't think it is at all wrong for celebrities to back political causes. We are thinking, taxpaying Americans with a say in the running of the country. By this I don't advocate using my every show as a platform, but I do say we should put ourselves firmly and personally behind our political convictions. This is a commitment we have to make individually to ourselves, whatever the cost. We own property, and our children go to school; some of us are still affected by discrimination, so we have to make a stand, and to some extent this has paid off.

Things change, even though they seem to take a long time. It's like the Chinese pebble which ends up in Malibu. It just keeps rippling along, century after century, but it gets there in the end, and when it arrives, you don't even notice it. I subsequently supported Richard Nixon because I believed he was going to do some good, both for my people and for the country in general. You must remember that when he got into office the second time, it was an absolute landslide. Most of the country was rooting for him in a big way. They tend to forget that now. In the history of American politics no other President received a greater vote of confidence from the electorate. The nation was promised a lot of things, and so was I, not only by the Nixon supporters but by the President himself. One of the projects Nixon promised me was that there would be a huge educational program in the ghettos. It was one of many pledges he made which I have no doubt were genuine at the time. Watergate came along and rewrote history, so we will never know.

I don't mind admitting I am still a little bewildered over the whole Nixon episode. I believed at the time I could still be a confirmed Democrat, yet vote for the guy because I thought then he could do the job better than anyone else around. I knew I had to get off the fence and commit myself. When we got down to the Republican Convention in Miami, I understood they were happy to have me along because I was both black and Jewish and in theory could get some of those votes going toward Nixon. But we didn't go along hat in hand to vote for the guy. We also wanted to demonstrate that the Republicans would treat blacks as true equals. That's why I kicked up a fuss when I found I wasn't given the facilities I normally have when I am on the road—a penthouse suite. Nothing new about that. I always have the penthouse suite. I wanted them to look after both me and my entourage as we always lived. They had to demonstrate that we blacks had equal status with anyone on the bandwagon, and to that extent we got what we wanted.

It is true that a lot of people in the black movement resented it when I hugged Nixon on a nationwide TV show. Some of them got nasty and voluble. The blacks stayed, mostly, lukewarm to Nixon, and very little I said changed their minds. But I had long talks with the guy face to face, and I must say, even now, he impressed me. He promised much more funding to black colleges and many new reforms. He had done away with the quota system, and generally speaking, the more he said, the more I believed in him. Watergate was still some time off when we were together in Miami. I did not check out all the political affiliations and relied only on what my heart dictated, as I always had. As I now know, that can sometimes lead you into trouble.

Hollywood was divided over the Nixon thing, at least before Watergate. Some guys, like Redford, had chips on their shoulders about Nixon, and Redford went all out to make *All the President's Men.* But he had come along in the wake of a great movement which had made political stands very popular in Hollywood. At one stage just about everyone campaigning for George McGovern was far better known than the guy himself. Some aspects of show business also rubbed off on the politicians. George Wallace, for instance, turned his rallies into revival meetings straight out of *Elmer Gantry.* The Kennedys loved nothing better than a star-studded Hollywood-style gala.

I think most stars were serious and conscientious about their electioneering. Paul Newman, for example, could support Eugene McCarthy but also take the Republican stand for Pete McCloskey because he thought the issues right. Paul, like me, had no party loyalties. He, and many other celebrities, thought of Washington as a whorehouse. If you've got to visit a whorehouse, you might as well try to find the best whore in the place. It was a cynical but widely held view.

Later, when Nixon had been discredited, many people started throwing the crap at me in a nasty way. They wagged their fingers and enjoyed pointing out how wrong I had been. The flak got so hot at one stage I think I was pretty close to a nervous breakdown. Murphy Bennett had to help me onto the stage one night, and I was very close to crying. It was a traumatic experience, but I finally won through. Time heals, eventually.

I got over it by reminding myself that my original motives, however wrong I have been proved, were honorable and seemed rational at the time. For a start, I believed Nixon was going to do something about Vietnam, and I was proved correct in that. Since I had been there myself and seen the conditions, I had sworn to myself that I would back anyone who felt he could pull America out of that bloodbath. Nixon had, in fact, cooperated fully and personally with my visit.

I didn't go to Vietnam because I believed in the war. I went because there were so many black soldiers there, and no one seemed to care about them. White entertainers were going over in droves. They were putting on good shows, but to the blacks, they belonged to the political system back home, and they were extremely disillusioned about it. There was nothing for the young black soldier to relate to.

I think we eventually succeeded, although it was quite a fight. When we got there, we put on the first show in Da Nang, and there were 18,000 black soldiers out front. I did the show as best I could but didn't realize the difficulties we had faced until I talked to some of the guys afterward. The cats told me that if I'd given them any kind of patriotic crap—or talked down to them— they'd have walked out en masse. They had it all planned. One condescending statement, and they'd have given me hell. They weren't in the mood for a preaching session. I must have said the right things because they stayed, and they came back to many other shows.

When we got to talking later on, they all wanted to know why I was there. The show itself became insignificant. Some of them liked it; some of them didn't—it was the issue that was important. What were my motives? They were highly suspicious. Was I after political kudos in Washington? Was I there for the publicity? Was I showing my fans what a patriotic guy I was? The questions came thick and fast, and I had to spend a long time warding them off. The mere act of telling them that I was there because of the black situation was not enough. Luckily I had the means to demonstrate my sincere feelings and motives. I had been warned that something like this might happen, and I had come prepared. It was the very reason why I had never been across with Bob Hope. I'd been on half a dozen special TV shows with the guy, and I love him dearly, but the Vietnam thing was a different matter. We stood on different political platforms, and we could never share the same stage on any real issue.

Patriotism was a fundamental part of the Second World War. But Vietnam was different. Anyone who went over there and said, "Hey, you guys, you're fighting for the great America," would be howled down with abuse. That little joke had lost its steam—even with the enlisted volunteers who went out to fight Pearl Harbor over again and thought they were jumping into a John Wayne movie. It didn't hold water anymore.

The "nonwhites" from all ethnic groups had the worst time of the war. They turned to drugs, and they were often trouble-makers. But I don't blame them for that. They didn't want to go near Vietnam in the first place and couldn't find a reason for staying once they had got there. Nothing improved. The Viet-cong hated them, but so did the Vietnamese. Their own white officers treated them like dirt. There was little thanks when they got home. Few black heroes ever got on television.

I caught the mood of disillusion on my very first day. I went out on a helicopter patrol, and we soon came across a massive area which had been totally devastated. Right in the middle, in its own seeming Garden of Eden, was a small plantation with a big white house sitting splendidly in the middle of it. It had been untouched by the war because it belonged to a Vietnamese who had influence. Later, while I was talking to the guys in the camp, they pointed out that the Vietcong was only a few hundred yards away. The area in between was owned by another local dignitary. They weren't allowed to cross it. Yet the Vietcong used the area for lightning raids whenever they felt like it. You simply can't ask a guy to put up with a situation like that for very long. I saw nothing but hell and frustration which had eventually turned into naked anger and bitterness. And when the black guys got bitter, they were yanked out and put into psychiatric wards. You only had to say, "What the hell am I doing here?" to be put on your ass. *Catch-22* had nothing on what really went on.

No war is nice, for heaven's sake, but I soon found Vietnam was something else entirely. Very few of the guys out there had any idea what they were getting killed for. What they soon did find out was the dreadful injustice of that kind of war. Most of the blacks didn't even hate the enemy. They saw the Vietnamese gov-ernment they were defending as hopelessly corrupt—at the cost of American lives.

The average Vietnamese was no different. When I first got there,

I was billeted in an officer's home, complete with housekeeper. She told me one day, "The French came and went. They couldn't handle it. Nor could the British. You Americans won't last long."

That's what the guys were fighting for, a spirit of helplessness pervading the whole scene.

Because of this, thousands of them turned to drugs. They got some kind of solace from them. They would lace their cigarettes with heroin, which they could buy openly, $5 for a little tube. The detoxification center grew and grew and became about the most disgusting and degrading place on earth. Many of the guys would rather have been on the front line than trapped in that place. It was meant to be a hospital, and some of the doctors knew they had a very large problem. But the guy who ran it, who immediately made me want to vomit, treated it as a prison. Guys going through withdrawal symptoms were trapped in tiny cells. The place was covered with barbed wire, the food was pure garbage, and guys with real medical problems were being treated like common criminals. It wasn't long before I had chosen the detoxification center as my special project. I decided I was going to give them hell back home.

When I originally planned my journey, I had a long series of talks with people at the United Nations. Over the years I had done many benefits for the UN children's program, and I knew most of the top officials by their first names. Before leaving I sat down with Kurt Waldheim, the secretary-general, and told him that I was going as an entertainer, primarily for the blacks, but that I wanted to do something more.

Waldheim and I had a very frank discussion about the possibilities. He quickly accepted my argument that I was not looking for medals or glory, and he began to explain areas where I might help. In fact, many of the people at the UN were trying to get conditions changed in Vietnam. They were seeking ways of exerting pressure to influence Washington. Waldheim made it plain that my influence would be "very welcome" in various directions. One of them was to talk to the blacks about drugs—not to spy on anyone, but to try to find out the extent of the problem. With this in mind he gave me a Dr. Jaffy as an adviser, and I immediately felt the project was worthwhile.

In the end we went as an official delegation. A member of Jaffy's Drug Abuse Center came along with me and a Nixon presidential aide. We met every day between shows to compare notes. Throughout the trip I went everywhere without any kind of fear, and I had a secretary trailing me, taking notes all the time. I talked to just about everyone I could find, and when I went into places where the white guys didn't like to go, I talked into a pocket tape recorder. At first the blacks were openly hostile. I was called everything by them. But I went on talking and listening, and gradually the word seemed to spread that I was for real. Soon the hostility ended, and we were able to talk face to face. The blacks took me into their confidence, and I shall never forget them. I had been taken apart piecemeal, and they gradually put me together again. For them, I had to go see things at their worst. If nothing else, I had a press conference to go to back home and TV shows to do. I wanted to tell the American people, as far as I could, what it was really all about.

When the tour came to an end, I had seen one hell of a lot of Vietnam. I also found that as an official delegation we had a strong voice on many, many subjects. We didn't exactly stop the war, when we got home, but we certainly made some changes. President Nixon put into immediate effect ten of the twenty proposals we had made. That was a start. The most vital one as far as I was concerned was that he changed the detoxification center immediately back into a hospital. Only a week later they pulled down the barbed wire, opened the place up, and flew in a professional medical team to deal with the situation. People who went over there later told me there wasn't a guard in sight. The drug problem began to be seen in Washington for what it really was—a dreadful symptom of a dreadful war.

When I think back now, I know we didn't change that much, but at least we put some wrappings around the cancer, and I had the chance, over a long period, of helping explain to the American people what the blacks really felt about the war. Because of that, I like to think I wasn't wasting my time. I hope I have never been wasting my time when I became concerned about a political issue, even if I have sometimes felt misguided. After all, the kind of racism that existed in Vietnam had always been reflected in Hollywood. It is another of the things that make me hot under the collar. I feel the same way about blacks in war movies as I do about Hollywood's interpretation of blacks in the West. I was curious as a child to find out why there weren't any black cowboys. I learned that as a people we had been "freed" by Lincoln, and I just wondered where the hell we had gone. There weren't many books on the subject in those days, and the movies ignored it. It wasn't until I found a book called *Negroes in the West* that I realized blacks had played such a significant part in the taming of the West. The book had five very worn pictures of black cowboys, and they began to fascinate me. Over the years I picked up little pieces of information until I had a fairly comprehensive knowledge of life for the black man in the nineteenth century. But picking up these little strands was very hard work.

The older I got, the more frustrated I became at the way movies pictured the early black movements. It was as if we hadn't existed. We were seen only as buffoons or humble servants. I am not opposed to the industry showing this side of black life because, God knows, in reality it was a very large slice of how we existed. But this attitude by no means tells the full story. OK, so there *was* the Mandingo syndrome, but give me something else to balance the picture.

The industry was so sensitive about keeping black issues out of the movies it wouldn't even tell the story of some of the early black heavies. I tried for years to play a gangster, but I was told, even by good friends, that it was far too controversial. If a black played in any film, he should have no significance as a person—good or bad.

I used to dream up all sorts of ideas which might help give black actors some work, but ideas are anyone's property in Hollywood until they actually become "properties"; even then there can be half a dozen versions going around at the same time. Everyone with an original idea in Hollywood eventually finds it has been stolen. I cannot remember all the times I've been sitting at the bar in my house, chatting away with all sorts of people—producers, directors, writers, even actors—and I've said I'd like to do something, or had an idea, and then forgotten about it. Months later I've been sitting watching TV and seen the identical idea come up. When the credits start rolling, you know who got moving on what you said. In Hollywood, even mediocre people can make a generous living by picking up ideas and selling them.

I could reel off several dozen ideas which legitimately originated from the bar at my house. For a long time, for instance, Rod Serling would be up there for an evening, and we'd gas away all night. He had a very creative mind, and we both loved dreaming up improbable situations for his *The Twilight Zone*. We would bounce things off one another, and it would be a lot of fun. Rod dedicated his last book to me as a gesture of our friendship.

One night I had a great idea about a bigoted white man who got a strange disease and woke up to find he was black. Rod was crazy about it, but the sponsors thought the subject was too sensitive and turned it down. The story went around to a lot of people, but soon I forgot about it. Imagine my surprise when I found everyone raving about the film *Watermelon Man* and saw my own idea on the screen, chapter and verse.

The making of a black *Dracula* was also almost certainly born in my house. My love for, and knowledge of, horror movies is well known. Putting the Count into the ghettos among the super-hip blacks had been a pet project of mine for years. I was always talking about it at the house. As it happens, I don't like claiming credit for the film which eventually came out. *Blacula* was such a waste of a good idea and was so embarrassingly bad I feel it must be done again properly.

Before the black exploitation movies came along, it was practically impossible to find a black in films who had a word to say for himself. In order for a black cat to fight a white man in any sense of the word, the white had to be seen on screen skinning pet poodles and screwing babies so that when the black guy tackled him, the audience wanted anyone to beat him, whoever he was.

Things have changed, and some say that blacks are now overexposed. I find it difficult to argue with that, though I am acutely aware of the dangers. I've seen good black actors driven to the grave because they couldn't find enough work. I can't really tell the guys who survived, "Don't be exploited," because they look at you and say, "I'm an actor, and I've a wife and baby to support. I'll do any work I can find." But many aspects of the present scene fill me with fear. Much as I love some of the guys around Hollywood today, I'm not going to start handing out medals. It's been a long, hard fight, and a lot of people have died along the way trying to make it so that today blacks can just walk into parts. Most of them have no idea of the blood which has been spilled over the years.

For a long time Europe put America to shame. Europeans were doing good pictures there with fully integrated casts more than twenty years ago. They didn't bother to argue about a black man's sexual prowess. They let him act like a human being, especially in France.

Blacks in America, even a few years ago, had to fight colossal battles to have their work accepted both in films and on TV. I can remember when a very sensitive writer wrote a part for the *General Electric Theater* on TV which he specifically asked me to play. It was a warm, noncontroversial story about a young kid who had attached himself to a black soldier. The story had nothing to do with the "black problem"; it was about basic human relations, and the soldier could have been any color. It was beautifully mounted and written, and at first the TV company gave the go-ahead.

However, when the sponsors saw it and realized it would be playing against Dinah Shore, they tried to pull out. We had a tremendous fight, and for a long time it seemed we were losing. We brought a hell of a lot of pressure to bear, mainly on artistic grounds, but the racial issue came into it. General Electric even threatened to pull out all its sponsorship on TV if the film went ahead. We fought on, and the company eventually relaxed a trifle. It gave us an ultimatum. If there was any controversial reaction which could be linked to it, it would then pull out. We went ahead.

We ended up with higher ratings than the competition and got rave reviews. I was nominated for an Emmy, and the *General Electric Theater* laughed all the way up the ratings.

I remember it now as a huge fight with fierce interplay between finance and politics—all to tell a simple, human story about a black soldier. For me the nomination was the prize because it made the whole fight worthwhile, but even that had its farcical side. As soon as the nomination came along, everyone started taking bows and claiming responsibility. GE said it was "an enlightened company putting out new forms of theater experience."

The immediate overreaction was typical and predictable. GE offered me half a dozen parts. It was buying up anything that came along which could be built around a black guy. The GE people didn't even read the scripts. They brazenly wanted to cash in on the success they claimed they had created. "Hey, look," they said, "the public bought it. We've made a buck. Let's go, Sammy." I saw them looking through scripts with white parts they could turn into black parts, and on that ludicrous note, I took my leave.

All this was long before *Shaft* came along and started the whole black exploitation boom. There was nothing at all wrong with that film except for the 10,000 lousy imitations which followed it. It was made in interesting circumstances. The backing company was predominantly black, using white business money. It started the film and, as often happens, ran out of funds halfway through. However, it had made enough of the film to persuade black East Coast businessmen to buy a share. MGM wouldn't put up cash but guaranteed it a release, which solved many problems. The final financing of the film became almost "street" business. Blacks decided to back it, and some cats were putting in $300 from their savings. Others were finding thousands. It was the only reason *Shaft* got finished. Luckily they've all made their money back dozens of times over.

At first the film seemed a poor choice. It had no established star, and the story was cornball. That kind of movie had been done a million times. But it had a look, a classiness, and an authenticity (as well as the Isaac Hayes score) which made it unique. As the original black gangster movie it will always enjoy a special status. But I occasionally regret what happened when the moviemakers woke up to find *Shaft* had been such a success. They had board meetings and said things like: "OK, they want to see blacks on the screen. Let's give 'em blacks on the screen—until they get sick of them."

To a certain extent this was excusable. The pressure had been building for years to force the industry into more black participation. Suddenly, after *Shaft*, it realized that black audiences had been starved for this kind of film. They had become, in fact, a significant financial power as an audience, and the companies decided to cash in on it. The black community got a big kick out of seeing one of their own playing James Bond with a flashy car and a beautiful doll on his arm. So the studios made films in which the black cat kills the head of the Mafia and all his henchmen and guns down a few crooked cops while he's at it. It was exciting because it was new. The audiences would leave the movie, saying, "We're getting even, baby."

Unfortunately, the novelty value of these films wore thin rather quickly. They had no substance and soon reached a saturation point. This is a great shame because, with less haste and more sense, black movies could have had a truly significant role to play. Now it too has been overdone to the point where it is a cliché, and the whole movement toward intelligent black movies was passed over.

Richard Pryor is one of the very few actors to have emerged in any significant sense from the black movement in Hollywood. He is also the first black actor to play the industry at its own game. Universal set him up in a multipicture deal and give him an office-bungalow next to Telly Savalas. Big deal. The $2 million price tag didn't even buy exclusive rights, leaving him available to sign with Warner's for a four- to six-movie commitment. He still has properties in the pipeline with Paramount and Columbia. He had blown his career with NBC-TV by being too outrageous. Yet his divorce from the studio was the biggest laugh in town. Under the contract they paid him $2 million not to appear on TV for five years.

Yet this guy, who can act his balls off, just as a sideline to his fantastic business deals, has played it his own way all along. When he appeared at a gay rights benefit at the Hollywood Bowl, he was so annoyed by the arrangements made for the black artists that he told the audience of 17,000 to "kiss my happy, rich, black ass," leading the organizers to shrug and say, "When you hire Richard, you hire Richard."

When you hire Richard, you hire a guy who not only can fill theaters with such films as *Car Wash* and *Greased Lightning* but also has the talent to be co-scriptwriter on Mel Brooks's *Blazing Saddles*. There isn't anywhere in the world that cat can't go if he wants to. I love Richard Pryor to the point of obsession. He is a comedic genius who can also play a beautifully sincere piece in *Lady Sings the Blues*. The scene in which he breaks down was completely ad-libbed. Richard is a black experience within himself. He's got it mastered. The freedom with which he works within his own sphere is unique and brilliant. I just hope they don't jerk him off into impotency as they have so many black artists.

Richard is riding high, but even he is unaware of the fight that went on before he was able to become acceptable as a screen hero. Possibly Stepin Fetchit made it a bit easier for Richard Pryor. Before you saw Elizabeth Montgomery and O. J. Simpson making love together, you had to have *Guess Who's Coming to Dinner*.

We have a tendency to forget quickly in Hollywood. Great strides have been made, but more often than not they were made up of tiny footsteps which pushed a little farther on each tread. It is no longer necessary to be a Willie Best. They could always leave Willie in a room with Paulette Goddard because he was around only to make people laugh. He was lazy, stupid, and ugly so it could never be even vaguely suggested that any white actress would find him attractive. Paulette would never have been left alone with Harry Belafonte, let alone Richard Pryor.

Much of the future is up to guys like Pryor. People in films owe me things, and I could make some more movies. But my scope is severely limited. Richard, on the other hand, is a hot property who can demand and get what he wants. He is in the lucky position to take a lot of people with him and explore much of the talent hanging around.

In recent years the big studios have started minorities programs to explore the talents of various ethnic groups, as well as blacks. The programs have faced many difficulties, not least of all rip-offs from the minority groups themselves. When the programs first started, the Black Panthers and several other militant groups tried to take them over for their propaganda value. The second problem was that some of the studios tried to exploit the talent they found. It was a way of buying it up cheap.

Despite these setbacks, many of the schemes have been successful. Universal, for instance, had a very positive attitude toward its program. It used to find individuals and artistic groups and use the UCLA film club as a nucleus to get people together from every walk of life. From this, talented groups emerged and not only provided university film clubs with a lot of material but got the films noticed where they mattered—by the industry itself. Small groups used the scheme as a springboard to try out their ideas. To this extent the programs have been very useful. America used to be almost completely without an experimental cinema, so there was a constant thirst for new ideas and concepts. The minorities programs have been virtually alone in filling the gap.

Generally, in the United States the healthiest aspect of the movie industry is the sheer amount of activity which is going on. There is always such scope. And because it is geared to profits, successes, when they do come, are phenomenal. I agree that

Hollywood seems to be excessively cautious in its real creativity. It scores a huge success with *Star Wars*, and immediately imitations spring up. But then along comes *The Deer Hunter*, and the picture changes overnight.

In some ways, TV is making much bigger strides than the movie industry. Even Mary Tyler Moore covered highly sensitive issues on her show. *Roots* was the ideal TV vehicle and would never have made it as a movie. There is a great deal of activity on the creative side of television. Several black actors have gone into directing on TV. Ivan Dixon, for instance, one of the cast of *Hogan's Heroes*, became a *Kojak* director. Georg Stanford Brown, one of the cast of *The Rookies*, became a director on *Charlie's Angels*. They are among a dozen good black directors presently learning their craft. Many of the advances being made behind the scenes date back to the explosion of the equal opportunities movement in the sixties. The corporations hired many token blacks and found, to their surprise, there was a great deal of talent around. Tokenism became a recognition of talent, and black advancement in the industry came surprisingly quickly.

Some of it was born out of genuine goodwill by socially aware people who recognized the need to change. People like Shirley MacLaine went out of their way to find work for blacks. If she couldn't find a wardrobe lady, for instance, she would hire an out-of-work black actress and teach her the job. She would often call me up and say something was available, did I know of anyone who wanted a job? That wardrobe lady may not be acting, but she is employed in the business, and because of her training, she need never be out of work.

I have got jobs for dozens of other people on the fringes to keep them in contact with films. The director Hal Ashby, for instance, lived at my place for a while when he was working as third assistant in the cutting room. He made his way up to the huge success he is today—by learning his craft from the bottom. Black actors don't get the opportunities, so they take anything that turns up. And if they have the talent, sooner or later it wins through. That is why I am still relatively optimistic about the future.

I have never retired from being in the middle of the black issue, but nowadays I take it a little more easily. I don't give lectures anymore, and I don't go on TV and rant about my convictions. But no black can ever stop being aware of what is going on in America, and to that extent I still consider myself involved. I am one of the few black entertainers, for instance, who have made it their duty to find out the situation outside the United States. I like to keep abreast of aborigine problems in Australia, and I have always been involved with what is happening in Europe.

One of the first things I did when I got to London was meet with Michael X, and it became one of the great pluses of getting to that lovely city. My dear friendship with this man will probably never be understood by the British, who saw only evil in him. At the time Black Power was an almost unheard-of concept. Michael began to challenge not only the white attitude toward blacks but the black attitude toward whites. He gave blacks their first real self-awareness and made them fight for a new identity.

My interest in Michael X was not necessarily to endorse his views, but merely to find out what was happening to the black movement in London. I would often go up to his small apartment in Notting Hill, and we'd gas away the hours on every subject under the sun. Inevitably we'd get back to black militancy. But I never saw the dark side of Michael X. He was deeply disturbed, but intelligent with it. He had a wide range of views on any number of different subjects. His knowledge of films was comprehensive. He was penetratingly bright and always concerned. He wanted changes quickly. I didn't necessarily agree with all his ideas, but they were profound. He was never the black militant with me. It would have been totally alien for me to sit in a London slum talking about "killing Whitey." He never sprung it on me. Consequently in all my dealings with the man I was never aware of the fact that he was an ardent militant with a few very outrageous ideas.

Michael was a very persuasive man, and I instinctively knew many of his arguments were right. He was almost a lone voice between the white and black communities, and I found he was desperate to unite the different black factions in London. I agreed to do a special benefit at the London Palladium with the intention of trying to get all the black communities in London under one roof. The theme was unification, and to the extent that every one of the black movements in London was represented, it worked.

His concept of self-awareness linked to a change in the status of blacks is something they have never achieved in England. If Michael X had been around longer, they might have got much closer by now. They are still ripping each other off, and I think England's black problem has probably only just started.

After meeting Michael, I was interviewed by BBC television and let it be known, gently, that I was thinking of giving up my so far moderate stand on civil rights in favor of the Black Power movement. I declared, "I am not a Negro—I'm a black man." It seems strangely subdued these days, but then it was considered a highly controversial statement. When I then accused the British of not understanding their own black problem, all hell broke loose. The papers printed miles of comment—some sensible, some abusive. One day I was called to the telephone at the Palladium, and a man said he would be in the theater that night with a gun and would murder me. For the rest of the trip I had a squad of Scotland Yard detectives trailing me wherever I went. It was necessary, but it was no fun.

Despite this, I managed to get involved with the black movement in Britain. Besides the Palladium show, we did six late-night cabarets at the Playboy Club and a charity concert at the Lyceum Ballroom in aid of the starving children in Biafra and Nigeria. We charged $25 a head, a very large sum then, and we packed them in.

I also handed over $12,500 of my own cash to the British Black Power movement. I made it clear I didn't want it spent on guns or any other direct militancy. Michael had taken me to many black communities and was trying to raise the cash for some kind of cultural center for blacks. They also needed a place where cats could talk to lawyers and welfare people when they got into trouble. I was happy to pay toward that. It was an important aspect of my long love affair with London, but by no means the only one. Before I was through with that city, I was able to acquaint myself with just about every aspect of its fascinating life.

Chapter 14

Golden Boy
in a White Rolls-Royce

One of the most satisfying things about reaching the top of this most peculiar trade called show business is that you never stop moving. I was born a natural gypsy, and I find it difficult to stay in one place for any length of time. Basically I'm a fidget, but most good entertainers need to stretch themselves continually to stay up there—and one way of doing this is to test themselves on new kinds of audiences.

A couple of decades ago I realized I had played just about every possible house of entertainment in the United States. It was time to move on. I was not going to be content until I had wooed them in every major concert hall elsewhere. Consequently the world has become my playground. With the exception of the downtown Moscow theater, which is permanently reserved for the Bolshoi Opera and Ballet, and the People's Hall of Culture in Peking (not to mention a few countries in southern Africa which I simply left off my personal map), all my ambitions have just about been realized.

I've whooped it up in Sydney, stormed through Paris, Berlin, Copenhagen, Rome—and a fistful of other magical cities—and

261

felt completely at home in Rio de Janeiro. I've got drunk with the draftees in bars in downtown Saigon. I've kissed the Wailing Wall in Jerusalem, and I've become acquainted with homemade tequila at the bullfights in Mexico City. I know the view from every major hotel in the Western world. I've been on film sets in every continent, and I've met one hell of a lot of wonderful people.

But there is one place for which I have a very special affinity, and for no reason that I can pinpoint, it has a special place in its heart for me. I love London more than any other place on earth. If my business people would let me, I'd willingly live there for the rest of my life. This is a genuine and lingering love affair with a city which, for me, has everything. As soon as I hit the tarmac at Heathrow Airport I feel at home. When I saunter through the terminal, all the cockney porters yell, "Hiya, Sammy, good to see you again." I can also walk the streets at night, something I would never do these days in the States.

My love for the city dates back to 1963, when I did my TV debut for BBC television. The show led to a $50,000 contract for all my London shows for the next three years. It seems a pittance now, but at the time this was something of a record, and my business people were in ecstasy. I was planning to spend a lot of time in Europe, and they were worried about how the hell I would pay for it. I first arrived at Heathrow complete with bowler hat and brolly and stepped smartly into a white Rolls-Royce. The British got a kick out of it and the newspapers gave me a very good time. The reviews were fantastic, and the Palladium was sold out almost immediately. The theater took in $50,000 in the first week, which again was a British record. It surpassed the previous holder, Danny Kaye, by about $12,500. And Danny had had royal patronage in the form of a teenage Princess Margaret to whom he was little short of God.

It was one of the busiest periods of my life, and if I had kept it up, I would have been six feet under long ago. I was doing two ninety-minute shows a night and then going to the recording studios until dawn. We were cutting an LP at the time. I was also doing charity shows right, left, and center, and we were always watching films at the May Fair Hotel. I snatched a few hours' sleep, usually from about 6:00 to 10:00 A.M., and then started all over again. There were parties everywhere, both day and night, and the British newspapers called me the Great Gatsby because they saw me throwing huge shindigs and then getting lost in the crowd. It was a habit of mine. You don't get trapped that way, and if you do find a young lady, it is easy to slip away without being noticed.

My special pals in London in those early days were Peter O'Toole, John Mills, and the comedian Dickie Henderson. If I didn't throw a party at the May Fair, one of the pals threw one for me. I invited all the kids from the show, and that always gave me a kick. When I had been on the boards as a youngster, we used to work our hearts out getting audiences warmed up for the big stars, and they would often cash in on the energy and electricity we had produced. But protocol, in the old variety idiom, stopped them from socializing with us. If they had a private party, we were never invited. So when my own time came, I made sure the folks in the show were first on any invitation list.

The following year I couldn't wait to get back to London with *Golden Boy*. It was during this trip that I met Bernard Delfont and, eventually, his brother Lew Grade, both of whom wound up in the House of Lords. Even then they were the whiz kids of British show business, with Bernie running most of the theaters. Our friendship is still going strong, and I never fail to see them, and do business with them, when I go to London. The rivalry between these two unlikely but immensely likable rogue elephants of entertainment has never failed to amuse me.

My first experience with Delfont, however, was not very happy. I wanted the world premiere of *Golden Boy* to be in London, and Bernie was more than interested. He loved the show, and we talked business. However, just as we were getting everything together, he backed out. We were going to do only six or eight weeks in London, and Bernie didn't like the short run. He felt he might not get his money back. London didn't get the premiere, but when Delfont saw the cash flow we had generated, he finally capitulated, and we arrived at the Palladium for a twelve-week run.

Nowadays the two brothers not only are the cornerstone of the British entertainment industry but are making a very big mark on the rest of the world. I saw Delfont recently, drumming up a magnificent deal; only that morning he'd sold some movies

to NBC for $100 million. He'd already got his money back
several times on the films in the package. The cream—which went
directly into his pocket—came from reselling to TV.

The two brothers have always vied furiously for position and
worked together only when it was silly to deal with someone else.
In a single decade Lew Grade has become a formidable force in
worldwide entertainment, and his brother is only a razor's edge
behind him.

I always try to call on Lord Grade when I'm in town, and he
never fails to amaze me. He has his first cigar at 6:00 A.M., in
the office, and his last when he leaves at 10:00 P.M. In between
he never stops wheeling and dealing. The most amusing hour I
spent with him was just after he had made *Jesus of Nazareth*,
the spectacular and highly praised Franco Zeffirelli version of the
New Testament. Grade soon had me falling all over the floor.

Apparently the Vatican had put a great deal of money into
the British/Italian production and had a large say in the final
cut. Zeffirelli had sent Grade the uncut version and a copy to
the Vatican. A few days after seeing it Grade got a call.

The voice at the other end identified itself as being just about
as close to the Pope as you could get. "It's wonderful, Lord
Grade," said the Vatican aide. "It's brilliant, sensitive, and the
color is superb. We felt throughout that the locations were exactly
as the Holy Land must have looked at the time. It is done
entirely with meticulous taste."

Lord Grade knew all this anyway, but he couldn't help puffing
himself up with the congratulations—until the voice paused and
said, in embarrassed tones, "There's just one tiny little thing
wrong . . ."

"Yes?"

"Well, Lord Grade, do you realize they've left out the Virgin
Mary?"

Lord Grade said, "Christ," and immediately apologized. "Don't
worry," he added, "I'll fix it. I'll get back to you within the hour."

As he had been speaking, he'd been writing a note to his
secretary: *"Get me Zeffirelli."*

Before he put the phone down, Franco was on the other line.
"You bunch of foreigners," Grade shouted. "You don't know a
thing about the Bible. Now I've got all the cardinals up my arse.
For Christ's sake, get the Virgin Mary back in my picture."

Zeffirelli had started the story after Jesus was born because he wanted the action to move faster and assumed everyone would know the background. After Lew's call he had to shoot much of the picture again—putting Mary firmly in her rightful place.

Grade told me this entire episode with a very straight face, but by the time he had finished I was choking to death and beating my head on the floor.

Later we watched the six-hour film together, and I was naturally very impressed. The whole thing was very much Lord Grade's baby. He was extremely proud of it, and rightly so. He seemed to want me to like it very much, and this puzzled me a little. When I asked him why he had selected me for a private preview, long before it would become a worldwide sensation, he got heated and said, "I am telling a fundamental part of the history of religion. In London I can get Jews, gentiles, Arabs, Buddhists, Hindus, atheists—the lot. And if they want to see it, so much the better. But where else, at this time of night, can I get a BLACK Jew to tell me how great it is?"

By the time we finally brought *Golden Boy* to the Palladium I had separated from May Britt. I was a free man about town after several years, and I wanted to go, go, go. It was on this trip that Bobby Kennedy died, and after the initial shock I wanted to drown all that sorrow in as much fun as I could find. But I worked hard as well because it seemed the only other therapy. I was on a big downer and stayed depressed and disillusioned for much of the time. The choreographer Lionel Blair managed to cheer me up. Even Lionel, however, couldn't buck me up when I found I had a tumor of the throat and faced an operation on my vocal cords. I thought it was cancer, and it was driving me crazy. I was plagued with illness during the whole London trip. I broke some ligaments in my foot; that naturally curtailed my dancing. I was tearing my throat to pieces and came down with laryngitis. On top of all this, suddenly one night a private detective jumped onstage and gave me a writ. Some guy had lost the designs for the clothes in the show and decided to get publicity and sue *me* for their return. Nothing was going right. But London was not always as bad as this.

Over the years I've been at the Palladium and other theaters many times and grown to love the place. I've taken a whole month off and sat in the Inn on the Park, relaxing and enjoying myself.

I've rehearsed in just about the most appalling rehearsal rooms in the world, facilities which no star would ever contemplate back in the States, drafty church halls where I worked out routines with Lionel Blair. But I wouldn't have changed a minute of it. It was all part and parcel of my gradually growing affection for that town. For instance, if I hadn't had to rehearse in those church halls, I'd never have discovered that extremely odd area called Notting Hill Gate.

"The Gate" is a sprawling, bustling, colorful, and cosmopolitan area of West London. It has such a complex of different identities it has ended up with a unique character. It is London's Greenwich Village with some of the city's greatest pubs, restaurants, street markets, artists, bohemians, general poetic riffraff, and oddball political anarchists. Almost incidentally it is also the spiritual headquarters for London's West Indian community, and on a Saturday night when the reggae is pounding, it is as near as many of the immigrants have ever been to downtown Kingston. It is the natural habitat of the night people, but when the sun shines, the whole place also turns into a sort of everlasting carnival.

To say the church hall in the Gate was tacky is a huge understatement. It was practically derelict. But Lionel Blair and I worked hard there and managed to have a lot of fun. Lionel and I were always talking films between rehearsals. He's an ardent movie buff. We were chatting one day about one of the great British films of that year, *10 Rillington Place*. Lionel suddenly remembered, "You know the house they used in the film? It's just around the corner."

I said, "Jesus, I've got to go see it." I couldn't wait to get the day's work done so we could slip around in the Rolls and take a look. When I had originally seen the film, it was one of the few thrillers which had stood my hair on end and sent goose bumps racing down my spine. Richard Attenborough played the murderer Christie in a brilliant *tour de force*. The film did for Richard what *The Boston Strangler* had done for Tony Curtis. It was not just the performance; it was that he established a feel for the chill of murder—down to the sordid stale breadcrumbs and sour milk on the table.

I had to see that house. When we got there, I got out of the car and stood looking at it for a long time. It was raining a light drizzle. Without the natural mood of film, camera gimmicks or music, this house just wallowed in evil. If the MGM people had spent $10 million on a set, they would never have been able to capture that same mood. The fact that I was working a few streets away from Rillington Place gave Notting Hill Gate an exceptional spot in my affection.

After many, many joyous visits to London, three Royal Command Performances, hobnobbing with the blacks in Notting Hill, establishing myself at the very core of British show business, and making various films with Peter Lawford, I began to feel I was getting to know the spectrum of life there.

It was the simple things about the place that I really loved, just walking around the West End or Knightsbridge or even popping into a pub. I once stopped the car at a roadside inn, and the boys and I went in for a drink—again, something I would never do in the States. The landlord stared a little when we trooped in but did not acknowledge us in any other way. He was so cool that for the first time in years I felt like asking if he knew who I was. He refused to be ruffled in any way but, as a concession, when we got up to leave, he told me, "You may keep the glass, Mr. Davis."

It is this kind of stoic politeness which always intrigues me about the English. It is why shopping in London is one of the last great experiences left on earth. As soon as my bags are dumped at the hotel, my hands start itching to spend pounds. The silly thing about this is that I hardly make a cent when I do a European tour. The economics of traveling and keeping the show going through several countries means that the tour just about breaks even. I visit Europe mainly out of love and a growing loyalty to those people who continue to want to see me. So each time I cross the Atlantic my accountants go into a cold sweat.

They know I simply can't resist all those aristocratic shops in St. James's and Piccadilly. They point out that I could get the same things, cheaper and quicker, in New York. They don't understand; it's simply not the same. I have never been to London without having a dozen shirts made by Turnbull & Asser. Then I drive over to Cartier and get a little knickknack I certainly do not need. I spend a few thousand at Asprey's before lunch at the White Elephant, and I buy a few baubles at Harrods on the way back to the hotel. I pack it all in the white Rolls—itself ostentatious, but, as I've always said, "If you got it, flaunt it"—and I saunter through town, thoroughly enjoying every second of it.

All the people in those London establishments are now old pals, and with British reserve, they treat me as such. They don't do badly out of this mutual affection, of course. I know a guy in Asprey's who started as an assistant on the floor. He's now way up on the managerial side, yet he always comes down to serve me personally as an old pal. We chat for a while, and then he says, "I've saved you a little something. I knew you'd adore it." And of course, I buy it.

I once went into Turnbull & Asser and asked them to make some shirts a special way. I still wear them a lot onstage. I wanted shirts with long, pointed collars. One day I met Bob Evans, the Hollywood producer, and he tried to do a sneaky one on me. He admired my shirt and, when he got to London, tried to get Turnbull's to make some for him. The man at the shop told me later, with great delight and aplomb, "We wouldn't dream of giving him your shirt, sir."

A few months later I met Bob at L.A. International Airport. I think he was coming and I was going. He was furious. "What the hell is this, Sammy?" he shrieked across the terminal. "You own Turnbull's or something?" We sped to the bar for a drink, and he ranted and raved in a good-natured way for twenty minutes about how he had to have those shirts. Bob Evans is not the kind of guy people refuse easily, and he just wasn't used to it.

After all, he could probably buy Turnbull's—and Sammy Davis, Jr., with the change. He couldn't understand that half the point of shopping at a place like that is its special kind of loyalty to its customers. So all the time we were having that drink I kept thinking of the shocked look on the guy's face when Bob wanted my shirts. That's what you pay your money for. As soon as Bob went off, I raised my glass to Turnbull's and said, "Here's one to you."

Bob, who was then married to Ali MacGraw, had been something of an actor himself. The only role he is proud of is the bullfighter in *The Sun Also Rises*. He has always had a soft spot for Ava Gardner. He tries to forget most of his other movies. Whenever a film of his appears on television, I call him and tell him I've just seen it. It drives him crazy. At one time he spent a fortune trying to buy all his old films so no one could see them. But he's got a great sense of humor and we have a lot of fun together.

Shops like Asprey's live in a whole different world, almost a last-century atmosphere. They have a kind of style money can't buy, it rubs off on you. You feel like a gentleman as soon as you go through the door. It has always been the same with the White Elephant Club. One day, during a particularly pleasant lunch, the manager came up and asked me very nicely if I could "pop round" after the Palladium show because he had someone special he wanted me to meet. Naturally I said I would. I often went there for a nightcap anyway. I turned up and found the sweetest thing. The staff were throwing a party for me, complete with a big banquet. They had managed to get hold of just about everyone I knew in London and had invited them and their wives and families. We had one absolute hell of a ball. The staff danced the night away with all the celebrities, and at the end of the evening they presented me with a gold credit card which Asprey's had made especially for me. It was one of the most touching points of my life. And it just goes to show when the British do talk about money, they do it in solid gold from Asprey's.

In 1972, after more than two years of marriage, Altovise and I decided we owed ourselves a honeymoon. We'd just never got around to it. So we finally left on the QE2 for Southampton.

My wife is no stranger to London. She was a dancer in the Palladium production of *Golden Boy*. In fact, we met during the show and married soon after. Next to Paris, London was her favorite haunt. For the first time, we didn't do anything on that trip but relax and enjoy ourselves.

My affection for the White Elephant Club was growing all the time. I knew the owner very well by then. In 1969 I had come to London to do my first European cabaret for ten years. I opened at the Talk of the Town. Billy Eckstine was then playing at the Empress Club in Mayfair, and naturally I took a party along several times to laud the old maestro. The club was owned by Alec Hyams, who was then married to the top TV producer Stella Richmond, who happened to own the White Elephant. By 1976, when I was back at the Palladium—this time with Billy Eckstine on the same bill, along with those whirling dervishes of jazz dancing, the Nicholas Brothers—the club had become my spiritual home.

Two other long-standing customers were Anthony Newley and Leslie Bricusse. Their songs and music have been the cornerstone of my professional success for many years, and consequently I have been able to give them a great deal of exposure where and when it mattered. We have naturally remained the closest of friends. Songs like "What Kind of Fool Am I?," "Once in a Lifetime," and "Who Can I Turn To?" have remained in my repertoire for two decades. They continue to be favorites with audiences and are always being requested. In 1961, *Stop the World—I Want to Get Off* made Tony into an international superstar, and he has been on the nightclub and cabaret circuit ever since. He had already been around for a decade.

Way back in 1948 Tony came out of the East End to go to the Rank "Charm School," the British version of the old MGM school which nursed such stars as Judy Garland and Mickey Rooney. While Tony went through his elocution lessons, Chris Lee was putting on his first makeup. They all had to walk around with books on their heads learning poise.

In those days Tony was what he called a "tear-arse," and he often got drunk on straight gin. Down in the East End he mixed with a dreadful crew of fags, prostitutes, con men, and gangsters. He would drink with them in the pubs every night and then report at the "Charm School" and learn how to say "How now brown cow" in impeccable English.

He made forty films before he was forty, but it was no thanks to Rank. They kept him there for only two years because he was such a bad influence on the others. When he played the Artful Dodger in *Oliver Twist*, he was invited to a party for all the Rank stars, but he had to be hustled out when he was discovered making love to a lady under the piano. Michael Redgrave and Alec Guinness were among the other dignitaries present.

Tony and Diana Dors were just sixteen. Newley thought she was the sexiest thing on two legs and fell crazily in love with her. In those days, Diana Dors was already being called the female Errol Flynn, and she really played up to it. They billed her as a glamorous Puss in Boots, purring down a cream telephone. She became the very first British homegrown sex symbol, and the original Diana Mary Fluck was even denounced by the Archbishop of Canterbury after revealing "all" in a British Sunday newspaper.

For years Britain had been trying to cash in on the big bust boom created by Marilyn Monroe and Jayne Mansfield in America. For a time it looked as if they had made it with Diana, who subsequently proved she could act as well. There were others who had nothing but big tits—girls like Sabrina, who admitted on TV that

she didn't have a single intelligent thought in her head. She was
an overnight phenomenon in Britain when her ample bosom became a cinema legend. Sabrina knew full well her breasts were
her only asset, and she would fiddle with them continually, as if
trying to make sure they were still there. One day a TV director
went crazy watching her and said, "We know you've got them,
darling. And they're absolutely super. They won't run away. Now,
will you please stop touching yourself up and just say your damned
lines?"

When she did *Yield to the Night,* Diana showed beyond doubt
she didn't share Sabrina's problems. Her biggest mistake was turning down *Saturday Night and Sunday Morning,* which won Rachel
Roberts an Oscar. She regretted it later, but at the time she said,
"Getting paid five hundred pounds to be seen aborting a baby in a
bath just wasn't on for me."

Her second big mistake was that she underrated Albert Finney,
who also starred in the film. Finney is one of the original British
geniuses both on stage and film. He was a brilliant Tom Jones,
giving the part a freshness and impetus which were unique. He
also played such a fantastic Hamlet that Olivier called him the
greatest actor of his generation. Not that he always received such
accolades. Charles Laughton went to see him years before, when
he was at the Birmingham Repertory Company playing Macbeth,
and he said he was "quite dreadful." In fact, Finney was then
learning his craft. The celebrated critic Ken Tynan had "discovered" him, aged seventeen, at RADA and had persuaded several
people to take a serious interest in the talented pupil. Finney
turned down two lucrative film offers to go to Birmingham.

When I first knew him in London, he was always going on
gigantic drinking binges with Peter O'Toole, Burton, and Nicol
Williamson. They must have made some quartet. He soon came
to London with the stage version of *Billy Liar,* which quickly established him as a rising star. Since then he has rationed his new
roles carefully and consequently has made very few mistakes.

The English have a great tradition in Hollywood. Since the
silent days they have crossed the Atlantic very successfully, but
the era of James Mason, Stewart Granger, and David Niven was the
richest. Stewart leaped to fame when Errol Flynn died and the
studios couldn't find anyone else who could wear tights. Granger
was a good-looking man with a glint in the eye who looked as if

he had been born in tights. Can you imagine Charlton Heston or Victor Mature climbing into a body stocking?

The next generation of English actors created another following, although it was never as potent as the Mason-Granger days. John Mills, Trevor Howard, Jack Hawkins, and Kenneth More bridged the gap before the reemergence of the second cult wave of Finney, Richard Harris, Oliver Reed, and Michael Caine. Of the second school, only Kenny More remained unknown in the States. He came over once to play in a western with Jayne Mansfield, couldn't stand the place, and rushed home as soon as possible. Everyone was saying, "Who's that guy?" By the time they found out Kenneth had gone. Hollywood just wasn't his scene.

It was in the sixties that the British film industry came into its own. Richard Burton and Michael Redgrave had been riding high for some time. Then along came the "kitchen sink" dramas like *Saturday Night and Sunday Morning*. Richard Harris arrived soon after with *This Sporting Life*, and the vogue was established. It was an odd choice for a cult movie because absolutely no one in America could understand rugby. Despite this, all you could hear for a while was: "You got to see this film; the English have discovered a new Marlon Brando." Harris was like an ape, so raw and rough. He spilled his guts into that picture. He transferred all the tension and violence of the game right into his relationship with Rachel Roberts.

Michael Caine's first film, *A Hill in Korea*, was so bad no one would employ him in a good part for almost six years; the only work he could get was as an extra in the Pinewood Norman Wisdom comedies. Then *Zulu* came along, and Stanley Baker cast him in the second lead. The producer Harry Salzman liked it and wanted him for *The Ipcress File*—which completely floored America. Caine was well on his way when he gave us the brilliant *Alfie*, then *The Italian Job, Sleuth*, and *The Eagle Has Landed*.

His attitude toward America is odd. Whenever he is in the U.S., he "guards his exit." However successful he becomes, he never wants to be forgotten at home. I can remember when he came up to the house one night and told me, "I haven't the vaguest idea what the fuck I'm doing here. I don't know what pictures I've made. I don't even know the title of the film I'm making right now. Whatever it is, they're buying it and paying me a fortune. I'm taking the bleeding money, and I'm running."

Michael York was another latter-day British wonder who took off big in this country when he played Liza Minnelli's bisexual lover in *Cabaret*. The director, Bob Fosse, immediately recognized his distinctive quality of elegant machismo and once told me it is his life's ambition to direct Michael as a real mean, gutsy bastard. York brought a certain brilliance to *The Three Musketeers* and has proved himself to be a director's actor. They all love him. When MGM came to make the $8 million *Logan's Run*, Michael was the only actor considered for the lead. They told his agent if he didn't make it, they would drop the whole project. That is what you might call confidence in an actor.

A producer once told me that the best thing that ever happened to Michael was when some guy busted his nose. He would never have got anywhere in Hollywood with a too-perfect profile. They would have dismissed him as being too sensitive-looking. That crook in his nose gave him a slightly awkward and therefore interesting face. He has a schizophrenic look, full of mysteries. One moment he is entirely sensitive, yet the next he is immensely tough. He turns both men and women on in the best sense of the term. Michael Anderson, the director of *Conduct Unbecoming* and *Logan's Run*, said he'd like to go on photographing his face forever. Anderson couldn't really fathom Michael when he first met him, and that added to the fascination. He discovered that the actor had great hidden depths which he could never reach down and touch. York left those little mysteries there, and the audience caught on. He is part poet and part pugilist, but at the same time, he is essentially a hardworking, very well-trained, and disciplined actor. The only major mistake in his life was turning down Ryan O'Neal's part in *Love Story*. He thought the whole thing was too corny but admitted later that he could have done a lot with it.

Oliver Reed was one of the hard-hitting new breed who soon became established in America. He has a brooding sensuality and a tough, sadistic streak. The violence seems to lie just below the surface, giving his roles a complex but complete excitement. He was making *Oliver!* for Carol Reed in England when Peter Lawford and I were doing *Salt and Pepper*. Lawford and I had taken only a small section of the lot. Reed and Co. had the rest. *Oliver!* was a very big, ambitious film for such a small studio.

Lawford and I had built a nightclub and filled it with gorgeous girls, a large part of the great fun of making the film. We had just about every young, beautiful, aspiring actress at our beck and call for weeks on end. Peter and I would turn up at the commissary with a couple of dozen lovely ladies and find Oliver Reed sitting alone in the corner, looking mean.

In normal circumstances he would have been a great turn-on with these girls, but the makeup boys had made him look so menacing none of them would go near him. The little dog in the film soon became the only creature he could talk to. Oliver wouldn't be parted from it. It was funny to see this tough, hard-drinking hell raiser feeding little delicacies to his pet pooch.

Since everyone steered clear of him, Oliver got more and more uptight, and the dog picked up his mood. When any of us did go over to chew the fat, it growled like hell and sent us away. Oliver's commitment to his work was real, but he couldn't help bringing some of that evil off the set with him. He was growling and snarling—as he did throughout the film. In the end only the dog seemed to understand.

Peter and I had come over hard on the heels of the rest of Hollywood. In the fifties just about every American actor went to London to make a war movie or a cops-and-robbers film. There was a big exchange of ideas and talents which had a profound effect on the industry later on. But top British stars often had to play second lead to sometimes mediocre American actors. These early films were called Aquascutum pictures because everyone wore one of those long gray raincoats.

There was a line which came up sooner or later in every one of these films. The British guy would turn to the American and say, "We do things rather differently over here." It was the most overused cliché in movie history. An inspector from Scotland Yard would say it to an American private eye. An army officer would lay it on an American scientist. You could always rely on that line's coming up. The British had a weird fear that American audiences wouldn't understand their way of life.

Very few of those films are worth remembering, but because they still keep showing up on television, many British actors are known here without ever setting a foot in America. There is a recognized school of British acting which is familiar to the American public, wholly through TV.

In the early days, however, many British films crept into America without getting a general release. Some of them became cult films without any major backing. The New York release of *The Angry Silence*, for instance, coincided with a dreadful snowstorm. The papers didn't come out, and the reviews were never seen. It gained its reputation by word of mouth, and it was, by any standards, an incredible film. Richard Attenborough had started his own production company with several friends. They figured they could make the film for $350,000. British Lion wouldn't give them a distribution guarantee unless they cut this to $250,000. Attenborough persuaded everyone to work for almost nothing and refused to take a penny himself before the film showed a profit. They did it for just $195,000, and it made its money back within days of its release.

The British have always had a fair share of filmmakers who have wielded tremendous influence in the industry. Perhaps only they could have invented a Ken Russell. People have always accused Ken of getting some kind of demented kick out of producing outrageous sex scenes. In fact, on the set he is about as clinical and methodical as a surgeon doing an appendectomy. He drives his actors hard and always tries to get something more from them. He believes, probably rightly, that most actors have four or five well-tested tricks up their sleeves and often rely on these for their performance. Ken will watch them perform for some time and come up with some tricks of his own.

He will start off a scene knowing they have already thought it all out. Then, just as the camera starts whirring and everyone becomes quiet, Russell jumps up and yells, "Who put that bloody chair over there?" The chair is moved, the scene starts again, and he yells, "For Christ's sake, move that table to right angles." By this time the set is a bundle of nerves; often the actor is so jumpy he gives a spontaneous performance without a trick in sight. It could be called nervous cinema. Whatever it is, it works for Ken.

One big difference between British and American filming is that the unions have a lot of power in England. The guys there either stop at 5:30 P.M. or go on overtime. They can play games to ensure they work past the deadline and so take home more money. In Hollywood they schedule a certain number of pages a day and keep shooting until they've done it. The actors and technicians could finish at 4:00 P.M. or go on to midnight. It's a great incentive to get things right as soon as possible.

The influence which British films have had on Hollywood is

phenomenal. Considering the acute financial problems, an almost total lack of decent facilities (even in the heyday of British film-making the studios were more like factory farms), a mere fifth of our own audiences, and that acutely depressing weather, the British contribution has been almost unbelievably high. You have only to look at the Academy Awards to see what I mean. Consistently, year after year, the Brits have more than held their own.

Yet, when George Brent went to England to play in *The Last Page*, he turned up at Bray Studios and thought the whole place was the set. He had just starred in a major production with Bette Davis and looked at the building and said, "So where's the studio?" When they told him this ramshackle place was it, he went into a state of shock. The conditions were so primitive that his hair turned white before he finished filming.

Primitive or not, studios like Elstree and Pinewood have a monumental place in the history of movies. Elstree has been rattling them out for more than half a century. Right back to Hitchcock's emergence with *The Ring* in 1926 and up to *Murder on the Orient Express* in 1974, Elstree has churned out classic after classic. A list of the stars who have gone through Pinewood Studios reads like a *Who's Who* of films. Pinewood is the younger brother of Elstree but has also had its heyday. Moira Shearer's *The Red Shoes* was made there; so were *Goldfinger*, *Genevieve*, and *A Tale of Two Cities*. These studios have nothing to be ashamed of.

The British film industry has certainly done things we could not have accomplished in America. They made those wonderful little mystery thrillers which we could never have mastered, creating a vogue in the forties.

We Americans were much more hard-boiled in our approach. We developed the gangster and detective movies, but we didn't have the elasticity to explore all the refinements. We spent decades looking for a Joe Losey who could recognize the subtleties and nuances of a role. We had no one, for instance, who knew what to do with Dirk Bogarde. Everyone understood there was something special there but didn't know what it was. Dirk's incredible performances were lost on our directors. He dealt with everything so sensitively. This had all our top directors scratching their heads.

Nowadays we have actors like Dustin Hoffman and Al Pacino who can be superbly subtle, but they can be handled only by the new-wave directors. It is a shame that the great directors of the forties and fifties can hardly get a job these days because their particular styles are completely out of fashion. They know every trick and camera angle, but they could never master the nuances.

This is a huge enigma for movie buffs because we still love looking at their pictures. I very much doubt whether many of the films being made today—even with their sensitivities—will have half the staying power of the old school.

But who knows? The interesting thing about motion pictures is that the kaleidoscope changes so rapidly and so drastically that I doubt whether we will ever be able to say, in all confidence, "That is the ultimate film."

Chapter 15

The English Way

The White Elephant Club's association with show business goes back a long way. In the old days all the out-of-work actors and actresses used a small coffee shop called, for some unknown reason, the S and F, in Denman Street in London's fashionable West End, guys like Laurence Harvey, Stanley Baker, Edmund Purdom, Richard Burton, Jack Hawkins, and Pete Murray. When one of them landed a part and had some money, he'd pick up the others and they'd all go to the White Elephant for a blast. The club soon found a special place in their hearts, and as each of them made it, they didn't forget it. When they'd been down on their luck, the club sometimes "forgot" to give them the bill. Nowadays it has been paid back ten times over.

I've had some great times at the White Elephant, but these days my visits are marred by a tinge of sadness, for all the great guys who aren't around anymore. Guys like Jack Hawkins, whose courage when he died from cancer of the throat became a legend on both sides of the water. He was one of those great British stalwarts whom you could always rely on for a brilliant performance. He made his last film with a tube in his voice box, and his friends needed every single bit of self-control to stop themselves from crying. They all knew what was coming when he filmed *The League of Gentlemen*. Richard Attenborough, who made the movie with him, can remember the exact moment when Jack realized he was finished as an actor. They had to shoot around him for several days. Then, Dicky told me later, "Jack got himself together and hurled all self-pity to the wind. We finished exactly on schedule."

We always caught up with all the news when we went to the White Elephant. In the great British tradition of finding money mildly vulgar, I never see a bill when I dine there. My manager, Murphy Bennett, my trusted aide for many years, picks up the tab at the end of my stay.

Days at the club are delightfully casual and refreshing. There is a stream of attractive, interesting people passing through the place, and over the years we have all got to know each other. Lionel Blair is one of the great regulars, and I often bump into Albert Finney.

It's a place for eating leisurely, gassing away, talking movies, drinking fine wines, and being superbly looked after: four-hour lunches with such people as Stanley Baker, for whom the club would make up a special plate of bacon and eggs.

Stanley had an immense talent but never quite made it into superstardom because he was never fully appreciated by his peers. They used to say that the only people who seemed to like him were the distributors and the public. Later he managed to set up a trend by being the only British actor who could play an authentic tough guy. He became known in *The Cruel Sea*, but he paid his dues as a working actor for years before the accolades came trickling in. It took Joe Levine, an American, to see his real potential and give him the cash and the go-ahead for *Zulu*. He later went on to make such good films as *Robbery*, and his parting shot as an actor was the TV series *How Green Was My Valley*, which he completed while he was dying.

When he died, of course, the critics raved about his great performances, and many people in the industry realized they had never used his varied capacities to their full extent. He was a tough professional who retained the respect of everyone who worked with him. His death sent a shock wave throughout the entertainment industry.

I had known the family for many years and am the godfather of his youngest daughter. Like everyone who ever had the pleasure of seeing Stanley with his wife, Ellen, I adored them both. Back in the days when Burton and Stanley were sharing a house in Hampstead—Burton going off each morning to star in another Elstree production and giving Stanley a lift for his occasional day's work—Ellen moved in to look after them. She married Stanley after a whirlwind romance, even though she had been told by another actress, "You don't want to become one of Baker's dozen, do you?"

Ellen was the first to learn from the hospital that he had terminal cancer. She told her husband immediately. Stanley was not the kind of guy you minced words with. He sat her down very gently and spoke to her about all the wonderful things they'd gotten out of life. At first she smiled, but later he found her crying. He put his around around her and said, "Don't do that. I can't get through it without you."

Baker loved acting, and he was a hard working natural. But he loved life more, and that made him the special kind of guy he really was. He was a hard drinker and an astute gambler. He managed to fleece Gregory Peck at one mammoth session of poker which lasted several days. Gregory is a brilliant and experienced poker player, but admitted he'd met his match. When Stan went on a drinking session, it would last for days. He and Burton learned how to drink together in the early days, and Stanley never forgot. When he died, Burton was so distraught he didn't surface for a week. When he did, he wrote one of the most magnificent obituaries I have ever seen.

Stanley was a hard man, and he liked his sprees. When he was making *The Angry Hills* in Greece, he went on a monumental binge with Robert Mitchum. The two of them hit just about every bar in Athens and drank ouzo until it was coming out of their ears. Stanley lasted for seventy-five hours before falling down. When he woke up a day or so later, he was annoyed to find Mitchum had gone on drinking for the rest of the night. Bob was fifteen years older. Stanley could never forgive himself.

But he had one golden rule: He put everything needed for his family to one side before he spent a penny on himself. He was fiercely loyal to his friends and family, and God knows, if anyone insulted them, there was hell to pay. But he had the soft belly of an alligator under that hard skin. He was tough on his kids because he knew the world outside could bruise them easily if they weren't prepared for it.

In order to live with the terrible realization that Stanley was not around anymore, Ellen had to get a grip on herself. At first she could hardly get up in the morning. She got rid of the staff so that she had to get up and do the cooking and cleaning for the four children. Stanley could never bear to see her in pain, and she found that one of the best painkillers was going to the movies. She would go to the multitheater ABC in London's Fulham Road and watch three or four movies on a Saturday.

A group of us were sitting around in the White Elephant, discussing the Bakers, when we realized we had a problem. Maybe Ellen wanted to be alone, but on the other hand, maybe she desperately needed cheering up. That is always the problem with the people left behind—they think they embarrass their friends. I decided that I had to make an attempt to get her out to lunch and a chat about old times. No one wanted to impose on her sorrow, but I decided, rightly as it happened, that I would not take no for an answer. We had an absolutely fantastic lunch together, and without hindsight, I realized that Ellen Baker was responsible for changing part of my entire philosophy of life.

She will hate me for saying this, but she is a brave woman who has the dignity and guts of a giant. I mean good, old-fashioned grit and determination. She is honest, pure, tranquil, and amazingly sensitive. Yet she has the same beautiful toughness that her husband had. There was not a trace of self-pity in her, just an honest appraisal of her situation, and how to deal with it, and still the overwhelming love for Stanley. She fully appreciated the support of her friends and was thankful, but she quietly let it be known that she could cope. She never once played the martyr, and that must have been doubly difficult because everyone was falling over himself to give her sympathy.

Our lunch started off very well as we talked over all the old times together. But an extraordinary thing began to happen. I found myself in such awe of her vitality and strength that I began to seek support from her. At the time, it was true, I was going through a bad downer in which a lot of divergent situations had come together to cause real personal problems. So we began to lean on each other.

Later, when I got back to Beverly Hills, I realized how small my own problems had been compared to Ellen's and what a fantastic example she was. Knowing her changed me in two ways. I will never again allow myself to wallow in any kind of self-pity. Nothing's that bad. The meeting also made me much less tolerant of other people's self-pity. Nowadays, when people come up to me and cry and moan because they didn't get the part they wanted or something, I think of Ellen Baker and say to myself, "What would you do with a real problem?"

If something doesn't work out, it is no longer the end of the world to me. We'll go on surviving. Ellen's example of strength strengthened me as a person, and I shall always be grateful to her for it.

The only other person who affected all the buddies in the White Elephant as much when he died was Laurence Harvey, who was poles apart from Stanley in everything but his career. Larry had been a good friend of mine for many years. We had known each other in London and crossed paths several times in America. But we cemented this friendship when he moved permanently to Hollywood. During both our up and down periods, we would always be in each other's houses. He'd drop by and see me at any odd hour, and he was very welcome. He was the kind of guy everyone loved having around. He was amusing, erudite, interesting, intelligent, and extremely affable. I personally enjoy my best relationships with people I can fool around with verbally, witty people who can match me jest for jest and quip for quip. This goes back to the Holmby Hills Rat Pack and was continued by the Clan. I never lost the habit. I love nothing better than having a verbal sword fight. As a sparring partner Larry Harvey was perfect. We'd sit by the pool and gas away for days. I was always saying things Larry disagreed with. My rather sentimental approach to show business was matched by his utter cynicism. When I started one of my eulogies, he would say in that ultra-English voice of his, "Sammy, dear boy, don't be so blasted gauche. It doesn't suit you." That was always the start of an hour or two of very funny semihostile conversation.

When he began to temper everything with that irritating raised-eyebrow routine, I used to impersonate him and accuse him of overplaying the sophisticated English bit. He would carry on as if he'd lost his monocle, gently sip his champagne, and think up the next insult. It was when I mimicked him adjusting his neckerchief and pretending he was Noel Coward that I finally scored points. "Oh, shit, Sammy," he would say in mock horror, "you've got to let me have some fun in this heathen place called Hollywood."

On the face of it we were unlikely pals. Larry played his sophisticated English bit to the very hilt, and the act was very popular with the Hollywood hostesses. But underneath he was a warmhearted, very hardworking actor with a subtle and brilliant sense of humor. We became natural buddies probably because our backgrounds were so different. Larry, for instance, was a crazy wine buff. He adored good wines. He was always telling me the inside story of how he had tracked down a rare vintage. Once he had found a California wine which lived up to his expectations; he bought the vineyard and had his own special "Harvey" labels made. Frankly I could take it or leave it. I have no objections at all to a fine glass of cold hock on a warm day, but if I am left to my own devices, I generally prefer something which has been through a distillery. This used to drive Larry crazy. He would open a favorite "find" and beg me to taste it. To be polite, I would always do so, but as soon as a respectable time had passed, I'd pour myself a large vodka and tonic. Larry got really frustrated when he found he couldn't convert me to his tastes. To Larry, good wine was a religion. He would sit there with his eyes closed, "experiencing" this great alcoholic beverage, and when he caught me at the vodka bottle, he would say, "You bloody cretin," and pop some more caviar into his mouth. So I was surprised when, one day, a crate of wine was delivered to me; it was the special "Harvey" wine marked "For a special occasion."

It was clear to us all that Larry was very ill. He had become gaunt and thin over a two-year period, and only his great sense of humor encouraged everyone to believe that he was going to make it. Even that grin of his, which remained slightly waspish with the cavalier twist, began to get a bit hollow. But he always seemed so stoic, cheerful, and witty that it was difficult to believe he was in pain and very ill.

I was surprised to find that his wife, Pauline Stone, was not at a dinner to which about twelve of Larry's close buddies had been invited. He sat at the head of the table, trying to look as resplendent as possible, but his lips were a little whiter than usual, and it was probably a much bigger strain than he was showing. Even so, he kept us cheerful until after the meal. Then he said in a debonair way that I still remember, "Well, pals, I have chosen you all very carefully for this auspicious occasion as I want to discuss a few things. This is the very last meal we will have together because I have only a few months to live, and I'm going off to enjoy them to the full. I don't want anyone to get all upset and maudlin. Please promise me before I begin that you won't start getting maudlin because I couldn't bear it."

Somehow or other we all managed to remain cheerful; in a funny way Larry had such presence that it was not difficult to do it all his way. His immense charm and acceptance of his fate rubbed off on us. He repeated in a matter-of-fact way that he was dying and had come to terms with the situation. He asked us, as his intimate buddies, to do the same. "Dear me, if *I* can do it, surely you can." At this point he wasn't playing the stiff-upper-lipped Englishman; he was just telling us as naturally as possible what the score was and asking us to bear it. He talked about his death as casually as he'd have discussed what theater we were going to in London in the old days.

"Now," he went on, "I have a few things here which are very, very dear to me, and I don't want them to go to anyone who does not love them. You are all dear friends, and I have chosen you because you would appreciate these little items. If they went to an open auction, it would upset me greatly. Things like this dinner service"—it was all gold and had everything down to the last teaspoon—"if this doesn't go to an old friend, I'll come back and haunt you all."

We knew the man was being serious, but he managed to pull it off with such casual and gentle good humor that, at first, the dark side of the tragedy escaped us all. Only later, when I really thought about it, did I appreciate the full bizarre significance of the event. There was the famous Laurence Harvey holding his own last supper—auctioning off his favorite personal possessions to his great pals—and we were sitting around the table being almost flippant about the affair. There were many items which he wanted us to have: several dinner sets, which were collector's items, a vase or two, some beautiful furniture, and so on. As he pointed them out, we sat there saying things like: "I'll have that one," or "I'll deal with that," until nearly everything had been earmarked.

The plan was that we would pay his wife their true value when we picked them up.

Later in the evening the two of us had a chat at the bar. All the time he was talking I knew it was probably the last time I would see that crooked smile and hear that languid voice. He asked me to buy his house and his art collection, or one or the other. Both were very dear to him.

"I want them to go to someone who will love them as much as I have," he said. "I have implored my wife to sell everything when I have gone, get rid of all traces of me, and get married again. She must do that. She must go out and start a new life. It's just the thought of an unknown someone living here that I can't stand."

I had unfortunately already committed myself to far more than I could actually afford. This worried me because we all were emotionally involved with his coming death and wanted to do everything we could to help. When I tried to explain this, he held me momentarily by the arm and said, "Oh, well, old boy, it was a good try. Let's join the ladies."

After that we settled down with drinks and just talked away an hour or two. He said he was going to spend the last few months doing all the things he'd always wanted to do but had never got around to. And that, a few days later, was exactly what he did. He went off on what can only be described as a rampage. He saw a lot of places, drank the best wines in the world, ate the greatest gourmet meals, looked up old pals he hadn't seen in years, and generally had as much of a ball as his health would allow. The funny thing was that from the time of the "last supper," he would not allow his wife to come near him. It was the Achilles' heel of his acceptance of death. He could not stand letting her see him die. So he banned her from his life. He went off on his own and was adamant about it.

By the time he came back from his binge he was clearly wasting away fast and knew there was not much time. He casually began to put his house in order. He had already seen his brother in London and talked about his parents in Israel. Back in Los Angeles he checked the hospital where he knew he would soon have to go. He paid his bills, reread his will, then calmly arranged all the details of his own funeral. All this was so that his wife would be spared the heartache when he died. But it was also because he wanted things done a special way. To the very last moment he wanted to be the stage manager of his final act.

The slightly bizarre thing about his remaining days was that he was still making plans for a new movie. It was wishful thinking, of course, but even he could not accept the finality of death. He just had to keep moving. Despite all the preparations for death, he could not sit down and wait for it. He wasn't trying to fool anyone else. He was just keeping the flag flying until the last breath.

The last words we ever had together were at the end of that evening, and they were typical of the conversations we had that night. When the time came to leave, I told him, "We won't ever forget you, Larry. I'm going to do one for you. We'll swing a great party, and we'll remember you for all the great times."

He smiled wryly and said, with the old Larry twinkle, "Well, for God's sake, old chap, make it a fun do. Have attractive people around. Have the whole place swarming with beautiful birds and handsome men. Don't let anyone come who is ugly or boring. And get tight, old boy, get as tight as hell."

At that moment I remembered the wine he had delivered and how it had been labeled for something special. I never did see Laurence Harvey again.

We opened that case exactly one year after he died. During the early evening I got together all the people who had been at the "last supper" for a special toast before the masses arrived. We opened the wine and poured it out. As we raised the glasses, I said, "Tonight we're going to have the one we promised Larry." We even had a medium there who swore Larry was around. So we filled an extra glass for him. We also remembered his one great eccentricity. He liked his bread and rolls burned to a crisp. In restaurants he was always getting the waiters to take the bread into the kitchen and burn it to a frazzle. So we burned all the bread in his honor.

Among the people in the "inner sanctum" of pals were Peter Lawford, Joanna Pettet, and Harold Robbins, who were naturally among the first to arrive. Soon after, the multitudes showed up. Larry had a formidable fan club, not only of all the celebrities but of people from every walk of life. He was the kind of guy everyone enjoyed knowing. His image was odd because he was, in fact, singularly unsnobbish and down-to-earth when it came to friendships. It was an absolute rule of the evening—no one was allowed to be maudlin. We all loved the guy, and we were upset by his death, but we were going to do it for Larry the way he had wanted.

When everyone had arrived and the champagne corks were sounding like a B western, I decided to propose a toast to set the mood. There was absolute silence as I raised the glass. I said in my most serious voice, "This one's for you, Larry." But before they could take the second sip, I went on: "And wherever you are, Larry, fuck you, too, pal."

I knew that old Larry was up there with his raised eyebrow waiting for someone to get emotional. He would have that sardonic grin on his face and the forelock of hair over the cynical gaze. He would be saying in that pukka voice of his, "Oh, what a lot of silly arses."

Naturally we proposed one hell of a lot of toasts to Larry that night, and we did exactly as he'd ordered and got as tight as hell. But even though everyone talked all night about his or her favorite Laurence Harvey stories, there wasn't a single tear or a long face in the house. There was a great feeling of affection, perhaps a tinge of sadness, much bantering, some little elements of remorse, but no one was maudlin, the word in any dictionary in any language that Larry could not stand. We ate a lot and drank more, and throughout dinner and on to the early hours we talked of Larry. We ended up showing *The Manchurian Candidate*, which was arguably his best performance, and even when we were all sitting watching the guy on screen, we managed to keep the spirits high. I don't think you could have done that with any other actor.

When the film was over and we were sitting outside with that peculiar hazy light coming up over Los Angeles, people still would not go home. Everyone wanted to sit around talking about the great guy. It was cozy and intimate, and fun . . . and if Larry Harvey had walked through the garden at that moment, I knew he would have approved.

I like to think we gave him the sendoff he deserved, one worthy of the legacy he left us on celluloid—and in all those marvelous memories.

Just as it was getting light, I raised my glass for the last time. I simply said, "OK, pal?"

I could see him somewhere up there, giving me a wink. It may have been a fading star, and it could just have been something to do with the amount of goodwill and alcohol which was swirling around the brain cells. Then I neither knew nor cared. But nowadays I like to think that that wink was what the movies are all about. If I can go on packing a little of it in my suitcase each time I leave home, it won't matter what town I'm in. Hollywood will be with me.